Presented to:

_____

From:

_____

Date:

_____

366 DEVOTIONS

New Beginnings

THE LORD'S MERCIES
ARE NEW EVERY MORNING

Christian art gifts®

Visit Christian Art Gifts, Inc., at www.christianartgifts.com.

New Beginnings

Original copyright © 2000 by Christian Art Publishers, RSA.

Published under license by Christian Art Gifts, Inc., Bloomingdale, IL, USA.

First edition 2024.

Written by Solly Ozrovech.

Designed by Allison Sowers.

Cover and interior images used under license from Shutterstock.com.

ISBN 978-1-63952-476-1 (DEV260)

978-1-63952-477-8 (DEV261)

Printed in China.

29 28 27 26 25 24

11 10 9 8 7 6 5 4 3 2

*Because of the L*ORD*'s great*
love we are not consumed,
for his compassions never fail.
They are new every morning.

Lam. 3:22-23

A WORD TO THE READER

My heart is steadfast, O God, my heart is steadfast;
I will sing and make music. Awake, my soul!
Awake, harp and lyre! I will awaken the dawn (Ps. 57:7-8).

There are thousands of people in our country who spend time with God in the early hours of the morning. It is a special time of silent seclusion that helps us to find the strength and inspiration for a full and busy day ahead.

This book, written in an accessible style that is easy to comprehend, wants to make a humble contribution to make this time with God meaningful and dynamic. Of course, the Scriptures are always the point of departure, and there is no substitute for the Word of God.

Therefore, I appeal to you first to read the passage from Scripture before continuing with the daily devotion and the prayer. We pray that, in this way, the Holy Spirit will open the Word to you. The best time to meet God is early in the morning so that we may devote the best of our time and mind to Him.

Soli Deo Gloria

January

PRAYER FOR THE NEW YEAR

Holy God, Creator of new things,
we thank You for the experience of the dawn of a new year.
Help us to discard the old ways of the old year and
to walk a new path in the new year,
waiting faithfully for Your blessing in solemn and
prayerful patience.
Together with the old year, we want to lay down our old sins.
In the new year, through the strength and mercy of God,
which we have experienced so often in the past,
we want to crucify the "old I" on the cross.
In the old year we have had many troubles, and therefore we plead
that in the new year You will grant us contentment with our lot
so that we will look forward to every new day with confidence
and venture forth with God at our side.
May Your bountiful blessings accompany us in the new year:
peace and quiet for our heart.
May there be flowers aplenty on our path and
may our joy as well as our grief be hallowed by God.
In the name and for the sake of Jesus Christ.

Amen.

IN SAFE KEEPING

"I am with you and will watch over you wherever you go...I will not leave you until I have done what I have promised you" (Gen. 28:15).

Here we find a wonderful, all-encompassing promise for the first morning of a new year. The old year is behind us with all its burdens of guilt and sin, its sorrows and disappointments, its dark days and difficult hours. Now, because of the eternal faithfulness of God, we may enter the new year with this declaration of the gospel, this joyful message, which continues to resound in our ears. May God allow it also to permeate our deepest heart.

We are heading towards an unknown future, and despite what we have left behind in the old year, we will not be free of troubles and worries. We are, after all, human children with much anxiety and little faith. This is why we stand terrified and weak before the unknown.

However, now the almighty God comes and reads the fear and worry in our eyes, and speaks to us as He did to Jacob, the one-time drifter: "Don't be afraid. I am with you. The promises that I have made I will keep." These words fall like heavenly music upon our ears.

Through Jesus Christ this God is our God. If we believe, we are God's redeemed children through Christ, and we will never have to doubt His eternal faithfulness. God has spoken these words, and each promise will be consummated in our lives if we wait patiently for Him.

I thank You, Lord my God, that regardless of whether I lie down or get up, You continually watch over me. When I venture upon unknown paths, You support me with Your strength. Thank You for always being faithful and that the night will never become so dark that Your light will become invisible to me.

DON'T LOSE YOUR WAY

Show me your ways, O LORD, teach me your paths; guide me in your truth and teach me, for you are God my Savior (Ps. 25:4-5).

There are very few of us who haven't been lost at some point in our lives, usually because we took a back road. It was Langenhoven who said, "Never take a back road, because there is a reason why the highway doesn't run along there."

Maybe we attempted an unknown road by car or foot and suddenly realized that we had lost our way. At that moment our greatest need is for a road map or a friendly helper to guide us back to the right road. If we refuse to accept advice in such circumstances, we run the risk of only worsening our situation.

It is the same in life. You set out on a project or an action that swiftly turns out to be mistaken; or you have to make a choice and it becomes apparent that you have chosen the wrong option. Or maybe you have to make a decision, but you can't, because your perspective is obscured and forces beyond your control make it difficult for you.

Throughout the journey of life, we must lay every decision we have to make before God. Then, wait in the quiet of His presence to give you guidance, so that you can be sure that you are setting forth in faith, and know that you are not alone because Jesus the living Christ will be there to guide you on the right path. It would be the height of folly to ignore this fact on your journey into the new year.

Lord Jesus, Governor and Finisher of my faith, help me not to follow my own heart, but to wait quietly for Your guidance so that I will walk the right path.

HOW WILL I KNOW
THE RIGHT WAY?

"I will instruct you and teach you in the way you should go;
I will counsel you and watch over you" (Ps. 32:8).

Who will need to grope their way in the dark if the faithful God will be our guidepost? Even if we have to pass through torment and strife, we will arrive at the right destination, as long as God's Word remains our truth: "I will teach you everything about the path that you must travel."

The question is whether we will follow the heavenly Guidepost; whether we want to be taught by Him. Unfortunately there are so many of us who do not want to allow Him to teach us, even if we piously say that we do. We have said it so often in the past, and yet we don't truly want to see the Guidepost planted in the ground before us. We want to walk our own path without any interference. Isn't it then understandable that we end up being disappointed with dashed hopes?

Today's text contains another powerful word of comfort: "I will keep watch over you." Is this truly a word of comfort to us? Will it be a relief to us, knowing that God's eyes are upon us? He pays attention to the path that we are walking. May the thought of this keep us from wandering onto a wrong path and prevent us from committing deeds and speaking words that do not demonstrate love.

The eyes of God will be upon us. May this, which is intended as eminent consolation, not become a sentence to us.

We praise and thank You, O God, that we may entrust the path
of our lives to You. When we call upon You in faith and trust,
You are always there to support us and show us the right way.

YOUR DEVELOPING PRAYER LIFE

*Grow in the grace and knowledge of our Lord
and Savior Jesus Christ (2 Pet. 3:18).*

Of the spiritual luggage that you will carry with you into the new year, prayer is one of the most important components. Some people maintain that prayer is easy. Others believe that it is difficult. If you are trying to develop a growing and meaningful prayer life, you will know that both these statements contain some truth.

With the best intentions in your heart you set aside time for a peaceful time of prayer, but just as you are preparing yourself, something intrudes upon these precious moments: a telephone call, a knock on the door, a sudden reminder of something you should have done. You can be sure that the Devil will leave no stone unturned to prevent you from praying.

It would be a good idea to take these things that distract you and enfold them with your prayers. Take the disturbances that the Devil places in your way and change them into subjects for prayer.

Prayer is not a static entity, but a dynamic, pulsating gift that needs to be used continually if it is to retain its power and fulfill its function of leading you into a more intimate relationship with God. If your prayer life is weak and ineffectual, you become like a motor battery that hasn't been used for some time: it cannot fulfill the task for which it was created. Recharge your prayer batteries through disciplined prayer and feel how God starts working in your life.

*Lord Jesus, let me discover the wonder and the power
of prayer anew through the inspiration of the Holy Spirit.
Sanctify my prayers and make me faithful in my prayer life.*

YOUR FAITH WILL BE TESTED

"However, when the Son of Man comes,
will he find faith on the earth?" (Lk. 18:8).

How will one be able to face the future without faith? As the writer of Hebrews says, "Now faith is being sure of what we hope for and certain of what we do not see" (Heb. 11:1).

In the final days of the old millennium, many things were said and written about the world as it is at present. Violence continually erupts and signs of permissiveness, lawlessness, and anarchy are commonplace. We often hear the clarion call reminding us that we live in the last days and that the second coming of Christ is at hand. There is nothing more that humanity can do to prevent the destruction of the world.

Regardless of whether there is any substance to these predictions, and despite the fact that chaos is rampant, we are not allowed to abandon the standards set by Christ. The fact that the world is in a desperate state does not give Christians the right or an excuse to give up in the struggle against the forces of the Evil One.

Our Christian commitment lasts for a lifetime. Despite the Evil One's efforts to undermine the Church of Christ, despite the pressures building up against the Christian faith, it remains your duty to exalt the name of Christ. Through His strength you must hold on to everything that He has taught, so that when He returns, you will hear these words from His holy mouth: "Well done, good and faithful servant!…Come and share in your master's happiness!" (Mt. 25:23).

When the days of trial come, Lord my God, strengthen me in
my faith so that I will not fail in truly being Your faithful witness.

WHEN THINGS GO WRONG, PRAY!

"I revealed myself to those who did not ask for me;
I was found by those who did not seek me. To a nation that
did not call on my name, I said, 'Here am I, here am I'" (Is. 65:1).

When things go wrong, there are always those who question the existence of God. In the midst of the chaos of personal tragedy we hear their cry of distress: "If there is a God, why does He allow such things to happen?"

The brutality of war or the death of a child is used as the basis of an argument in which the love of God is denied. Time and again God stands as the accused, as if He is simply allowing the tragedy to happen. God's love is denied and the skeptics flourish by using these arguments to drive people further and further away from God's protective love.

God's immutable promise to His children has always been, and will always be, that if they only turn to Him in prayer, He will hear their voices and answer their prayers. Jesus promised, "Whoever comes to Me I will never drive away" (Jn. 6:37). The almighty God challenges His children and says, "Return to Me with all your heart…Rend your heart and not your garments. Return to the Lord your God" (Joel 2:12-13).

Whatever your worries, however desperate your situation, turn in sincere prayer to God and gratefully accept His guidance.

When I am tired and overburdened, weak and unbelieving, Lord Jesus,
I turn to You in prayer so that I may receive new strength and vigor.
Help me in this through Your Holy Spirit who prays for me.

THE GLORY OF TODAY

This is the day the LORD has made;
let us rejoice and be glad in it (Ps. 118:24).

We can't change the past, and the future is a mystery to us. Therefore, the present is of crucial importance. By living in the moment we can bring homage to the past and prepare ourselves for the future.

People realize the importance of the present in different ways. Some people are continually involved in big plans that they want to accomplish at some point in the future, and any sacrifice in the present is worthwhile because the future is bright with possibility. The serious student will sacrifice his sport and social life to realize his dreams. But wise is the student who manages to keep his eyes fixed on future ideals while enjoying the accumulation of knowledge for the sake of the satisfaction that it provides in the days of his preparation.

There was a time in the history of Christianity when the present was scorned and only the future was of any value to the serious believer. It was a "pie in the sky when you die" approach to life and faith. Currently, this religious philosophy is on the wane, and the truth is dawning increasingly on people: Jesus Christ, who is our perfect Master in the art of life, is not only involved in the heaven after life, but wants to establish heaven in the hearts of people here and now.

When you venture forth on the path of this new year with Jesus Christ, the present is filled with His glory and life becomes indescribably beautiful and good.

Heavenly Governor, though the future is unknown,
I confidently place it in Your almighty hands,
so that I may enjoy the present.

WHAT DO WE
OWE ONE ANOTHER?

*Let no debt remain outstanding, except the
continuing debt to love one another (Rom. 13:8).*

If we consider the matter carefully, we all have so much to be grateful
for to the Lord. Despite the fact that we become dejected and pessimistic
when things go wrong, we must realize that God's mercy and love for
us are infinite. He granted you life and the freedom of choice to do with
this life what you wish. You may be blessed with a happy family who
loves you deeply. Even the most dejected person will, if he ponders the
matter seriously and honestly, inevitably find something for which he
can thank and praise God.

How do you prove your gratitude to God for the bountiful grace
in your life? No money, no commodities, no hours of service can be
sufficient payment for His love. He bestows all these benefactions upon
you and then ultimately sacrifices His life for you.

Love can never be repaid sufficiently, because it is an article that is
simultaneously precious and priceless. You cannot measure the magnitude of it; it cannot be weighed to determine its value. Love can only be
passed on and shared.

Here you have the only way in which you can acknowledge the great
love that God has for you: by sharing it with each person whose path
crosses yours on your pilgrimage into the future.

*O Holy Spirit, help me to understand the lesson of true love
as God has taught it to us through Jesus Christ. Grant that
my every thought, word, and deed will be an act of love for You.*

FOR DAYS WHEN EVERYTHING GOES WRONG

*"To whom do you belong, and where are you going,
and who owns all these animals in front of you?" (Gen. 32:17).*

When the one drab, humdrum day follows the other with tedious regularity and it seems as if your life has no meaning or purpose, it is easy to develop the attitude that nothing in life is worthwhile.

If this is your unfortunate experience, it proves that you are busy losing your grip on life—or that you have already lost it. Life must have purpose and significance if you are to live meaningfully. How is it possible to develop such a depressed attitude? Maybe you have been doing the same work for years, and as far as you can see, you will be doing it for many years to come. What, you may justifiably ask, is the use of thinking that circumstances will change? You feel as if you have reached a dead-end street.

One of the facts of being a born-again Christian is that it changes your attitude towards life. While you previously lived without hope or expectation, Christ now plants new hope in your heart and makes all dejection and despair disappear. When you truly start living in Christ, you look with new eyes of understanding and love at life.

This new concept of life that is conveyed by Christ gives life meaning, so that you will never again have to ask, "Is it worthwhile to live?" When the powerful thoughts of Christ fill you and the Holy Spirit's strength saturates your spirit, you realize the rich quality of your faith, and you will never again question the meaning of life.

*Lord Jesus, You came so that we may have life in abundance.
Let me come to You in dark days, so that my life may be
infused with significance and meaning once again.*

WHAT WOULD JESUS DO?

*Therefore, brothers, we have an obligation—but it is not
to the sinful nature, to live according to it (Rom. 8:12).*

The temptation to act in a normal, human manner in any given situation is always present. Consequently, the sharpness of the tongue will also always be inclined to make a painful and caustic remark.

Cruelty will inevitably manifest itself, with the sole purpose of winning points. A prolonged feud may result from a refusal to forgive some trifling matter. It is fairly accurate to say that most of the world's ills have their origins in the weakness and faithlessness of human nature.

To overcome the temptation to take revenge or to react in a way that will damage your relationship with someone else, first calm down and think before you act. Consider how Jesus would handle the situation. The Scriptures contain many instances of the hostility, ridicule, false accusations, humiliation, and rejection that He had to suffer. And despite this, He said and did nothing without love.

Regardless of how strong the temptation is to react in anger in any situation, stop for a moment and allow the Spirit of God to flow through your heart and spirit. In so doing, you will know that you will not be the cause of someone else's hurt. Through the love that you show you will emerge from the circumstances as a victor in Jesus Christ.

*Heavenly Teacher, help me through the Holy Spirit
to restrain my tongue and my emotions.
Grant that I will always manifest Your tolerant love.*

WHAT ARE YOU
STRIVING FOR THIS YEAR?

"But seek first his kingdom and his righteousness,
and all these things will be given to you as well" (Mt. 6:33).

Stories of people who started out with nothing and made a great success of life make for inspiring reading material. People tend to find immense satisfaction in their achievements, but the fact remains that they are part of the human race and have therefore been created in the image of God. It is only by admitting this fact that they may avoid foolish conceit. Successful people need salvation just as desperately as those who have made mistakes in life.

Have you noticed how success can change a person's entire personality? If financial success becomes an obsession to the extent that all other things are excluded, people lose the ability to understand and love their fellow man. Of much greater importance than acquiring success and money is developing an honorable character.

The most reliable builders of character are the laws of God, as portrayed by the living Christ. If you share your life with Him, your character will be formed after His image. An old hymn declares: "I want to be like Jesus, so humble and so soft. His words were always friendly and His voice was always soft."

This should be the goal of every child of God, be he rich or poor, successful or unsuccessful. To aspire to the highest and best in Christ is your calling and responsibility in the year ahead.

Merciful Master, I praise You for the fact that the
more I live in You, the more I develop a balanced
set of values and a pure spiritual consciousness.

ENCHANTED BY THE PEACE OF CHRIST

"Peace I leave with you; my peace I give you...Do not let your hearts be troubled and do not be afraid" (Jn. 14:27).

At some point in our lives, we all yearn for peace and inner calm. The general uncertainty of our world creates a sense of restlessness; illness, death, insecurity, and domestic disturbances cause worry and strife in our minds. The list of our troubles is endless, but the results are always the same: anxiety and stress.

Many people who experience such emotions seek professional help. The psychiatrist's couch and sedatives become an accepted way of life for them. Others, who lack willpower, turn to drugs and alcohol in an attempt to erase the reality of the present. Still others suffer in silence while life slowly loses all its meaning and significance for them. They continue living in a void that is bereft of everything worthwhile.

The only way to handle all the pressures and tensions of life is to possess a faith that is firmly anchored in Jesus Christ. Your relationship with Him cannot be a transient matter or a question of convenience. You have to practice a permanent experience of unity with Him in your entire way of life.

Hold on to God in all situations; talk to Him, however desperate you may be; know for certain that He is always with you. Even though it may be difficult for you to understand His peace, you will recognize it when it flows through your being, relieving all your fears.

Help me, Lord Jesus, to hold on to You, thus receiving Your peace in every situation in my life. Let your peace flow from me to all my fellow human beings.

THE HOLY SPIRIT IS OF CARDINAL IMPORTANCE

"The Spirit gives life." (Jn. 6:63).

Every human being develops physically. What is not as common as physical development is intellectual development. It requires effort and discipline. There are those who refuse to accept the challenge to develop mentally, simply because of their laziness. While all people do not have the same intellectual ability, there are many people who do not optimally utilize their abilities. The spiritual dimension is neglected or ignored because it cannot be determined or analyzed that easily.

And yet the spirit that is in you is of cardinal importance. If the spirit in you is strong, your physical and mental powers are influenced by its vigor. A strong spirit stimulates the intellect, and physical shortcomings may be regulated and even overcome through its power. Such a powerful spirit is the result of a living communion with Christ. To live in harmony with Him and to grow in the awareness of His living presence develops your thoughts and spirit and allows you to grow spiritually. This is pre-eminently the work of the Holy Spirit.

Jesus Himself developed spiritually, intellectually, and physically. If He had to go through this process of growth, how much more do we need to go through it? The tragedy of modern Christianity is that many disciples who have accepted Jesus Christ as Savior have stopped growing, because they have not given the Holy Spirit a central place in their spiritual lives. Stagnation results in spiritual death. Through the Holy Spirit we must continue to grow in Jesus Christ.

God, help me never to stop growing spiritually. Make me mature in body, thought, and spirit by remaining true to You.

FOR DAYS OF SORROW

The LORD will be your everlasting light,
and your days of sorrow will end (Is. 60:20).

There is nothing that we, as powerless humans, can do when God decides to take away a loved one from us through death. Regardless of how strong you are spiritually, you always experience profound sorrow during those moments of utter powerlessness and loss. Despite the fact that the Scriptures assure you that the death of the body is the passageway to the eternal glory of God, your human feelings of sorrow and loss dictate your grief at that moment.

In moments like these God lovingly calls to you to turn to Him and find peace in Him. The living Christ, who assures you that you will ultimately be reunited with Him, waits to lead you tenderly from your sorrowful darkness towards His wonderful light and the house that He went to prepare for you and your loved ones.

While it may be true that words sound hollow in your deep sorrow, it is just as true that the Spirit of the loving Christ can and will comfort you if only you would open your heart to Him. Allow Him to support you in your sorrow and to lead you on His path. Invite Him into your life and He will light your way and fill you with His peace. Then you will be able to start living on the sunny side of life again.

Thank You, Lord Jesus, that You conquered death and that
me and my loved ones will also be resurrected because You
were resurrected. Let me not grieve like one who has no hope.

TO DO GOD'S WILL
ACCORDING TO GOD'S WAY

Teach me, O LORD, to follow your decrees;
then I will keep them to the end (Ps. 119:33).

There are many servants of the Lord who diligently serve Him, but who keep the love of their hearts from Him. These people serve the Lord in many different ways, but often these are ways of their own choice. When they are challenged to a form of service that demands more sacrifices, they merely work harder and are more dedicated at their own choice.

While all work done for the Lord benefits the one doing it—no one can work for the Lord without being blessed—the only work that is truly beneficial is the work done according to His holy will.

The problem is to know what the will of God is for you. However, if you have compassion for others' physical and spiritual problems and needs, it will help you to understand God's way better. When the suffering of others compels you to compassion as well as action, you are most surely acting within the will of the Master. Christ was always profoundly touched when witnessing other people's suffering, especially the suffering of the innocent. If you become aware of someone else's spiritual distress and you offer your heart, thoughts, spirit, and voice to God, asking Him to enable you to help, you will be astonished at your own responses while God is using you in His service.

I am willing, Lord, to do Your work according to
Your way. Let Your Holy Spirit guide me not to follow
the path of my own heart, but to wait prayerfully so
that I will know the path on which You want me to go.

INTO THE FUTURE
WITH CHRIST

"Be strong and courageous. Do not be terrified; do not be discouraged, for the LORD your God will be with you" (Josh. 1:9).

We usually step into the new year with mixed feelings. Aware of the failures of the past, you go towards the future with a certain degree of hesitation. Will the failures of the past be repeated this year, and will that soul-destroying monotony remain with you this year?

What the new year holds will depend largely on yourself. You may try to side-step its challenges and continue in the same old rut that you have been in for so many years. Alternatively, you can jump at the opportunities that the new year presents you with and start with a completely new lifestyle and approach to life.

There are two ways of handling the challenges of the new year. You can approach it in the same way as in the past: resolute to do better, but in your heart convinced that you will be back in the same old rut of unfulfilled expectations and doleful failures before the end of January. Alternatively, you can go to meet the new year with the full realization of who you are, but also with the conviction that you serve a wonderful God who desires only victory and fulfillment for you.

God invites you to enter into a partnership with Him. He offers you not only the gifts and grace of an intensified spiritual life, but also the privilege of being a saved child of God through Jesus Christ. If you step into the new year with trust and faith in Jesus Christ, nothing in the future can hold defeat or failure for you.

Holy Lord Jesus, because You have given me Your Spirit,
I can face the future with courage and confidence.
For this I praise and thank You from the depths of my heart.

THE LIGHT ON YOUR WAY

God said, "Let there be light," and there was light (Gen. 1:3).

When a year has rushed to its end and we look back upon the road traveled, we tend to only see things like adversity, violence, disasters, and strife. When we then look towards the future everything seems gloomy and pitch dark, and we fear the future. There is no getting away from the fact that the past leaves much to be desired. As a result many people feel that they can expect no better from the future, and this hopelessness makes them despondent.

If this is your heart's disposition towards the new year that stretches ahead of you, it is very likely that this will happen. What we expect in our hearts usually happens to us. You must think positively and believe in order to obtain positive results. As you journey through the new year, you will have to live on the reserves of your faith. You must call into remembrance all the great deeds of God throughout the centuries and place your trust in Him to lead you on His perfect path.

The prayer of your heart should be every day: "Lead me, O Light of the world!" Even today Jesus Christ is still the Light of the world, and He has promised that those who follow Him will never walk in darkness. There is no darkness that He cannot illuminate. He invites you to continue this year's journey in His company. Take His hand in faith and trust and experience Him as the light of your life.

God of light and truth, thank You that Your Son has illuminated my life so that I may walk towards the future in faith and trust. Be my light, even when darkness falls around me.

A LIFE OF VICTORY

For everyone born of God overcomes the world. This is the
victory that has overcome the world, even our faith (1 Jn. 5:4).

Maybe you are one of those people who find life in its entirety an immense struggle. Everything you undertake ends up in frustration and possibly in failure. This unhappy situation may lead to diminished self-confidence, so that you shrink back from new endeavors and start accepting the false perception that nothing you undertake will succeed. Even before you have started you have given up on yourself.

Self-pity is like a consuming cancer in your life. It destroys your belief in yourself and in what you can achieve. When you pity yourself, you are your own worst enemy. Self-pity creates self-centeredness, and once this disease pervades your thoughts and spirit, your whole world becomes centered on yourself. Such a person is usually egotistical and fails to find the purpose and meaning of true life.

The only way to avoid a life of self-inflicted limitation is to accept the discipline of faith. It is inspirational and elevates you above self-interest, thereby imparting a deeper and broader perspective on life. It enables you to admit that it is only through the strength and influence of the living Christ and through the Holy Spirit that lives in you that you are able to constructively deal with the problems and failures that come your way.

Through faith in Christ you can live on conquered ground from day to day. Do this, and the beautiful flowers of the new year will unfold before you.

Holy Master, I thank You that I may live victoriously because
I believe that You are my Savior and that the Holy Spirit
lives in me. I thank You for every victory that I win over myself.

Read Job 8:1-13

DO NOT SCORN THE DAY OF SMALL THINGS

"Your beginnings will seem humble,
so prosperous will your future be" (Job 8:7).

Many people are so excited by the big and important things in life that they fail to see the apparently unimportant matters that carry the seeds of true greatness. There are many industrial and business ventures that originated in a backyard or a simple kitchen. They all started with an idea, were inspired by knowledge, and made possible through hard work and an iron will to succeed. Never in the history of mankind have there been more true tales of humble people, motivated by an idea, who created something out of nothing.

There are people who find shelter in the false perception that everything worthwhile has already been thought of by people who are cleverer than they are, and that it is therefore not worth the trouble to start something new. Nothing could be further from the truth. The world is full of ideas that are waiting to be discovered. But how?

Many people find it strange to think that contemplation is the channel for creative thought. True Christianity is involved in every facet of life, and if it is to be effective it must encompass your entire life. True Christianity can never be confined to the inside of the church. All constructive ideas have their origins in God, the great Creator. Those who wait for Him in a spirit of excited anticipation, who are sensitive to His guidance, will receive new ideas. This will lead to a practical manifestation of our faith and to spiritual growth.

Father, make me sensitive to Your perfect guidance, in my spiritual as well as practical life. Fill me with holy idealism, only in Your honor.

DON'T TRY BARGAINING WITH GOD

"Do not test the LORD your God as you did at Massah" (Deut. 6:16).

You cannot try bargaining with God. There are people—some in complete innocence—who in their prayers tend to offer God something in exchange for the fulfillment of their requests. Despite the fact that there may have been instances where people did receive what they had asked for, it remains an undesirable practice that can easily have a negative influence on your faith.

It is imperative that you realize and accept the fact that everything you are and everything you have comes only through the grace of God. Because He loves you He provides in all your needs according to the wealth of His mercy and the all-powerfulness of His will.

It is also essential for you to accept that you belong to Him. You have been redeemed through the sacrifice of Jesus Christ on the cross, and now you belong to Him. From these facts it becomes clear that you cannot bargain with Him on the basis that you will do something for Him if He will give you something in exchange.

The right approach is to lay all your concerns and requests before Him and then to wait faithfully. Accept that whatever He ordains for you will be good, and acknowledge it as being within His will.

If this is your attitude in your prayers, you will experience the peace of God that flows from faith in and acceptance of the will of your heavenly Father.

> *Your will for me, O Father, is only good. Therefore I will wait patiently for Your answer to every prayer I pray. Keep me faithfully at Your feet so that Your plan for my life may come to fruition.*

SCRIPTURAL RELIGION

"Why do you call me, 'Lord, Lord,'
and do not do what I say?" (Lk. 6:46).

Why is it that so many good, churchgoing people today experience a sense of disappointment and failure that borders on despair? They have faithfully attended church throughout their entire lives and honestly feel that they truly love God in their own way. Despite this they suffer from spiritual malnutrition. There is something important lacking in their spiritual experiences.

The answer may lie precisely in the fact that they love God in their own way, instead of in the scriptural way. They have created a form of Christianity that fits neatly into their lifestyle. This private and personal version of Christianity turns them into masters of compromise. They find excuses not to forgive; they are selective in who they want to love; their business negotiations are controlled by whatever suits them at that moment and not by scriptural principles.

Scriptural Christianity starts with an act of repentance and confession. This implies a complete turn-around and an awareness of the presence of the living Christ. Scriptural Christianity means complete obedience to God and to the standards set out by Christ. These standards are found in the New Testament, and the Master commands us to keep them.

Such demands are not unreasonable, because when He calls us He also equips His disciples with His Holy Spirit. When we are empowered in this way, Jesus Christ guides us into the fullness of life.

Thank You, Lord Jesus, that You came so that
we may have abundant life. Keep me from seeking
my spiritual salvation outside the Scriptures.

DIVINE PROTECTION

They remembered that God was their Rock,
that God Most High was their Redeemer (Ps. 78:35).

There have been countless occasions in history when it seemed as if all was lost and all hope was gone. People and even nations were forced to admit defeat in an unequal battle against the superior numbers of the enemy.

Even so, there have been even more cases in which deliverance came to people and nations in answer to their prayers. God has saved people and nations from obliteration in miraculous ways and has enabled them to overcome dangers, transforming defeat into victory.

These cases, both personal and historical, should serve as a constant reminder of the victorious omnipotence of God in all spheres of life. No circumstances are too small or too big for Him, and no prayer will remain unheard or unanswered. This is the extent of God's unfathomable love for His people and His world.

Where you now go to meet a new, unknown year in which adverse circumstances may threaten to overwhelm you, or fear may make your heart tremble, remember that Christ has given His life for you. Turn to Him and lay your fears at His feet, because only in Him will you find deliverance from your distress.

Lord my God, You are a safe fortress to me; a shield
against every calamity that threatens to befall me.
You promised to be my keeper who will not slumber or sleep.
In this knowledge I step into the unknown with confidence.

GO WITH GOD

When his master saw that the LORD was with him
and that the Lord gave him success in everything
he did, Joseph found favor in his eyes (Gen. 39:3-4).

It seldom happens that two people experience the presence of God in their lives in exactly the same way. It is one of the great mysteries and joys of the Christian faith that the triune God manifests Himself in so many different ways to His children, to each according to his personal situation, circumstances, and needs.

The Christian disciple is often discouraged when hearing of the refreshing and astonishing experiences of others who have felt the touch of Jesus in their lives and who have experienced unforgettable moments of ecstasy in which they knew without a doubt that they were in the presence of the risen Christ.

If you have experienced these feelings of discouragement, which can so easily make you despondent, don't allow it to influence your relationship with God negatively. You are a very special person to God. Not only are you His unique once-off creation, but you are His child, and as your heavenly Father He knows your needs better than you know them yourself. As a result the omniscient, loving Father will always be with you in a special way to fulfill your unique needs.

All that is expected of you is to wait quietly for Him and to know that He is God.

Faithful Father, I find peace and quiet with You
and rejoice in Your lasting presence in my life.
May I step into the future with Your loving
hand upon mine and with faith in my heart.

HE KNOWS AND HE UNDERSTANDS

He did not need man's testimony about man,
for he knew what was in a man (Jn. 2:25).

Because Christ understands your weaknesses, it doesn't mean that He excuses your sins. He, who was tempted like us in all respects, has called you to a life of victory through the strength of His immanent Holy Spirit. Unfortunately those things which people call "weaknesses" for convenience's sake, and which are really just sins, rob our spiritual lives of their growth and vigor. These things create an obstacle between our spiritual lives and Christ.

As far as Christ is concerned there are no insignificant sins, because all sin separates the human being from the Master. As soon as there is a weakening in people's relationship with Christ, they will always find trifling excuses to defend their missteps.

Christ never tries to gloss over sin. He understands human weakness and frailty, offers forgiveness, and purifies us, saves us, and gives us the spiritual strength to live victoriously.

Christ looks beyond man's sin and sees what he can become through the power of God's Holy Spirit. He does not see us as struggling, failed and imperfect beings, but as channels of the grace of God who do His will in the sphere of life where He has placed us. Because He knows what people are like, He knows their potential and desires to lead them to the perfection that God has ordained for them.

> *Holy Jesus, please look beyond what I am and inspire*
> *me to be what You know I can be. Let me never hide*
> *behind my weaknesses while Your Holy Spirit is available.*

BE WARY OF FALSE PROPHETS

They want to be teachers of the law, but they do not know what they are talking about or what they so confidently affirm (1 Tim. 1:7).

There is increasing confusion in the thoughts of the average Christian. He is confused by the variety of interpretations of the Scriptures. All over the world there is a conflict of opinions among the leaders of denominations, churches, and sects, who place their own interpretations on the Word of God and preach their religious convictions accordingly.

For example, much is written and read about liberation theology, or the sociopolitical gospel. The issue of surrendering to Christ differs from one group to the next. In this situation there is a real danger that the man on the street will become so confused and disillusioned that he will soon be completely lost for the church of Christ.

The foundation of our Christian faith is God's love for us through His Son, Jesus: "For God so loved the world that He gave His one and only Son, that whoever believes in him shall not perish but have eternal life" (Jn. 3:16). The unavoidable requirement of the Christian faith is complete surrender to Jesus Christ, because a love so divinely wonderful demands all—body, mind, and spirit.

Any doctrine that is not founded on love and surrender, is not centered on Christ, and does not give all the glory to God, is false and only worthy of rejection. The Scriptures seriously warn us against false prophets. Let us pay heed to this warning.

*Lord and Master, amidst conflicting doctrines
I commit myself inextricably to Your pure gospel of love.*

THE MIRACULOUS POWER OF PRAISE

My heart is steadfast, O God; I will sing and make music with all my soul. Awake, harp and lyre! I will awaken the dawn (Ps. 108:1-2).

We often use prayer to thank God for what He has done for us, to lay our needs before Him, and to confess our sins and shortcomings to Him. It is sad, but true, that we often neglect to express our praise of Him in prayer.

Never underestimate the power of praise in your prayer life. If someone impresses you, you speak words of praise towards the person. Good artists, professional athletes, musicians, and singers are showered with praise. There is always a rapport between the giver and the receiver of praise.

Why shouldn't we then shower the benevolent God with praise? Think of all the remarkable things that He has done; the miracles that flow from Him; the extraordinary extent of His love.

Ponder for a moment the wonders of the universe and creation; of human life and achievement—and praise and glorify God. More than anyone He is worthy of our love and thanksgiving.

If you concentrate on praising and glorifying God, you will create a very special relationship with the living Christ, which will transform your prayer life and intensify your love for Him. Through your praise you will become a stronger witness for Him.

Great and wonderful God, we want to exalt Your name without end, and praise and glorify You for all the wonders of Your love and grace that You give to us even though we don't deserve it.

Read Psalm 111:1-10

WHEN KNOWLEDGE BECOMES WISDOM

The fear of the LORD is the beginning of wisdom; all who follow his precepts have good understanding (Ps. 111:10).

Knowledge is a wonderful thing, and one can never have enough of it. Anyone who specializes in a particular field of knowledge in order to serve others more effectively deserves our gratitude and appreciation. The collection of knowledge keeps the mind active and vigorous. The Scriptures declare that the Lord is a God of profound knowledge (see 1 Sam. 2:3). A thirst for knowledge is actually a yearning for a deeper understanding of God and His ways.

Knowledge in itself is insufficient unless it is aligned with God; not necessarily in a purely spiritual manner, but with an all-encompassing love for life, which transforms knowledge into wisdom as a consequence of an intimate understanding of God.

Unfortunately there are people who are intellectually brilliant, but who fail to create meaningful relationships with other people. They cannot control their behavior and emotions and are often poor partners because they lack understanding and appreciation.

The Word of God teaches us: "The fear of the Lord teaches a man wisdom" (Prov. 15:33). To honor God and to build an intimate relationship with Him through Jesus Christ is the first step in transforming knowledge into inspired wisdom. Therefore, maintain communion with God through prayer, Bible study, and contemplation.

God of wisdom, make me wise in Your ways, through the Spirit. Let me wait for You constantly so that I can develop an intimate relationship with You. Preserve me from knowledge without wisdom.

ARE YOU SEEKING JESUS?

But Herod said, "I beheaded John. Who, then, is this I hear such things about?" And he tried to see him (Lk. 9:9).

In our time there are many people who, like Herod, tirelessly search for Jesus. They seek Him in worship, contemplation, prayer, and Bible study. People go into retreat and seclude themselves from the world, or attend conferences, seminars, and workshops in an attempt to encounter the Son of God. Thousands attend evangelical gatherings in the hope of finding Christ in the ecstasy of worship or in the drama of divine healing and conversions.

There are also those whose living faith has lost its fervor, and who feel the need to renew their attempts to get back to the Christ who meant so much to them before. Many achieve success in this mission and enjoy the wonder of new communion with the Master. Others fail and their spiritual lives remain barren, stark, and desolate; their faith fades and they drift further and further away from Him.

If you sincerely and earnestly seek Jesus, there is one certain way of finding Him: seeking Him among people. Wherever there is distress you will surely find Him, and He will be with you in any deed of compassion that you perform. The Christ that you seek lives in the hearts and minds of people and in the smile of gratitude which you receive when you bestow love and compassion on others. It is here that you will meet the Master you are seeking.

Beloved and compassionate Master, it is when I serve others with love that I am repeatedly surprised by meeting You. Thank You for manifesting Yourself in this way to insignificant human beings.

BE A JOYFUL CHRISTIAN

Do everything without complaining or arguing (Phil. 2:14).

The Christian's life is a life of service and submission. It may be that you are called to work among people in distress or that your calling is administration, preaching, or another form of service. Whatever it is, it will demand that you sacrifice your time and yourself in the service of Christ.

Unfortunately many people have the habit of performing their tasks for Christ with a negative attitude. They will do their work and often do it exceptionally well, but they are unpleasant people with poor interpersonal relationships. This spoils the quality of their deeds, which should have been manifestations of compassion or mercy in the name of Christ. The result is that people hesitate to approach them because of the attitude that they encounter.

You must always remember that whatever task you are assigned to do for Jesus is to be done in His name, and therefore your attitude will have a positive or negative influence on the Christian faith. To ensure that you reflect the glory and love of God in everything that you do, you must do it in the strength of the Holy Spirit.

Follow the example of love, compassion, understanding, and humility that Christ set in His ministry. In this way your discipleship and service will be fruitful and effective, and fulfill its ultimate purpose to exalt God.

Master and Guide, I newly dedicate myself and my strength to Your service. Make me a joyful servant because I find my joy in You.

LIVE ONE DAY AT A TIME

"For today the LORD will appear to you" (Lev. 9:4).

We all tend to get impatient with ourselves sometimes. You may have been a Christian for many years and occasionally thought about deepening your prayer life and being more earnest with your Bible study. However, other things came up and claimed your attention. Your noble aspirations failed and were eventually pushed so far into the background that they were almost forgotten.

It was not your intention for this to happen, and on numerous occasions you were determined to do something positive and constructive about it. But despite your best efforts you slipped back into the old rut, once again tasting the bitter taste of failure and disappointment.

If you are determined to reaffirm your spiritual goals, don't start by making impressive vows that you know will be difficult to live up to. Learn the secret of living one day at a time and offering your very best to God throughout that day. Even then you will still have a sense of dissatisfaction because your best seems so inferior next to God's holiness and perfection.

The secret of living one day at a time for God is to do so in the strength of the living Christ. Put aside time for Christ in the early hours of each day and utilize this time optimally. It will place the entire day in the right perspective, and you will discover that as you experience every day in His presence, your spiritual life will grow and become meaningful.

Holy God, I want to live each day in Your holy presence so that I may grow spiritually and become stronger every day.

GROW THROUGH HUMILITY TOWARD CONFIDENCE

Rather think of yourself with sober judgment, in accordance with the measure of faith God has given you (Rom. 12:3).

We will never really know how many people harbor a negative opinion of themselves. If they serve on a committee or take part in a discussion, they are reluctant to express their opinions. Ideas are held back because they fear what others may think or say. Because they feel that they are inferior, they restrain their initiatives and live their lives filled with unspoken ideas—and the world is the poorer for it.

In the eyes of God you are of immeasurable value. God does not create nobodies. It is your privilege and your duty to develop your character and personality to its fullest potential. But how is it possible to be liberated from inferiority and to live free from limiting fears?

Accept the scriptural truth that it is possible to live in harmony with God through Jesus Christ who lives in you. Once this truth has taken possession of your mind and has become a motivational force in your life, you will be renewed to the point of understanding what life really is.

You will no longer retreat from daily challenges, because you will know that this new strength that you possess is not of your own making, but the product of the Spirit of Christ that works in you. Through your humility you will grow towards God-centered self-confidence and your life will be filled with thanksgiving and praise.

Thank You, my Savior and Friend, that I may rejoice: I can do everything through Him who gives me the strength. I want to sing Your praises!

February

Eternal God and Creator-Father,
the winter brings its own enchantments and its own apprehensions.
Thank You for rain and cold and time to read and contemplate;
for nature that waits slumbering for new growth.
Master, teach me this winter to make time for You and
to become quiet in Your presence;
to sometimes slow down to ponder
the essential matters of life;
to gather strength for a new time of growth.
The winter's cold also brings deep concerns, O Lord:
the poor and the elderly who are dying of hardship
while I sit snug and warm before the hearth;
the unemployed who do not know
where tomorrow's bread will come from;
the hungry who walk past me with beseeching eyes;
the homeless who must endure the cold outside
and feel the chill of heartless people in their bones.
Help me to care with love and to lend a helping hand.
Warm our wintry world with the glow of Your love.
In the name of the Great Merciful One, Jesus Christ.

Amen.

PUT CHRIST FIRST

So I say, live by the Spirit, and you will not
gratify the desires of the sinful nature (Gal. 5:16).

If we were truly honest with ourselves, very few of us would be able to deny that it is extremely difficult to live a good Christian life and to act in the way that Jesus expects. As a matter of fact, it is written in the Gospels that our Master Himself said this, and He never promised that it would be easy to follow Him. He explicitly warned us about the problems, dangers, and opposition that His disciples would encounter.

One of the greatest obstacles on the Christian path is our human nature with its desires, accepted practices, presumptions, and many other things that monopolize our time and attention. These things sneak into our lives, and whether we realize it or not, they relegate Christ to an inferior place in our lives.

It is needless to point out that this is an unacceptable state of affairs, and no person who bears the title of Christian can allow it. And yet, in his own deceptive and cunning way, Satan continues to tempt us to follow our own desires, to the detriment of our faith.

To resist temptation it is essential to open up your entire life to the influence of the Holy Spirit. Deliberately invite Him to take control of your life. He will undoubtedly assist you in overcoming all evil and help you to live the Christian life to which you have been called.

Lord Jesus, from experience we know that if we wait prayerfully
for You, Your Holy Spirit will give us the strength to resist
every temptation. For this we thank and praise Your holy name.

GOD STILL PERFORMS MIRACLES

Still, many in the crowd put their faith in him.
They said, "When the Christ comes, will he do
more miraculous signs than this man?" (Jn. 7:31).

Is your religious mind broad enough to expect miracles? One of the great tragedies of modern Christendom is that it has become so ordinary that it is no longer expected that miraculous events will occur. People attempt to explain everything in terms of logic, and we deny the reality and worth of a childlike faith.

Miracles happen every day—it's just that many people prefer to call them coincidences. Sick people recover as a result of faithful prayers; guidance is given in unexpected ways; a trouble maker is transformed into a law-abiding citizen through the acceptance of spiritual powers that he cannot fully explain; great distress is relieved in miraculous ways. Many people witness God's work in the lives of human beings. This truth is so genuine that only those who refuse to acknowledge and praise God for His goodness fail to see these miracles.

Jesus Christ is still an essential force in this world. Even though there are those who wish to relegate Him to only the spiritual and religious life, He is still the Lord of all life. He manifests His full glory in every sphere of human thought and action. Those who acknowledge His reign and who place their trust in Him experience the miracle of the workings of the Holy Spirit of God in their lives. In doing so, you too will discover that the time of miracles is definitely not over.

Holy Father in heaven, because You bestowed Your Holy Spirit
on me, I daily see all the miracles that You perform.

WHO CONTROLS YOUR LIFE?

You, however, are controlled not by the sinful nature but by the Spirit, if the Spirit of God lives in you (Rom. 8:9).

Are you in control of your own life, or are you controlled by changing circumstances, variable moods, and other forces beyond your comprehension or control? It may be possible that you say and do things that are not true to your nature. Paul says, "When I want to do good, evil is right there with me" (Rom. 7:21). This is a very common human experience. You therefore need an external force that is larger than yourself to control you when you cannot control yourself.

The nature and temperament that you have inherited is often a slave to destructive habits, and when you are constrained by such bonds, your whole spirit is in slavery. Even though your spirit tries to assert itself, it finds that it cannot enjoy the freedom which it intuitively knows to be its birthright. However, here is a wonderful truth of Christian principles and experience: "Where the Spirit of the Lord is, there is freedom" (2 Cor. 3:17).

When the Holy Spirit of God takes possession of your life and expresses Himself through your spirit, you will discover that your life gains new meaning and significance and is filled with spiritual strength that enables you to grow to maturity in Him.

Thank You, Lord Jesus, my Redeemer and Savior, that when Your Holy Spirit fills my life I am governed and guided by Him.

FAITH IS PRODUCTIVE

"According to your faith will it be done to you" (Mt. 9:29).

There are people who manage their faith as if it is a commercial product; something of which they either have a lot or have little, depending on the circumstances of the moment. In times of stress and tension they yearn for more faith but don't quite know where they can acquire this miraculous trust.

However, the fact is that you have faith and that your need is not for more faith, but for a change in the quality of the faith that you already have. Perhaps you have had faith in the wrong things for too long. Perhaps you have had more faith in failure than in success; you long for inner victory but are convinced that you will fail. Your actual faith isn't really a religious question; it is what, from habit, you expect life will give you. This daily expectation, which is merely another facet of faith, is what really becomes evident in your practical life.

You will agree that it is important to maintain an attitude of expectation in life: to expect only the finest and the noblest in the secure knowledge that what you expect will be realized in good time.

How is it possible to expect the best when standards are dropping so quickly and the outlook on life seems so grim? Only the person who has faith in God and His plan for the final redemption of the human race can step into the future with courage and tranquility of spirit. This enormous truth brings a reassuring purpose in your life and enables you to go towards the future with confidence.

With steadfast faith in You, my God and Father,
I step into the future with confidence and peace of mind.

WORK WITH GOD

But as for me, it is good to be near God (Ps. 73:28).

Every one of us desires what is best for us. We feel that we have a right to receive that which belongs to us. Unfortunately so many of us have never tried to define exactly what it is that we regard as our "right," and as a result we are often unhappy and complain throughout our pilgrimage through life.

This inner desire that seems to be so unattainable, and the awareness that there is something that we seek but cannot define consciously, makes us lower our expectations of life, especially regarding that which is our "right." "I have the right to happiness," and "I have the right to financial independence" are but two of the rights claimed.

Often these demands are made without stopping to think about how they may be achieved through personal involvement. Many people demand happiness, without giving it; others demand financial independence without being careful in their financial transactions. In the fulfillment of our expectations and demands, God surely has the right to our cooperation as well as our prayers.

Our Scripture verse for today contains an amazing and practical truth. When God occupies the first place in our lives and His laws govern our daily lives, the demands of our lives become of secondary importance. Then it is no longer a question of what you demand from life, but rather what you can contribute to the fulfillment of His holy will in your life. Then you will experience a life of profound joy, freedom, and lasting satisfaction.

While I seek Your gifts with a yearning heart,
O Father, I offer You my humble and willing
cooperation in the fulfillment thereof.

ARE YOU THE JUDGE?

"Do not judge, or you too will be judged" (Mt. 7:1).

Most of us tend to jump to hasty conclusions and consequently also often judge other people. A simple comment may be misunderstood, or someone's behavior may be interpreted inaccurately. You may try to avoid an unkempt person because you think that he is a drunkard who is begging again. A snippet of news that is recounted incorrectly grows as it spreads and soon the issue or person concerned is discredited. It just goes to show how easily human nature tends towards condemning others.

In some cases it is sensible and necessary to judge others. However, it is of crucial importance that you do so very carefully. You must investigate the surrounding factors in every situation and judge fairly.

In all likelihood you will find that things are not always what they seem, and that the person who is being condemned is not always entirely to blame for his faults and errors, or that he is not the person you imagined him to be. There may be a completely natural explanation for his behavior or actions, which calls for your understanding and love.

In all your interactions with people you should look for positive and commendable aspects and try to place yourself in their position. Try to act towards them as Jesus would have done. Then you will not judge somebody wrongly.

Loving Lord Jesus, help me always to look at my fellow human beings through Your eyes and with Your love.

SERVICE YIELDS FULFILLMENT

Today, if you hear his voice, do not harden your hearts (Ps. 95:7-8).

Many people in the world today are dissatisfied with their lot. Some feel that life is merely monotonous existence; others complain that they achieve nothing in life; yet others are so busy finding fault with everything that they fail to see the good things in life; and then there are those who are only interested in themselves and consequently become lonely.

The one sure path to fulfillment is to serve God among His people. There are people who need a helping hand, who seek companionship, or a friendly word of advice. There are others who yearn for encouragement or recognition. A few moments of your time can make an immense difference in their lives. Opportunities to serve God in this way come along all the time. All you need to do is open your heart to God and remain sensitive to the voice of His Holy Spirit. He will touch your conscience and guide you towards those in distress.

When this happens you should not hesitate. People often refrain from acting because they fear that they are incapable, or that their helpfulness will be misinterpreted. If you are willing to allow the living Christ to use you, you can also be sure that He will lead you to those He wishes you to serve lovingly. In addition, the Holy Spirit will put the words in your mouth and grant you the abilities to perform your task. In this way your life will become dynamic and meaningful.

> *Fill me with Your abundance, O Holy Spirit of God,*
> *until my heart overflows and streams towards those*
> *who need my ministry. Lord Jesus, keep Your love burning*
> *in my heart, because without it I cannot do Your work.*

CHRIST LIVES TODAY

"He is not here; he has risen" (Lk. 24:6).

Here we find a dynamic truth that imbues the Christian faith with strength and life. A gospel without the resurrection of Christ may be a beautiful philosophy, but it will lack the essential ingredient that elevates Christianity from a religious philosophy to the positive experience of a living faith.

When Jesus walked the earth with His disciples in the glory of His resurrection, it was not a passing mystical experience only granted to a privileged few. He promised to be with His disciples through every generation. The Spirit of Christ is just as alive and present in your life today as in the lives of the first disciples. He is the timeless Christ.

The first disciples had the privilege of knowing Him in His physical presence. Modern disciples do not have this privilege, but He becomes a living reality to those who discipline themselves and wait patiently and in silence, with their thoughts focused on His presence. This experience of knowing the living Christ is more than a psychological or emotional response to an intense, religious longing, although both these dispositions may be present believing you are in the company of Christ fills you with a presence and strength that is real and pertinent to your life.

If you live in the awareness of Christ's presence, you become increasingly sure that life is not a drab and lonely pilgrimage, but an exciting and satisfying adventure that you share with your living Master.

I thank You, risen and glorified Lord Jesus, that I may experience Your living presence and share my life with You. It gives me courage and strength for every day.

DON'T BE PARTIAL

"Do not show partiality in judging;
hear both small and great alike" (Deut. 1:17).

In your public or business life, is your judgment influenced by social status? Are you more interested in people who occupy positions of authority than in those who are typified as "ordinary people"? When you are confronted with the opinion of an important public figure as opposed to the opinion of a relatively unknown person, whose interpretation are you more likely to accept?

These questions speak to the conscience of every honest and sincere person, because there are few people who can say in all honesty that they are not in the least influenced by the opinions of important people. The opinions of a prominent businessman are newsworthy while the opinions of ordinary folk are completely ignored.

By getting caught in this trap you deprive yourself of learning the full truth. You owe it to your fellow human beings and to yourself to consider all viewpoints and to give equal attention to both sides. Otherwise you will not be able to make a well-balanced judgment.

Jesus Christ gave no exclusive preference to anyone and He had time for people from all walks of life. No one is greater than the all-seeing, all-knowing God, Jesus Christ. If the Master could do it, how much more do we owe it to each other not to be partial?

Help me, impartial Lord Jesus, to keep an open mind and
to listen to all people, regardless of their social status or wealth.

GOD IS IMMUTABLE

He set the earth on its foundations; it can never be moved (Ps. 104:5).

In every sphere of life it is essential that something will remain constant in order to ensure stability. This applies to the fields of mathematics and science, but also to your everyday life where you need a standard upon which to base your lifestyle. The lack of something constant will inevitably lead to confusion and chaos.

As far as the day-to-day life of mankind is concerned, the Lord Himself established something constant. Through the prophet Malachi He said, "I the Lord do not change" (Mal. 3:6).

People come and go; times change; fashions are in vogue one moment and passing fads the next; moral standards, behavior and principles appear to vary from one generation to the next. As a result, there is a very real danger that you will become confused and find it difficult to know how you should live your life and what exactly is expected of you.

Follow the way of the Master to overcome this problem and to free yourself from feelings of doubt and guilt. He set an example for your entire life, and if you hold on to it, you can be assured of a life of peace and fulfillment.

Holy and almighty God, help me to build upon the Rock of ages, because all other soil is uncertain and nothing but sinking quicksand.

THE MIGHTY HAND OF GOD

For the wisdom of this world is foolishness in God's sight (1 Cor. 3:19).

Throughout the ages people have claimed the honor of making the greatest discovery of all times. Looking back we see the wheel, fire and the power of steam, followed by electricity, the telephone, radio, and television. Great leaps of progress have been made in the spheres of science, mathematics, medicine, atomic, and nuclear power, and now we live in the age of the computer.

While we should by no means disparage the wonders of these discoveries, it is essential not to overlook the omnipotence of God in this world of so-called human achievement.

It would be worthwhile to take a little time to quietly ponder how mankind would have fared without the assistance of the Lord. Just as He created people, He also provided them with knowledge and abilities. The expertise of scientists, engineers, and doctors did not appear out of nowhere but is the result of God-given talent. In the same way the omnipotence of God can destroy anything which man undertakes (or abuses), if it is against His holy will.

Despite all the excitement over human achievement throughout the ages, we must never forget the mighty hand of God in all things.

Holy Father, throughout the ages Your almighty hand protected and guided Your flock. Thank You that we may experience Your presence and omnipotence in everything.

LIGHT FROM THE DARKNESS

When all the people saw this, they fell prostrate and cried,
"The LORD—he is God! The Lord—he is God!" (1 Kgs. 18:39).

Today, as in the days of Elijah, it takes an earth-shattering experience for some people to recognize the existence and omnipotence of God. People become used to a way of life that has little or no space for the Lord: they immerse themselves in their work or their chosen lifestyle.

Regardless of this, God moves in mysterious ways to manifest His wonders. These ways may be drastic. Therefore we should not judge the Lord with our senses, but trust Him for His mercy. Behind the severe ways in which He sometimes acts lies a heart full of unfathomable love.

Perhaps you have experienced adversity or tragedy, or maybe your burden seems unbearable and your problems irresolvable. At times like these, don't give in to the temptation to throw in the towel, but turn to the living Christ in faith. He was a human being just like us. He knows all about your situation, understands your distress, and is waiting to come to your assistance.

To draw people to Him, Christ underwent the torment of crucifixion. As He did then, He who leads you out of distress still sometimes uses negative circumstances to draw you closer to His heart. Accept this assurance and live in peace under the certainty of His love.

Blind disbelief is doomed to destruction, O Father.
Everything that it does is in vain. But You, wonderful
God and loving Father, have a perfect plan with every life.

GUARD AGAINST SUBTLE TEMPTATIONS

"Be careful that no one entices you by riches;
do not let a large bribe turn you aside" (Job 36:18).

The extremely dangerous consequences of compromising on your principles can never be overemphasized. Time and time again one hears of people who give in to temptation and as a result lower their moral standards. The consequences are usually disastrous, for themselves and for their families.

Initially the suggestion to compromise on your principles may appear quite innocent. You accept a small gift for an apparently insignificant favor; a suggestion that you bend the rules somewhat or turn a blind eye may be made in jest at a lunch or dinner to which you have been invited as guest.

When the suggestion that you deviate from the right course is made or even just insinuated, you should be on your guard. What starts as a trifle may soon start growing covertly, and before you know it, it will have become uncontrollable and you will find yourself in a trap from which you will struggle to escape.

Jesus made it clear that He will not tolerate compromise. He set the example for a good and virtuous Christian way of life. Follow in His footsteps and resist everything that is contrary to His principles. Only then will you live in tranquility and peace of mind.

Holy Spirit of God, help me to stand firmly against
the temptation to lower my Christian standards.
Let me live according to the will of the Master.

DON'T PUT
YOURSELF DOWN

*No, in all these things we are more than
conquerors through him who loved us (Rom. 8:37).*

There are people who constantly degrade the gifts that God has given them, so that these gifts eventually become useless. Others bemoan the fact that they are so ordinary that they have no gifts at all. Both these attitudes cause God great sorrow.

God has given each person at least one gift. It may initially be barely noticeable, but it is there and waits to be discovered and developed. You have the responsibility to first discover that gift which God has given you, and then to develop it to its fullest potential.

Initially you will experience problems and you will find numerous excuses why these gifts cannot be utilized: you are too busy, there is no time, you are under too much work pressure. But the main reason may not be immediately apparent to you. The truth of the matter is that you are scared of starting to work on God's gifts, in case you fail and cannot complete your task. Someone whispers in your ear that you are not up to the challenge, and you accept this lie at face value, without even attempting to prove it wrong.

God would never give you a gift that you cannot bring to fulfillment through effort and dedication. At first it may seem to be beyond your natural abilities, but God grants you the grace and the strength to become spiritually strong, and to develop and fully unfold the gift that He has given you.

*Thank You, Lord my God, that You foresee everything I need
to develop the gifts that You have given me to their fullest potential.*

GOD IS IN CONTROL

Then Job replied to the LORD, "I know that you can do all things; no plan of yours can be thwarted" (Job 42:1).

In every sphere of society and in every successive generation, you will meet hardened pessimists who find little or nothing that is right with this world. They see no hope for the future, and wherever they go they create an atmosphere of gloom and dejection. This attitude finds precipitation in their personal life and as a result they become mean-spirited and negative.

In the midst of this atmosphere of despair, it is beneficial to take a few minutes to ponder the greatness of God. Look back over the years and you will find example upon example of the wonderful ways in which God has transformed despair into vivacious hope; changed sorrow into joy; allowed victory to grow from defeat.

Of all these examples the one that towers above all the others is the way in which God used Jesus' crucifixion to manifest the wonder of His forgiving love in the glory of the resurrection. To those of little faith Golgotha was the end of a sorrowful road, but Easter Sunday ushered in the beginning of a wonderful new life: God's plan for the redemption of mankind had been completed.

When things around you appear dark and terrifying, hold on to the promises of God. Remember the mighty deeds that He has performed, and continue in confidence and with the certain knowledge that He is wholly in control.

Almighty God and loving Father, my heart's knowledge that You are in control allows me to be courageous even in dark days. Guide me on Your path and keep my faith strong.

UNITE BEHIND JESUS

Is Christ divided? (1 Cor. 1:13).

In an era in which the church of Christ is under constant threat, there are two main problems within the Christian community: indifference and dissension. The Evil One undermines the principles of Christ in many ways, as is evident from the manifold instances of dissipation, immorality, drug addiction, and violence in our society.

At a time when Christians ought to unite against such evils, there are indications of poorer church attendance, to such an extent that some churches have to be closed down. Doctrinal and denominational differences are driven to extremes, to the detriment of the united voice of the churches.

The church has been under fire throughout the ages and will be for as long as Satan attempts to destroy the living Christ's work of redemption. Time and time again he has made vicious attacks on the church averted only by a small but valiant band of Christians.

Until Satan is finally destroyed, as prophesied by Scripture, you can be assured that he will not abandon his attempts. Therefore it is imperative that those who call themselves Christians will stand united against the Devil. Instead of fighting each other, we should fight him.

It is the duty and privilege of everyone who bears the Master's name and who is fortified by the strength of the Holy Spirit to be diligent in their worship, to set aside all their differences, and to stand united against anything that is intended to disparage the glory of the triune God.

Lord, grant that Your followers on earth will stand united in our attack on the evil forces that threaten us. Help us not to allow insignificant differences to divide us, thus allowing the Evil One to reign supreme.

STRENGTH IN CHRIST

*My flesh and my heart may fail, but God is the strength
of my heart and my portion forever (Ps. 73:26).*

There are a variety of factors that may cause you to feel despondent, weak, and helpless. These factors cover a wide spectrum of issues, but their effect on your mental, spiritual, and physical wellbeing can be very destructive, should you allow circumstances to overwhelm you.

There is no getting away from the fact that Christians must endure problems and setbacks. Indeed, Christ warned us of this, and most of His followers were severely tried when their faith was put to the test.

The joyful assurance that you receive from Christ is that He will never abandon or forsake you. In addition, He will provide you with the ability to successfully cope with your circumstances through His strength.

To some people this may sound like an unattainable and idealistic dream, but you can transform it into a glorious reality. You have the assurance that the heavenly Guide will always be with you. All that is expected of you is to accept His Word in faith and to remain in His company. Lay your fears, worries, and hopes before Him. Do this, and you will experience the peace that surpasses all understanding.

*Holy Lord Jesus, my ability to handle my problems
emanates solely from my unconditional faith in You.*

ARE YOU EASILY HURT?

"Remain in me, and I will remain in you" (Jn. 15:4).

Perhaps you are one of those people who go through life being continually hurt by other people. You may have become so sensitive to what others think that your life has declined into a wretched existence.

If you allow this state of affairs to continue, it may have serious consequences for your whole personality. The challenge lies in the fact that you are responsible for deciding whether this situation will continue or not.

God left you with the responsibility of choice. You choose your thoughts and attitudes. You decide whether you are going to live on the pinnacle of true life or in the valley of despair. It may be that you mistakenly think that these circumstances are created by matters beyond your control. However, in reality it is the power of your thoughts that make you the person you are.

This thought could seem overwhelming if it wasn't colored by the realization of a higher power. As our thoughts control our deeds, so the Holy Spirit can also control our thoughts. If you allow the Spirit of Christ into every aspect of your life, He takes control of your thoughts, and you discover that the petty remarks and possible insults that have been thrown at you no longer have the power to hurt you.

The strength of the Holy Spirit in you is more powerful than any torment or insult hurled at you.

Thank You, Lord Jesus, that You live in me through Your Spirit, and that You give me the strength to stand steadfastly against the small-minded insults that I have to endure. Help me always to stay in You.

IS SANCTIFICATION YOUR GOAL?

"I am God Almighty; walk before me and be blameless" (Gen. 17:1).

Throughout the world the focus is on excellence and perfection. In the arts, science, and business, everyone aspires to ways of perfecting methods and machinery in the name of progress. In many cases perfection in terms of material things has become such an obsession with human beings that they have allowed moral and spiritual standards to decline or to be abandoned altogether.

The beauty of God's Creation is ravaged by pollution and waste materials while human machinery just keeps rolling on. Deadly weapons are manufactured because one nation wants to rule over another. Personal and ethical values have taken the back seat to monetary profit. This is the price exacted by progress.

There is only one kind of perfect life that is worth living, and that is the life that Christ sets out for us. Nothing else can give you true fulfillment and satisfaction, because life in Christ is eternal and constant.

Whatever your task, if you aspire to true excellence and perfection, you have to ensure that God is your guide in all your endeavors. Dedicate everything you do to Him; remain within His will; maintain the standards that Christ has set. If this is your goal, you will achieve a degree of excellence that nothing and no one else can offer you.

Lord God, You who are consummately perfect
and who want Your children also to achieve perfection,
grant that I will never relinquish the ideal of perfection,
because Your Holy Spirit works in me constantly.

LIVE IN FELLOWSHIP
WITH CHRIST

God, who has called you into fellowship with his Son
Jesus Christ our Lord, is faithful (1 Cor. 1:9).

God has given you a wonderful privilege. He has called you to share in the life of Jesus Christ. When the full meaning of this divine gift dawns on you, the implications are almost too great to envision.

To share in the life of Jesus Christ implies unlimited possibilities, but also great responsibilities. Connected to so much omnipotence and wisdom, your understanding of God is deepened, your vision of what your life can be is expanded, and you become aware of the enduring presence of Christ. But such intimacy with the Master creates certain responsibilities. The quality of your life has to be in accordance with the expression of your faith. The characteristics of God must be reflected in your life through love, honesty, unselfishness, and purity of purpose.

To express the Spirit of Christ to the best of your ability, you should develop a vision of what you can achieve for the Master. You are no longer restricted by secret fears and uncertainties, but can move confidently forward in the empowering strength of the living Christ.

Christ offers Himself to you so that you may share in His life and share your life with Him. But this offer only becomes a reality when you accept it in faith. You may have the knowledge of this glorious truth, but until you have made it your own, you will not experience the strength and joy of the presence of Jesus Christ in your life.

Lord Jesus, I invite You anew to come into my life
and to do Your work on earth through me.
I now open my heart and life to You.

THERE IS A LESSON TO BE LEARNED IN EVERYTHING

It was good for me to be afflicted so that
I may learn your decrees (Ps. 119:71).

Despite all your positive thinking and creative prayers, things still happen to you that you would rather have avoided. Consequently, you start wondering where you failed and what you did to land yourself in such a situation.

This can be a time of futile self-accusation in your life, and you may feel that either God disappointed you or that your faith wasn't strong enough. The psalmist has a unique way of looking at his tribulations. He believes that God wishes to teach him lessons through these hardships and that God has a message for him in every situation. As a result he uses his time to search for the lesson rather than pitying himself or complaining about the circumstances through which God wants to teach him the lesson.

Of course, when tribulation strikes in your life, you should do every-thing in your power to remedy it, and not simply foolishly and passively regard it as the will of God. This is the difference between calamity and blessing. It is often in moments of tribulation, when negative forces threaten to overwhelm you, that you discover a new facet in the loving character of God.

You learn that a short spell spent in the valley of despair can enrich your life in a wonderful way through positive and constructive thoughts and meaningful conversation with God.

Master and Guide, thank You for the lessons that I have learned in tribulation. Sustain me through every situation in life, be it prosperity or adversity, and let me embrace the lessons that You wish to teach me.

WHAT WORDS CAN DO

Nor should there be obscenity, foolish talk or coarse joking,
which are out of place, but rather thanksgiving (Eph. 5:4).

The language you use reflects the quality of your spirit and is the measure according to which others evaluate you. If your words fortify and inspire others, you will always have friends. People will enjoy your company because of the blessing that they receive from your words.

Never underestimate the power of the spoken word. Not only does it manifest who you really are, but it also has an immense influence on others. If bitterness and hate dominate your words, or if you are driven by a compelling need to hurt and humiliate others, words become instruments that can inflict irreparable damage.

There are people who cannot speak their thoughts except in vulgar or blasphemous terms. God's name is taken in vain. Such utterances not only indicate an impoverished mind, but also an immature spirit.

By using words in the right way, you can help to heal injured hearts that have been battered by inconsiderate people. When communicating with others you should always choose your words carefully. Using the following miracle-working words every day can make a world of difference: "I love you and I appreciate you."

Set a guard over my mouth, O Lord; keep
watch over the door of my lips (Ps. 141:3).

PEACE IN THE MIDST OF CHAOS

But in keeping with his promise we are looking forward to a new heaven and a new earth, the home of righteousness (2 Pet. 3:13).

In times of crisis there are people who tend to lose all courage and hope, and threaten to collapse in what they perceive to be a lost battle against insurmountable problems. This experience may take place in your personal life or be prompted by the state of your country or the world. The causes are numerous, but the results are always the same: the future always seems dark and hopeless.

To everyone who believes in Him, Jesus offers a life of abundance. This promise encompasses your situation here and now and until all eternity. Because He conquered sin and death, Christ has prepared a place for all the faithful in the eternal glory of the kingdom of God.

In your present life the Lord offers you His Holy Spirit to everyone who trusts in Him. It is His Spirit who gives you the ability to handle life's problems successfully in the certain knowledge that He will not forsake or abandon you. As Paul says, "If God is for us, who can be against us?" (Rom. 8:31).

Whatever your circumstances may be, remember that Jesus is always at your side to guide and help you. Put your trust in Him as He leads you, and remember that He is busy guiding you towards God's eternal kingdom where there is only harmony and peace.

> *Beloved Leader, I know that this life's struggles and problems will soon pass, and then I will enter into the eternal peace of Your Kingdom.*

THE REWARD OF
THE RIGHTEOUS

*Do not fret because of evil men or be envious of those who
do wrong...Trust in the LORD and do good (Ps. 37:1, 3).*

Many disillusioned people believe that it is not worthwhile to do good.
This may concern their own lives or the lives of others, but they can quote
example after example to justify their standpoint: someone who always
managed his business honestly and is a person of impeccable integrity,
who is now experiencing serious financial trouble, while others whose
business methods are particularly dubious are prospering. The death
of a loved and only child, while so many other children grow up to be
honorable citizens despite the carelessness of their parents.

Never lose sight of the fact that life does not begin and end with the
earthly existence that we are experiencing now. The tribulations and suffering that you experience now, the way in which you conduct yourself,
your attitude towards others—all these things prepare you for the eternal life that still lies ahead.

Whatever happens here and now, always remember that the ultimate judge is the almighty God. Always aspire to satisfy Him and behave in ways that are agreeable to Him. Even though you will suffer
for a while, you can be sure that God will reward you for the way in
which you lived here on earth and the way in which you reflected Jesus
in your everyday life.

*Lord and Master, I will hold on to the guidelines and standards
that You have set for my life, so that I will please You in all things.*

THE POWER OF
THE SPOKEN WORD

A word aptly spoken is like apples of
gold in settings of silver (Prov. 25:11).

A single word can make a vast difference to a person's life, and it is therefore of the utmost importance how it is said. Some people have a gift for words. By saying the right word at the right time, they can radically change someone else's life by filling them with a sense of pleasantness and well-being.

However, it is equally true that an inappropriate word at an inopportune moment can have a destructive effect on a person's life.

There are times in people's lives when they yearn for a sympathetic or encouraging word, when the display of loving interest and compassion can make an immense difference and brighten their dismal day. A word of appreciation or advice is never wasted; even constructive criticism or a loving reprimand can be beneficial to the recipient.

It is important that you will never be afraid to speak, but at the same time you must, through the strength of the Holy Spirit, choose your words and your timing very carefully.

Be sensitive to the mood of the person you are talking to, guard against unnecessary flattery but also against crassness, be sincere in what you say, and say it with the love of Jesus in your heart. In so doing you will infinitely enrich not only the person you are talking to, but also yourself.

May the words of my mouth and the meditation
of my heart be pleasing in Your sight,
O Lord, my Rock and my Redeemer (Ps. 19:14).

DO YOU SOMETIMES FEEL UNSAFE?

Surely God is my salvation; I will trust and
not be afraid. The LORD, the LORD is my strength
and my song; he has become my salvation (Is. 12:2).

We are all under some kind of pressure. The state of the world has penetrated all of our homes and has created a fear of the future. It seems as if the world is heading for disaster, which nothing and no one can prevent. This external pressure causes internal tensions, and feelings of fear and insecurity become an integral part of countless people's lives.

God's omnipotence and redemptive power are much more than mere religious clichés. It is an experience that may be enjoyed by all who place their faith and trust in the living Christ and entrust their lives unconditionally to His care. To do this is not an act of self-denial or an unwelcome discipline that adds to the burdens of your life, but a voluntary act that gives you confidence and diminishes fear.

If your faith is focused on Christ and you are guided by His principles, you not only conquer all destructive fears, but you also become aware that He equips you with spiritual power and strength. It is unnecessary to feel weak and insecure if you know that He loves you and promises you His assistance.

Always remember the promise of the Scriptures: "The eternal God is your refuge, and underneath are the everlasting arms" (Deut. 33:27). Hold on to this promise: God will never disappoint you.

I place my trust in You completely, Holy Father, and it fills me
with confidence, which banishes all uncertainty and fear.

WHEN YOUR CONSCIENCE SPEAKS

"I heard you in the garden, and I was afraid because I was naked; so I hid" (Gen. 3:10).

There are times in our lives when we are bowed down under the burden of guilt, and many of us find it exceedingly difficult to reconcile with our consciences. The causes of this are too numerous and varied to mention.

The most common are those deeds containing half-truths, deception, jealousy, and falsehoods, to name but a few. Some of these are very insignificant and yet the human conscience will remind the wrongdoer in no uncertain terms of his transgression.

Because it is connected to feelings of guilt and shame, many people will try to conceal their mistakes by instinctively turning their backs on them and trying to shut them out of their thoughts. Others try to justify their behavior. They think that this will help to calm the storm that is so often the result of wrongdoing.

One thing is absolutely certain: however hard you try, you cannot hide your transgressions from God. Regardless of the steps you take to conceal the offense that shames you, you can be sure that the blinding light of Jesus Christ will uncover it before your all-knowing Father.

Never try to hide from God. Be assured of His love and confess that which you are ashamed of or fear in prayer before Him. Gratefully receive His forgiveness and the peace that goes hand in hand with true contrition.

Lord Jesus, through experience I am assured of Your love and forgiveness, and therefore I expose my soul before You time and again. Thank You for Your forgiveness and love.

LIFE PARTNERS

"I no longer call you servants, because a servant does not know his master's business. Instead, I have called you friends, for everything that I learned from my Father I have made known to you" (Jn. 15:15).

It is only when you have earnestly requested the risen Christ to become your life partner that you realize the full impact and implications of your Christian faith. A partnership implies the shared responsibility to achieve a common goal. When Christ is in control, your life undergoes change and transformation as a result of the partnership in which you now find yourself.

The purpose of the ministry of Christ is to unify you with the Father. He asks your cooperation to achieve this, by acknowledging His sovereignty and His redemptive power in your life. If you do, you will experience a growing awareness of His presence in your daily life, because you are following the path that Christ has mapped out for you.

Such a wonderful partnership, which is connected to such a magnificent goal, may sound idealistic and impractical, but it is the pinnacle of wisdom. To live your life in partnership with God and with a focus on spiritual matters brings an exceptional balance to your life.

With Christ managing and controlling your life, you possess a code of conduct inspired by the Holy Spirit. You will not be a sleeping partner, but will be eager to manifest the partnership in your life at all times. It is your essential part in this wonderful partnership.

My Lord and Master, in partnership with You I will live and work in victory. I thank You for Your love and grace.

THE PRICE OF DISCIPLESHIP

*"If anyone would come after me, he must deny himself
and take up his cross daily and follow me" (Lk. 9:23).*

Prompted by today's verse from Scripture, let us use this day for introspection through contemplation and prayer. Let us do so with Christ's sacrifice and love in mind. "Self-denial" is not a word that falls easily on the ears of sinners. Hearing about "taking up the cross" is definitely not music to our ears. But we are called to do so because Jesus has made the incomparable sacrifice for the sake of redeeming us.

Jesus sacrificed His life for us on the cross. His offering was complete and total, because He gave his everything for mankind. While you continue your pilgrimage through life, you should recall and commemorate His sacrifice. Think of His unfathomable love that urged Him to this sacrifice. Then you will realize that you and all of humanity owe the Redeemer infinitely more than you could ever give.

Only complete and unreserved surrender to Jesus Christ can, in a minor way, be compared to His sacrifice. This will call and urge us to a life of relinquishment, cross-bearing, and self-denial for everyone who calls himself a Christian. If we bear our cross with joy, we will discover that we carry the instrument of our own redemption. And then every act of cross-bearing and self-denial becomes worthwhile.

*Lord Jesus, when I fix my eyes on the cross I realize that my life is still
filled with pride and self-interest. I know that nothing could possibly
compare to Your sacrifice for me, but help me to dedicate myself to
You—body, soul, and spirit—in answer to Your wonderful love.*

March

Creator-God, in this month of spring we worship You
as the loving keeper of Your Creation.
We praise Your holy name for the beauty of spring
that erupts everywhere around us.
Thank You for trees that until recently were bare and dry
and are now suddenly breaking into growth like giant bouquets,
displaying their splendor to glorify You.
Thank You for a thousand shades of delicate, crisp green leaves
that are appearing all around
as if You spoke the words of Creation just now!
Your earth is awakening and exults in new life; the winter is past,
the time for singing has come.
Savior, please touch my heart and life too:
bring new growth to my heart.
Let a surging song of praise for Your salvation sound gratefully in
my heart.
Praise the Lord, O my soul.

Amen.

PRAISE THE LORD FOR THE MIRACLE OF NEW LIFE

For by him all things were created: things in heaven and
on earth...all things were created by him and for him (Col. 1:16).

We so easily fail to notice the beginning of spring simply because our love of life has faded. When this happens, it is usually a good time to come to a standstill, take stock, and rediscover the mysticism and meaning of life. If your spirit is no longer moved by the beauty of a sunrise or the sounds of soothing music; if you no longer find joy in the company of trusted friends; or if monotony has destroyed all your ambitions, it has definitely become time to deepen and broaden your concept of life.

To accomplish this it is imperative to deepen your knowledge and experience of the creator God. A tried and tested way to do this is to cultivate the art of thanksgiving. Look around you for something to thank God for. It may be something small and unimportant that you have accepted as a given through the years. When you start praising and thanking God, your eyes open to the grace all around you.

This praise and thanksgiving should not remain an emotional experience alone. Find someone who is going through a difficult time and offer your assistance. In this way your own life will be enriched beyond your wildest expectations. Count your blessings and thank God for them, be a blessing to other people, and you will rediscover the true spring beauty and vitality of life.

God of new life and growth, help me to discover the
true meaning of life by being a blessing to other people.

LIFE-ALTERING LIGHT

"Can his forces be numbered? Upon whom
does his light not rise?" (Job 25:3).

One of the most wonderful phenomena in this world is the way in which beauty may be experienced in the most unlikely places. An arid desert landscape may be transfigured by the rays of the rising or setting sun. Dreadful precipices may suddenly lose their austerity when they are illuminated by the light of the rising moon. In many parts of the world the barrenness of the land is transformed, almost overnight, into a fairyland of color and exotic blooms after the spring rains have fallen on the apparently dead earth.

Such is the wonder of God's omnipotence while He continues to watch over His creation. In this way He proves time and again in so many ways that all things are possible for Him. In the same way that He created light from the darkness in the very beginning, so He can still today transform the darkest night into dazzling morning light. Here and now.

These divine wonders are not limited to nature. Jesus also moves in the lives of people and is prepared to illuminate your darkness if you are only willing to turn to Him and trust Him. In spite of your circumstances you can be sure that the living Christ is prepared to lead you from the darkness of your circumstances into the wonderful light of the presence of God.

Jesus, Light of the anxious heart, You appear
and command the darkness to disappear,
thus spreading the beauty of Your heavenly light.

WHEN JESUS COMES
INTO YOUR LIFE

"Blessed is the king who comes in the name of the Lord!
Peace in heaven and glory in the highest!" (Lk. 19:38).

When we read the account of Jesus' triumphant journey into Jerusalem, we cannot fail sensing the joy and excitement of those who offered Him such a sincere welcome. He was the long-awaited Messiah who would usher in an era of peace, joy, hope, and liberation: "Blessed is the king who comes in the name of the Lord!"

Throughout the ages this same feeling of wonder, awe, and joy has been experienced by people who welcomed Christ into their lives. Jesus said that He came so that you may experience the fullness of life (see Jn. 10:10). This means that you can live in peace and calm in the certain knowledge that He is with you at all times.

Just as the people of Jerusalem were a captive nation under the hated yoke of the Roman oppressors, so today many people are enslaved by habits that are extremely detrimental to their well-being. The living Christ offers to liberate you from these habits. Similarly, there are many people seeking love, grace, and compassion in a world that can be very cruel at times. This is exactly what Jesus still offers today to those who accept Him as their Redeemer and Savior.

Welcome the Master into your life with the same joy as the people of Jerusalem did and experience the joy that Christ brings.

Redeemer and Friend, in love and compassion You
came to claim my heart and soul. I sing a hymn of
praise to Your glory, because by Your grace You raise me
from sin and shame, so that I may be Your joyful child.

PERSEVERE IN PRAYER

After he had dismissed them, he went up on a mountainside by himself to pray. When evening came he was there alone (Mt. 14:23).

To our Lord and Master prayer was an essential discipline. When He was at the peak of his popularity, thousands followed Him to hear Him preach and to learn from Him. But even when He was denied by all His friends and had to endure the humiliation of seeming defeat, He found His strength and inspiration in prayer.

Unfortunately many of His modern disciples only pray when they feel like it, and they forget that prayer does not depend on your emotional state. If you only pray when you feel like it, the time will finally come when you will not pray at all.

At times all Christians experience spiritual drought when it seems as if God is distant and remote. Consequently, their love for Him cools and their spiritual life loses its luster. During these times it is difficult to pray, but it is precisely then when prayer is crucial. Even though it might seem as if the heavens are insulated with copper, continue praying, because it is your only channel to God. Job says, "Though He slay me, yet will I hope in Him; I will surely defend my ways to His face" (Job 13:15). This is what ultimately impelled Job from his sorrow, and guided him to a renewed awareness that God's blessing rested upon him.

Discipline yourself in prayer so that you may triumph over your prayerless times and so experience the supportive love and strength of the Master in your darkest and most vulnerable hour.

I thank and praise You, Lord my God, that I may experience the supportive power of prayer in my darkest hour.

KEEP YOUR COMMUNICATION CHANNELS OPEN

Do not forget to do good and to share with others,
for with such sacrifices God is pleased (Heb. 13:16).

The cause of the disintegration of many of our relationships is a lack of communication. So many of our relationships lapse into a monotonous rut, and the difference between a rut and a grave is merely a question of depth. We owe it to our fellow human beings to give something of ourselves in every relationship that we become involved in. It is essential that we should take stock of the quality of all our relationships.

In our spiritual lives the disintegration of creative communication with the Master is a sure way of detaching ourselves from Him. When prayer becomes the repetition of meaningless phrases piously spoken, true communication dies. Then prayer becomes words without content, and communion with Christ is no longer an enriching experience.

Meaningful communication does not happen easily or as a matter of course. It has to be cherished and developed. The husband has to share his experiences with his wife, because by talking to each other their love and understanding are strengthened.

In prayer and communication with the Master, in our service to our neighbor, in the good deeds that we do in His name, we are making sacrifices that please God. Talk to your Redeemer as you would to a friend; tell Him of your hopes and fears; tell Him that you love Him. This will keep your communication with others alive and strong.

O Holy Spirit, prevent my communication with God and with others
from becoming meaningless. Make my prayers meaningful,
so that my human relationships can also be healthy.

A LESSON IN HUMILITY

While he was in Bethany, reclining at the table in the
home of a man known as Simon the Leper (Mk. 14:3).

According to the Gospels Jesus was, at this point, on His way to Golgotha, to glory. He was thoroughly aware of everything awaiting Him in the fulfillment of His divine mission. He knew that soon after He would rise from the dead exalted, having conquered the Evil One for all time. He would have finally affirmed that He is the Son of God, the Redeemer of the world.

The average person's response to such a situation would in all likelihood have been to revel in all this glory and comfort in the company of those sharing in this glory. But with Jesus it was different. He sought the peace and quiet of a house where He knew that He would be left alone; a house that most people hesitated to enter and that was avoided by the community: the house of Simon the Leper.

If there is any incident that manifests the humility of Jesus, surely it is this one: the Son of God, on the threshold of exaltation, turns away from the brilliance of popularity to seek out the hospitality and fellowship of a family cast out by society.

This is a quality of sincere humility that is very touching. It is not weak or servile. It is brave and strong without being oppressive or arrogant. It is a characteristic that every Christian should develop through the grace of God.

Lord Jesus, deeply aware of who I am and where I come from, I pray
that You will keep me truly humble after Your own holy example.

YOU ARE A CHILD OF ROYAL BLOOD

You are all sons of God through faith in Christ Jesus,
for all of you who were baptized into Christ
have clothed yourself with Christ (Gal. 3:26).

You should never feel spiritually inferior. Perhaps you see how others are asked to be involved in congregational activities while you are passed over. It seems as if your friends are bubbling over with the joy of Christ, while your journey with Christ seems drab and uneventful.

In prayer and study groups other people speak and pray, but you keep quiet. Others' knowledge of the Bible is so much more comprehensive than yours that it leaves you feeling guilty and inadequate.

You must always remember that when God accepts you as His child He doesn't do so on the basis of your knowledge, work, or worthiness. It depends solely and purely on your faith in Jesus Christ and your acceptance of Him as your Redeemer and Savior. You will remember that the one criminal on the cross was assured of his acceptance not because of his achievements, but purely because of his faith in Jesus and by the grace of God.

Jesus accepts you for who and what you are. All He asks of you is that you believe in Him and accept Him as the Lord of your life. In the gospel of John Jesus says, "Do not let your hearts be troubled. Trust in God; trust also in Me" (Jn. 14:1). Joyfully respond to this invitation and experience the grace and love of your divine Father every day.

Holy God and through Jesus Christ my heavenly Father, thank You
that I may, through faith, claim the privilege of being called Your child.

DECISIONS, DECISIONS, DECISIONS

So whether you eat or drink or whatever you do,
do it all for the glory of God (1 Cor. 10:31).

To make decisions can be a cumbersome task, because it often goes hand in hand with great responsibility. What you decide can, and often does, have far-reaching consequences for your own life as well as for the lives of other people, especially those who are dependent on you. It is precisely for this reason that so many people try and avoid their responsibilities. On the other hand, there are also those who make decisions recklessly or with only their own interests at heart.

To ensure that you do not become ensnared in these traps, you should take all your concerns in prayer to God. Lay your problems, doubts, and fears before His feet and talk to Him about your plans and thoughts regarding the future. Leave the matter to Him and ask Him to lead you in every decision that you have to make, so that you may remain within His will.

This may seem very impractical to you, but provided that you are willing to trust the Lord unconditionally, you will find that He will open doors to you in His own wonderful time and way, and will guide you on the path that He has chosen for you.

Remain in the presence of the living Christ and the Holy Spirit, and continually aspire to please God. In so doing you will find that you make the right decisions because God lovingly guides you.

Holy Lord Jesus, I want to lay every decision that I have to
make before You. Grant me the guidance of Your Holy Spirit
so that I may live and make decisions within Your will.

MAKE SOMETHING OF YOUR LIFE

But one thing I do: Forgetting what is behind
and straining toward what is ahead (Phil. 3:13).

In the human personality there are many forces at work, all of which seek recognition and fulfillment. In every person the characteristics of parent, financier, politician, moralist, religious person, student, and many others contribute to the complexities of the human nature. In different phases of your life you move, sometimes reluctantly, from one category to the other, and you fluctuate between those forces that strengthen, coordinate, and motivate your daily life.

The people who achieve success are those who realize the importance of specialization. They choose their goals and strive after them with unremitting zeal. They dedicate themselves to the fulfillment of their ideals. Therefore, ensure that your goals are worthy of the best that is in you. You will never find satisfaction in life if you aim too low.

Some people aspire to excel in the academic world, others in business or the arts. Regardless of the sphere in which you move, you must live life to the fullest. If you are a disciple of Jesus, you want to leave the world a better place than you found it.

The highest goal that you can aspire to is to become like Christ. This may sound too idealistic to be practically possible, but such a goal speaks of true wisdom. Christ calls you to the most exalted life conceivable. However, not only does He call you, He also enables you to achieve heights that you never would have reached in your own strength. Make your life worthwhile through the strength of your Master.

Through Your presence in me, Lord Jesus, I will
achieve the goals that You have placed in my heart.

HOW DO YOU HANDLE REJECTION?

"All that the Father gives me will come to me, and whoever comes to me I will never drive away" (Jn. 6:37).

Rejection is one of the great tragedies of life. The loneliness of being excluded from a group can be extremely painful. Many people undergo the distressing experience of being passed over for promotion or even dismissed from their jobs because of their age. It is difficult to have your sound advice rejected, while knowing that the path followed can only end in disaster. Examples of rejection are rife and can have devastating consequences for your personality and emotions.

When you find yourself in such a situation, turn to Jesus who knows and understands only too well what it means to be rejected. He was sent by God to bring the message of God's love to humanity. Yet He was despised and forsaken by people. However, despite His physical, mental, and emotional suffering, they could never break His Spirit or cause His faith in God to falter.

In your loneliness and dejection, always remember that the living Christ promised never to forsake or desert you. Whatever you may suffer because of people's unpredictability, Jesus' love for you remains true. Hold on to this immovable truth, and through Jesus Christ you will be able to deal with your feelings of rejection and feel how His love fills your life and your heart.

O Lord, let my soul be quiet, because I know that You watch over me and will never forsake me. Help me to bear all suffering and sorrow with patience and to surrender my entire life to You.

WHICH WAY?

Whether you turn to the right or to the left, your ears will hear
a voice behind you, saying, "This is the way; walk in it" (Is. 30:21).

It is not easy to resist the temptation of drifting with the current. It is
especially so when you, perhaps for the first time in your life, become
part of a group of people with whom you will share your life and time for
a shorter or longer period. In the days ahead you may be reliant on them
not only for your happiness, but depending on circumstances, even for
your life.

If you feel that what others are doing is wrong, you should never be
afraid to say so. There will undoubtedly come times when you will have
to decide whether to agree with the majority or to stand up for what you
know to be right. Don't compromise your principles. Regardless of how
difficult it may be or how unpopular you may be at that moment, hold
on to what you are convinced is the right way.

Remember that there was a time when your Master and example was
extremely unpopular, but despite rejection, humiliation, and even death,
He stood firm in His beliefs. If you do the same, you will in time earn the
respect of your colleagues, and you will know that you had the privilege
of being in the company of Christ—even when you were rejected.

Heavenly Father, through Your strength and grace
I will choose Your way in everything that I do.

FIND YOUR INSPIRATION IN CHRIST

"Were not our hearts burning within us while he talked with us on the road and opened the Scriptures to us?" (Lk. 24:32).

Jesus' disciples were devastated. The humiliation and crucifixion of their Master destroyed all their hopes and aspirations. Their lives had become meaningless. Their dreams of a new era being ushered in by the Messiah were dashed to the ground. They were reduced to a small group of uncertain people consumed by fear. Then Jesus appeared once more and their lives gained a new and meaningful dimension.

The hope and inspiration of Easter can be transferred to every negative situation in life. When you are afraid or worried; when your plans fail; when you experience setbacks or disappointments: you can either give up hope and be overwhelmed by despondency, or you can turn to the risen Savior and receive new inspiration from Him. The choice is yours, as it was for the disciples.

The friends and followers of the Master developed such an intimate relationship with Him during His lifetime that when He rose from the grave they were newly inspired by His presence, and hope flowed through them once more.

This can be your experience too, despite the disappointments of life, if you open your life and heart to the living Christ. You too will experience His influence and inspiration that will urge you towards a better and more confident life in His name.

All my hope and trust are anchored in You, risen and glorified Savior and Lord. Thank You that You inspire me time and again when I find myself in the dark.

LET LOVE INSPIRE
YOUR SERVICE

"Does the LORD delight in burnt offerings and sacrifices as much as in obeying the voice of the LORD?" (1 Sam. 15:22).

Before Christ came to the world, people attached great importance to making sacrifices to God. Over the years these acts began to be performed without devotion: their significance and meaning were lost as the people offered sacrifices with unrepentant hearts. Sacrifices were no longer acts of worship, but procedures that were followed mechanically and thoughtlessly.

Christ clearly and irrefutably showed that obedience to the commandments of God is of cardinal importance in your life as a Christian. No amount of material or financial offerings can ever be an adequate substitute for the love that you should show towards others. You can dedicate a great deal of time to serving the Lord, but unless it is inspired by and linked to His love, it will be of little value to His Kingdom.

The Master set the example for an effective Christian life, and He demands absolute obedience to God's commandment that we should love one another. Whatever you do in the service of God can only be to the glorification of His name if it is founded on the love of Jesus Christ.

Help me, O Lord, to continually love You more, so that I will also increasingly serve my fellow man in love.

MAKE TIME FOR THIS

I looked for sympathy, but there was none,
for comforters, but I found none (Ps. 69:20).

It cannot be denied that we live in a fast-paced world. People run around in an attempt to meet an ever-increasing amount of demands. We have less and less time, and the pressure on the individual becomes so intense that it becomes increasingly difficult to spend time worrying about the hardships of others.

Even the briefest overview of the life of Christ as reflected in the Gospels convinces us of the fact that He too lived under immense pressure. He was in demand as teacher, preacher, comforter, and healer. His day was filled with requests to serve others in some way or another.

Wherever He went crowds followed Him. He was also aware of the fact that He had limited time at His disposal to complete the work that God had instructed Him to do. Evil forces were perpetually trying to disrupt His ministry of love. Regardless of this, Christ had time for everyone.

There are so many people today who long for a sympathetic smile or a comforting word; people who are experiencing a crisis in their lives; people who are lonely, scared, and unsure. Always be sensitive to the distress of others and be prepared to lend a helping hand at any time. It doesn't matter how busy you are, make time for this, so that you may carry the joy of Christ into the lives of others.

Help me, O Holy Spirit, to carry the love
of Jesus Christ into the lives of other people.

YOU CAN'T SERVE
TWO MASTERS

"If you are returning to the LORD with all your hearts,
then rid yourselves of the foreign gods and the Ashtoreths and
commit yourselves to the LORD and serve him only" (1 Sam. 7:3).

Many people claim that they are seeking God and that they are trying
to establish a more intimate relationship with Him. Few of them would
admit that idols hold sway in their lives and exercise a significant amount
of control over them.

In their search for a new life in Christ, people stream to gatherings,
seminars and retreats; they study the Bible and other Christian literature;
they attend Sunday services as well as prayer and study groups. Despite
all this, their enthusiasm is often disappointed, and their search appears
fruitless. Consequently they begin to question the promises of Christ.

If you are seeking a meaningful relationship with the risen Lord, you
may be certain that the Redeemer is waiting for you to invite Him into
your life so that He may be in charge of it. However, before He will do
this, you are expected to banish every non-Christian matter from your
life. Jesus has to be the focus of your existence if you expect Him to fill
your life with His joy and fullness.

You have to give preference to Him above all the habits and ways of
life that you have become accustomed to. Do this, serve only the Lord,
and you will experience His peace and joy in your life.

Lord Jesus, I dedicate my life to You anew, in the
knowledge that You will give me life in abundance.

Read Luke 11:27-32

THE JOY OF LIFE IN CHRIST

*"Blessed rather are those who hear
the word of God and obey it" (Lk. 11:28).*

Many people's attitude towards their religious principles is one of reluctant submission to a tiresome yet necessary discipline. Tiresome because it limits or subdues our pleasure, but necessary for the well-being of the soul.

This should never be the attitude of the Christian believer, because Jesus came so that you may have life in all its abundance. He wants you to have a life of purpose, vigor, and joy. The entire Christian experience centers around a caring heavenly Father who wishes only the best for His children. His love is so incomprehensibly great that He sacrificed His Son. Jesus offers you forgiveness, redemption, and the hope of eternal life. Through His Holy Spirit He enables you to live in trust, confidence, and victory.

What more could anyone ask of life? Here you have the promise of the very best that life can offer and all that God expects of you is to accept His sovereignty in your life. Surely this is little enough to ask in exchange for a life of fulfillment and joy?

Lord Jesus, I rejoice in the knowledge that You redeemed me and granted me a life of joy and fulfillment. My heart sings in praise and gratitude.

WHAT AN AMAZING THOUGHT!

We have the mind of Christ (1 Cor. 2:16).

Even if the Christian faith were no more than a beautiful philosophy, it would still have been applicable to every sphere of life, because it expresses the great human need for love and fellowship. Imperfect people still aspire to perfection, and every heart and mind contains the seeds of the quest for God. Until man has found union with the Father, he will feel incomplete and frustrated.

The Christian gospel offers a unique way of life when it speaks of love for God and surrender to His will. In the gospel this is of much greater value than academic achievement. Such achievements are praiseworthy, and those who possess them can offer God a greater spectrum of services, but it is not essential in order to experience the fullness of the Christian faith.

To believe that God is true to His word, that He will do everything He promised, is the greatest stimulus that you can have in your spiritual life.

If you have this, you become a channel of His divine love, conveying it to the world in which you live. To allow your mind to be possessed by Christ is not only a religious experience but also a revolutionary act of faith that brings spiritual forces to the fore in every aspect of your daily life. Through the Spirit of Christ you realize the true splendor of life.

Jesus, my Lord, let Your Spirit govern my thoughts and my spirit so that I may gain a new appreciation for life's potential.

SOMETIMES THE ANSWER IS "NO"

Answer me when I call to you, O my righteous God. Give me relief from my distress; be merciful to me and hear my prayer (Ps. 4:1).

We often hear people complaining that God does not answer their prayers. They declare that they prayed extensively and earnestly, but nothing happened; they prayed for some or other specific thing, but did not get it; they asked for God's guidance on a particular path, but nothing came of it. The result of these prayer experiences is that many people's faith wanes because they maintain that God does not listen.

However, nothing could be further from the truth, because in the Scriptures we are assured that God hears and answers the prayers of His children. But we err in forgetting that God does, upon occasion, say "no." We focus so much on asking Him for those things that we want that we lose sight of the fact that Jesus assured us that He would provide in all our needs, and no one knows better than Christ what our true needs are.

True prayer does not consist of telling God what you want or what you are planning to do and then asking Him to place His stamp of approval on it. Prayer consists of opening up your life to God, laying your needs before Him, and trusting Him to lead you on the right path.

Lord Jesus, You are my Guide, my Leader, and my Friend. Therefore I submit obediently to Your will, even though You sometimes say "no" to me. Lead me according to Your will until the end of my pilgrimage.

DEATH IS NOT THE END

*Brothers, we do not want you to be ignorant
about those who fall asleep, or to grieve like the
rest of men, who have no hope (1 Thes. 4:13).*

Time and time again we meet individuals or families who have been plunged into the depths of grief by the death of a loved one. To these people it appears as if life has lost its purpose and meaning. They are powerless and inconsolable in their grief. In their state of paralyzed shock, the future seems empty and meaningless.

On the day after the crucifixion of Jesus Christ, His close friends and family must have experienced the same feelings. The Scriptures describe them as a sorrowful, terrified, and lost little group of people shocked by the death of their beloved Master.

And yet they were at the threshold of a miracle that would change the entire concept of death for all time. Instead of an ending, death suddenly became a beginning. With His resurrection Christ confirmed that He lives eternally and that those who believe in Him will never die.

When a loved one is taken from you by death, don't despair. Christ has gone to prepare a place for us in the kingdom of the Father. Hold on to His promise that He will come again and take you to Him. In Christ you will be reunited with your loved ones who trust the Lord. Do not be afraid and distressed: Christ lives and therefore we too will live.

> *I rejoice in Your triumphant resurrection from
> death, Lord Jesus. I exult in the knowledge that
> all of us will be together once more with You.*

WASHERS OF FEET

*After that, he poured water into a basin and began
to wash his disciples' feet, drying them with
the towel that was wrapped around him (Jn. 13:5).*

Much has been written and said on the topic of love and humility. Many have tried to explain the true meaning of their application in life. Despite all the profound statements, the fact remains that the world still has a desperate need for the demonstration of true love and humility, so that the illnesses of this world may be healed. Everywhere we turn we are faced with examples of behavior that is in direct contradiction with everything that God expects of His people.

Jesus, in His ordinary and truly earthly way, provided us with a practical demonstration of what is required by God's standards. On the eve of His crucifixion and glorification, He took the role of servant upon Himself with the humble task of washing His disciples' feet. He proved that humility and love can conquer all things.

In these days there is a great need throughout the world to let the humility and love of Jesus conquer pride and hatred. Instead of washing each other's feet, we tend to berate each other. Humility and love is the only path to lasting relationships. For this Christ died on the cross. Let us therefore become washers of feet for Christ.

*Holy Master, we want to take You at Your word
and follow Your example. Grant that there will be more
sunshine in this world because of my humility and love.*

THE EXCITEMENT
OF NEW IDEAS

The heart of the discerning acquires knowledge;
the ears of the wise seek it out (Prov. 18:15).

Don't believe it when someone tells you that the world is bankrupt of new ideas or that it is no longer possible to make exciting discoveries. It is said that 80 percent of our current knowledge has been discovered in the last 80 years.

Every day new and exciting discoveries open paths to even greater discoveries. If you can hold on to the truth that the greatest painting is yet to be created; that the most inspiring prose is yet to be written; that music as never heard by the human ear is still waiting to be composed, then you will place your mind and spirit in a state of readiness for the wonders that the future holds.

God's ideas are not spent, but He is looking for dedicated people through whom He may express Himself, so that His will may be manifested to mankind. To be prepared in all spheres of life for this inspiring service, we must cultivate a disposition of unity with God. This is not only a mystical experience but also a very practical one.

While you are building a uniquely personal intimacy with God, flashes of inspiration will penetrate your mind. Even though some of these may seem foolish to you, follow them and they may lead you into exciting spheres of thought and service.

Heavenly Father, only through complete obedience to You
can I share in Your divine thoughts for the world in which I live.

THE FORGOTTEN MINISTRY

*Joseph took the body, wrapped it in a clean linen cloth, and placed it
in his own new tomb that he had cut out of the rock (Mt. 27:59-60).*

Great emphasis is placed on the special and loving ministry to the ill
and dying and their loved ones, and quite rightly so. When a person is
seriously ill and his family is surrounded by sympathetic friends offering
their assistance and prayers, these tokens of concern are praiseworthy.
But what happens when death comes?

The needs of a family who has lost a loved one to death are just as
great, if not greater, as during the illness. Now is the time to support
them in a variety of ways. There are many things that have to be done
and many details that need attention. And these are usually unpleasant,
time-consuming matters that are not in the foreground.

To undertake these tasks for the sake of the grieving family calls for
special dedication to a ministry that is difficult but also worthwhile. This
is a time when the family is still paralyzed with shock, and they need
sympathetic, sound advice as well as a strong shoulder to lean on.

Never shrink back from this ministry, because through it you will
perform a deed of Christian love that is beyond words. You will gain
the immeasurable appreciation of those you have ministered to, and
through it you will honor your Lord and Master.

> *Loving and understanding Lord Jesus, grant that when
> the sorrow of death strikes a family that I know,
> I will not hesitate to bring the ministry of comfort to
> those who are grieving, not only in words but also in deeds.*

PROUD INHERITANCE

"I am he," Jesus said (Jn. 18:5).

Are you proud to be a Christian? Are you at all times ready and willing to stand up and be counted by professing Christ's sovereignty in your life? Or are there times when you keep quiet and are ashamed to profess your religion because you fear that you will not be accepted by a certain group of people?

There are many occasions when a Christian must identify himself with Christ: when the moral behavior of someone needs to be questioned; when someone's language or jokes turn filthy; when someone airs blasphemous commentary. These are but a few examples of times when it is required that a Christian distance himself from the general inclination, even if it means that he will be unpopular or be ridiculed.

When Jesus was at the point of being arrested and there were people looking for Jesus of Nazareth, He made no attempt to deceive them. His answer to their question bespeaks sincere honesty and surrender and obedience to the will of God. Without hesitation He says: "I am he." His answer demonstrates the quality of His courage, because He knew only too well of the humiliation, rejection, and suffering that would follow.

Follow His example and draw strength from Him. Be assured that when the time comes, you will also be able to profess with humble pride that you are a Christian.

> *Crucified Savior, please keep me from ever*
> *being ashamed of professing my Christianity.*

THE HONESTY THAT GOD DEMANDS

"Now then, you Pharisees clean the outside of the cup and dish,
but inside you are full of greed and wickedness" (Lk. 11:39).

God amazes me by never decreasing in patience in the face of all the excuses that we offer Him for the neglect of our spiritual lives. Some of the excuses are so clumsy that we would not even offer them to a friend. Social events take preference over worship; laziness is often called relaxation; uselessly running around in the name of God takes the place of becoming quiet before Him. It is easier to be active for the Master than to become quiet before Him and to learn His will.

When you are involved with God, it is necessary to be completely honest with Him. He knows the true reasons for your spiritual neglect; why then would you try to hide anything from Him? When you are honest with God two things happen in your life. You open up the channel between you and Him that had been blocked for so long by hypocrisy, false excuses, laziness, and other spiritual obstacles. You ask for forgiveness and experience the feeling of freedom that only God can give to you, a feeling that makes you spiritually sensitive so that you may grow in love once again.

A healthy spiritual experience is based on faith and not on feelings. Nevertheless, a feeling of great joy will fill your spirit if you are honest with God. Once you have broken through the obstacle of sin that separates you from Him, you will increasingly experience a sense of unity with Him.

Holy Father, grant me the desire and the
courage to be honest with You, so that my
relationship with You may be enriched.

DO YOUR MEMORIES
NEED HEALING?

But one thing I do: Forgetting what is behind
and straining toward what is ahead (Phil. 3:13).

Memories are an extremely important factor in your life. They can create inspiration, despair, or peace of mind. Your memories of the past will without a doubt influence both the present and the future.

Unpleasant and distressing memories have a tendency to persist and to become even more distinct with the years. You may remember an unkind word or an act of abuse that you fell victim to many years ago. However, to continually revisit this memory will influence and poison your mind to such an extent that a bitter, unforgiving spirit will take root in you.

The eradication of these disturbing and destructive memories depends on your ability to forgive. This is one of the most difficult aspects of the Christian faith. To hate those who have hurt you is entirely natural. It may be natural, but it is not Christian. The Christian way is the path of reconciliation and healing. To refuse forgiveness is to sow a seed that will eventually destroy your spirit and harm you physically.

You can only forgive others if you yourself have experienced the forgiveness of Jesus. To accept God's forgiveness through Christ enables you to forgive, thus purifying and healing your memories of all damaging influences.

Holy Spirit of God, heavenly Teacher, teach me the
ministry of forgiveness so that I can purify my
mind and spirit from all destructive influences.

BE HONEST

He who conceals his sins does not prosper, but whoever
confesses and renounces them finds mercy (Prov. 28:13).

The proverb that states: "Honesty is the best policy" contains an irrevocable truth. However, there are many people who find it difficult to submit themselves to it. Some of them ignore it on purpose, while others, caught in a web of doubt and fear, suddenly find themselves in a situation where they are unable to handle the consequences of honesty.

As a result they try to conceal their shortcomings or failures. In the process they sink deeper into new problems until it eventually seems impossible to disentangle themselves.

Such behavior inevitably leads to mental anguish and stress, because the emotions and nervous system of the average person cannot cope with the negative influences caused by deception. Consequently you suffer mentally, physically, and spiritually, and your life becomes nothing but a torture-chamber.

At one time or another, we all make mistakes in varying degrees. Christ, who lived among flawed people, is aware of and sympathetic to human fallibility.

If you did something wrong, don't try and hide it with a lie. Trust in the love, forgiveness, and courage that Jesus offers you. Acknowledge and confess your error and try to correct it. This is the only path on which you will find peace for your soul.

Thank You, Holy Spirit of God, that You taught me
that I may live in peace by being honest at all times.

LONELY, BUT NEVER ALONE

How great is the love the Father has lavished on us, that we
should be called children of God! And that is what we are! (1 Jn. 3:1).

The love of family and friends is always a great source of comfort and
joy. To have someone to whom you can turn and with whom you can
share your life experience is one of God's greatest gifts of grace. It is
therefore no wonder that parting with or saying farewell to a loved one
always fills us with deep sorrow and loneliness.

However, you are never alone, because as Paul said, nothing in all
of creation can separate us from the love of God in Jesus Christ (see
Rom. 8:38-39). The Lord assures us that He will never abandon or
forsake us and that He will be with us in all our days (see Heb. 13:5 and
Mt. 28:20). These are promises that you can hold on to and draw courage
and strength from in all circumstances, especially when tragedy strikes
and you are at your most vulnerable.

To take full advantage of the assurance of God's promises and presence you must often spend time in His presence through prayer and
contemplation. Share all your fears and worries with Him, as well as
your loneliness and vulnerability. Christ is not only the Lord of your life
but also your Friend, and therefore you must remember that He chose
you to belong to Him through His grace.

God of love and grace, those who experience Your love can never be
lonely. Help me to walk with You and to talk to You as with a friend.

THE TEST OF
TRUE DISCIPLESHIP

"By this all men will know that you are
my disciples, if you love one another" (Jn. 13:35).

The majority of Christians are attached to some kind of discipline or credo. This is essential, because without such anchors they become drifters without a safe harbor.

The weakness of these different convictions becomes clear when every association or church believes that only one is right and that all the others are wrong. Then an "anti"-spirit becomes prevalent, antagonism reigns supreme, and discipleship becomes ineffective.

The Christian faith must center around the living Christ. By accepting Him as your Redeemer, you pledge your faith to Him and submit yourself to His demands. It involves every aspect of your daily life and requires a high quality of dedication. Love is the most important sign of discipleship and without it no one can be His follower. Therefore the litmus test of true discipleship is not which theological conviction you believe in, but whether you lead a life of true Christian love.

This truth may cause some people to hesitate to accept the challenge and responsibility of discipleship, because who can love when surrounded by bitterness and hatred? The demand of love that Christ places on us is impossible for mere humans to obey, but if His Spirit fills your life, the impossible becomes possible. Then love becomes the main ingredient in your life and enables you to become a true disciple.

Loving Lord Jesus, let Your Holy Spirit take possession
of my life so that I may share in these gifts of the Spirit,
and so that love may become the motivating force in my life.

THE KINGDOM OF GOD

"The kingdom of God does not come with your careful observation, nor will people say, 'Here it is,' or 'There it is,' because the kingdom of God is within you" (Lk. 17:20-21).

The kingdom of God can be found in the hearts of those in whose lives Jesus Christ reigns as king. It is the kingdom of good relationships, because you are reconciled with God and live in harmony with Him. This takes place through the power and love of Jesus. As far as possible you then should live in peace with your fellow human beings.

Unfortunately political and social digressions have caused many people to end up on a side-track, and they continue trying to reach the kingdom without opening their hearts and lives to the merciful occupancy of Christ's holy presence. Only when the risen Lord reigns supreme in the lives of people can His Kingdom be established in their thoughts, spirits, and emotions.

Belonging to the kingdom of God demands unconditional obedience to the King. He must be assured of your faithfulness and you must strive to do His will. This faithfulness is not a one-time vow made in a moment of intense emotion, but a daily devotion to Him, regardless of your emotional state.

When the King of this inner kingdom lets His power be felt, you experience His strength, joy, peace, and all His blessings in your daily life. The greatest joy of life is the steadfast knowledge that you belong to Him and He to you, because He lives in you through His Holy Spirit.

Come, Lord Jesus, and reign as supreme King in my heart and life. Grant that the world will know where my citizenship is.

WHO? ME, LORD?

"Will a man rob God? Yet you rob me" (Mal. 3:8).

The average person would feel affronted if called a thief. The mere thought that you may be guilty of robbing God is so repulsive that it is almost indescribable. And yet, if we were to be honest with ourselves, there is an element of truth in these words that God directs at us through His prophet.

The commandments of the Old Testament form the foundation of the lifestyle that God expects from His people. Thereafter, with the ministry of Christ, we are shown indisputably and exactly what He requires of us as His children; namely, to comply with His demands. Jesus Himself calls all Christians to bear fruit in honor of God the Father (see Jn. 15:8).

When you seriously think about your faith and discipleship, you will realize that you are now God's ambassador in the world. It is through the effectiveness of your testimony that souls will be won or lost for the Master's cause. People will keep a close eye on your life, and if they see in your lifestyle something that is alien to the principles and example of Christ, they will turn their backs on Him. The church of Christ is judged according to the testimony of His disciples.

If you are guilty of this, you derogate from the glory of God and thus hinder His work of winning souls to His kingdom by manifesting the love and example of Christ in your life.

> *Holy Spirit, my Leader and Guide, help me to win and not lose people for God's kingdom through my way of life.*

ETERNAL LIFE THROUGH JESUS CHRIST

For this very reason, Christ died and returned to life so that
he might be the Lord of both the dead and the living (Rom. 14:9).

Most people fear a lack of security. A child who leaves home for boarding school; a person changing jobs; the loss of a life partner; all these things leave you with feelings of uncertainty and nervousness. You fear what the future holds for you.

Even worse is your fear of death and the uncertainty that goes hand in hand with it. There are many people who brood over this whenever they think of the unknown. In their uncertainty they fall victim to anxiety and tension. They worry about the dark, unknown future that will follow their physical death.

For the Christian believer there is a glorious truth that emanates from the life, death, and resurrection of Jesus Christ: in the Spirit He is with you right now to lead you through life with all its problems and fears. He also went to prepare a place for you in God's heavenly kingdom. In this way He assures you that when your earthly life is over, you will be with the Lord eternally (see Jn. 14:1-4).

Instead of being consumed with fear and worry, hold on to the promises of Jesus Christ. Place your faith and trust in Him and rejoice in the fact that because Jesus lives, you too will live eternally.

Risen and glorified Savior, through faith I know
that You live and that therefore I too will live eternally.
Praise the Lord! I know that my Redeemer lives!

April

O Lord, our Lord, how majestic is Your name (Ps. 8:2).

We worship You in this month as Christ the Conqueror!
You conquered death on Golgotha.
You have broken the power of Satan.
The Lord has truly risen! The tomb is empty!
Let the heavens proclaim His glory!
Thank You, triumphant Jesus, that You were obedient to death and
that God has exalted You to the highest glory;
that You sit at the right hand of God and intervene on my behalf.
Thank You for taking me with You on Your
triumphant journey through time and eternity.
I am assured that, because You were resurrected from death,
I too can be freed from death to a life of victory.
Lord Jesus, because You are the resurrection and the life
I can enter into the eternal home You went to prepare.
Let me never forget Your living presence;
assure me once again that there is nothing and no one
on earth that can separate me from Your love.
Forgive me, merciful Lord Jesus, if I sometimes live
as if You are not alive.
Let me live every day of this month and all the days of my life
in the glorious comfort of Your promise:
"Remember, I am with you in all your days!"
In the name of my risen and glorified Savior.

Amen.

LIVE FOR CHRIST

His divine power has given us everything we need for
life and godliness through our knowledge of him
who called us by his own glory and goodness (2 Pet. 1:3).

In this month we once again hear the call to live a Christian life, but some of us are so overwhelmed by the immensity of the task that our faith falters.

We tell ourselves that in our human weakness we cannot meet the standards that God expects of us. The sad consequences of such an attitude is that you lose courage and refuse to even try. In this way God is robbed of yet another disciple, and you deny yourself the joy of serving the Master.

The mistake that you make is to rely on your own abilities to serve Christ when you should actually from the outset devote yourself to Christ with absolute faith in your heart and trust Him to enable you to walk His path.

On your Christian pilgrimage you must remember that Christ will not call you to any form of service without equipping you for it. He has set the example, and all that He expects of you is to follow Him. If you dedicate yourself to Him and put your trust in Him, He will provide you with everything that you need to truly live.

Heavenly Father, I dedicate myself to Your service anew in the certain knowledge that You will provide everything that I need to live for You.

LET CHRIST RELIEVE YOUR LONELINESS

"I will not leave you as orphans; I will come to you" (Jn. 14:18).

The anguish of loneliness is an experience that is difficult to describe or explain; it must be experienced before it can be understood. Of all the forms of loneliness, the worst is that which results from the death of a loved one, because the separation in human terms is so final.

This profound loneliness may lead to inconsolable sorrow and deep unhappiness, unless you pull yourself together and take positive steps to fight your despair.

On the eve of His own death Jesus promised His disciples that He would not leave His children without a Comforter. Through His Holy Spirit the Savior undertakes to come to you and be with you at all times, as long as you trust Him for the forgiveness of all your sins and turn to Him in repentance.

When death strikes there is always a tendency to abandon all hope under the burden of sorrow. It is precisely then when you need the help and consolation of the Holy Spirit. In your sorrow turn to Jesus and lay your fears, sorrow, and pain before Him.

He is always there, ready to share your sorrow with you by giving you His peace or by using someone as an instrument to support and comfort you. He will manifest Himself to you in His healing love and in this way take the unbearable pain out of your sorrow.

Be quiet, my soul, the Lord is on your side.
Thank You, Lord Jesus, that I may say this from experience
and conviction, because You have given me a Comforter.

IT IS PERFECTLY NATURAL TO PRAY

He will respond to the prayer of the destitute;
he will not despise their plea (Ps. 102:17).

Most Christians regret the fact that they do not spend more time in prayer. They realize the inadequacy of their prayer lives, but when they do try to pray with depth and meaning, their good intentions are defeated by wandering thoughts and a restless spirit.

Prayer is a completely natural act, despite opinions to the contrary. You may set apart little time for God and live without giving Him a single thought, but deep inside you there is a core that cannot be explained without God. In moments of silent contemplation you will think about the meaning and significance of life, but without God there is no answer to its purpose.

Prayer is the heartbeat of the soul. You may understand nothing of schools of prayer or methods of contemplation, but every time you think of God there is something deep inside you that yearns for a reality that you cannot explain. This hunger of your soul and your seeking thoughts are, as a matter of fact, a humble form of prayer.

While prescribed prayers and orthodox methods of prayer may help you to enter into the presence of God, it is the cry of the troubled heart, so often expressed in confusion and despair, that moves the loving heart of God. Every time you invoke His name, He is there to meet you. Every time you think of Him, you are busy praying. Therefore do not feel discouraged if your prayer life seems inadequate. Every thought that is directed at God is a prayer that connects you to Him.

O, Hearer of prayers, I praise and thank You for the
natural prayer that carries me into Your holy presence.

THE TRULY
ABUNDANT LIFE

*He who has the Son has life; he who does not
have the Son of God does not have life (1 Jn. 5:12).*

One often hears the expression: "This is the life!" Usually it refers to
the enjoyment of material things and creature comforts. While we do
not wish to deny people their right to leisure and even a little bit of
self-indulgence, it may, if left uncontrolled, lead to self-centeredness
and selfishness.

Such pleasure in any case leaves one with a feeling of bored dissatisfaction and the need to seek out other forms of sensual gratification.
Eventually there is no way to find joy and life becomes meaningless.

Whatever your methods of relaxation and life enjoyment, you must
never lose sight of the fact that Jesus Christ came so that you may have
life in all its abundance (see Jn. 10:10). However involved you may feel
in your work or relaxation, you will never experience full satisfaction
before you have found the living Christ.

Don't make the mistake of limiting your life with Christ only to the
spiritual aspect. Always remember that He offers to be part of every
aspect of your life.

If you open your life to Him completely and allow His Holy Spirit to
work in you, your life will take on a completely new dimension. Invite
Christ into your heart and allow Him to transform your existence into
abundant life.

*Redeemer and Master, since I have surrendered my life to You
and allowed Your Spirit to rule my being, my fetters have
fallen away and my heart has been liberated to live in abundance.*

OLD AGE IS A TIME OF GRACE

"Even to your old age and gray hairs I am he,
I am he who will sustain you" (Is. 46:4).

As you grow older your attitude towards life changes. Aspects that you were sure of before are closely scrutinized under the searchlight of experience. Your approach to issues of which you were dogmatically convinced is blessed with a deeper and more sympathetic understanding.

It is unfortunately also true that the progression of age does not necessarily bring with it an increase in wisdom. Sometimes it results in a narrow-minded spirit becoming even more hardened in its views. The subsequent obstinacy can be an obstacle to inspirational ideas.

As a disciple of Christ your mind and spirit must remain receptive to the inspiration and guidance of the Holy Spirit, so that He can lead you deeper into God's protective love. Your faith must continue growing, and it involves the rejection of narrow-mindedness and pettiness.

As someone who lives in the love of God, you ought to be liberated from all prejudice and fanaticism. Aware that Christ's love is His special gift to you, you will become increasingly aware that you are one with Him. Whatever changes may take place in your life, you will live in an increasingly deeper and more realistic relationship with God. However, this only happens if you are guided by the Holy Spirit.

God's love will intensify your respect for others who love God, even though they might worship Him differently.

Thank You, Lord my God, that with the passing of the years I also grow in spiritual understanding and thus become liberated from all jealousy and prejudice.

WHEN THINGS START GOING WRONG

I will instruct you and teach you in the way you should go;
I will counsel you and watch over you (Ps. 32:8).

Life is very unpredictable. For a while everything may go well and everything you set out to do turns out successfully. And then suddenly, for some inexplicable reason, everything starts going wrong.

However hard you try, you cannot manage to achieve your goals; success evades you and it seems as if failure is one step ahead of you the entire time. Such a change in circumstances does not occur without cause. It may be difficult to accept, but its cause lies within you.

You may discover that your thoughts have switched from the positive to the negative; your prayer life may have lost its foundation of trust; complaining and grumbling may have become your attitude towards life. Unconsciously you attract every negative influence towards you.

When things start going wrong, it is time for you to isolate yourself with God. Cease all complaining and grumbling and enter the presence of God in humility, in the conviction that nothing is beyond His control. Surrender yourself to Him and He will lead you from this dark country. In Him you will find a divinely inspired path and things will once again start going right.

If your world is threatening to go to pieces, hem it with prayer to prevent it from fraying at the edges. Through Christ and the Holy Spirit, God will grant you the courage and guidance in your confusion and uncertainty.

Grant me the wisdom, O Lord, to wait for You
in prayer when things in my life start going wrong.

RECONSIDER YOUR RELATIONSHIPS

"Therefore, if you are offering your gift at the altar and
there remember that your brother has something against you,
leave your gift there in front of the altar. First go and be reconciled
to your brother; then come and offer your gift" (Mt. 5:23-24).

There is always a danger that religious convictions, backed by strong emotion, may overshadow the core of the message of Jesus Christ. When your Christianity becomes so personal and limited that it ignores human relationships, it becomes a mockery.

However excited you are in your acts of worship, however enthusiastic you are about the kingdom of God, your worship and enthusiasm become ineffectual if you harbor an unforgiving spirit towards another person in your heart.

It will be impossible for you to know the true freedom of worship inspired by the Spirit, because you cannot appreciate the joy of the living Christ if there is bitterness between you and another person.

Perhaps there is a separation or estrangement not caused by you in your life. If you have done everything in your power to mend the breach and the other person still withholds forgiveness, make sure that you don't cherish any vengeful thoughts.

Make sure that you have not only forgiven that person, but that you also still pray for him. When the time comes for your prayers to be answered and the breach to be mended, you will experience great peace and joy because you have proven once more that there is healing power in Christianity.

Lord my God, through forgiveness and praise I can live
in peace with You, my neighbor and myself. I thank You for this
through Jesus Christ who has redeemed me from an unforgiving spirit.

SHARE YOUR BURDENS WITH CHRIST

Cast all your anxiety on him because he cares for you (1 Pet. 5:7).

Someone in the business world, who was going through a difficult time, was once asked how he managed to sleep with all the worries that he had. His response was that he relinquished all his problems to God, saying, like the psalmist: "Indeed, He who watches over Israel will neither slumber nor sleep" (Ps. 121:4), and therefore he saw no point in the both of them staying awake all night.

Frivolous as this may seem, it emphasizes our obligation to trust God under all circumstances. Jesus undertook never to abandon or forsake us (see Heb. 13:5). He invited those who are weary and overburdened to come to Him for rest, and He assured us that He would never send away those who came to Him.

This does not necessarily mean that God offers you an instant solution to your problems, or that all your problems will disappear simply because you pray. It does mean that if you place your faith and trust in God and confide in Him in prayer, you will experience the peace of mind that will sensitize you to the guidance of the Holy Spirit.

He will enable you to think clearly and act positively. In His strength you will be able to handle your problems in accordance with the will of God.

Soothe my restless heart, O Holy Spirit. Calm the tempestuous ocean and the storms that rage. Lead me to waters where there is serenity so that I may experience peace of mind.

THE CORNERSTONE
OF YOUR FAITH

And now these three remain: faith, hope and love.
But the greatest of these is love (1 Cor. 13:13).

The Christian faith has many facets because people view and interpret Christ from many perspectives. This is understandable, because each denomination has its own traditions born from its unique history.

However, when you refuse to accept the authenticity of someone's faith because it differs from yours, serious problems may enter your spiritual life. This refusal causes a fanatic and narrow-minded attitude that will ultimately destroy the beauty of your living faith.

The test of your faith is the amount of love towards your neighbor that it generates—especially towards those who have a different perspective than yours. Such a love finds its roots not in ignoring the teachings and traditions of those who think differently from you, but only in living so close to Christ that His love flows through you. Your love for Christ envelops everyone who loves and serves Him, even though you cannot agree with them on every level.

Love is the most crucial factor in the Christian life. This love isn't always even-tempered, because there are moments when it challenges and admonishes. It makes you humble so that it may exalt you to great spiritual heights; it empties you of yourself so that you may be filled with the life of Christ. Love is an active agent that helps you to grow in the understanding of your heavenly Father, thus also increasing your appreciation of your fellow human beings.

Lord God, I worship You as the source of all true love.
Let Your love manifest itself in my life. Grant me an ever
greater understanding and appreciation of my fellow human beings.

PURIFY YOUR MEMORIES

Why are you downcast, O my soul? Why so disturbed
within me? Put your hope in God, for I will yet
praise him, my Savior and my God (Ps. 42:5-6).

Your memories are of your own making. When you recall times and deeds of which you are ashamed, your conscience will probably be disturbed and uncomfortable. It is at times like these that you wish that you could erase the memories that torture you so.

If you sincerely repent of the sin that is the cause of the memory, you can be assured of forgiveness through Christ. He forgives and repairs through His redemptive love. Then you will be able to live in peace and harmony with God, yourself, and others.

Today you are busy creating memories for tomorrow. Therefore you should be sensible and wise and create happiness for your future through your deeds and thoughts. A sure way of doing this is through a constant awareness of the living Christ.

Live a day at a time for Him; trust Him at all times, even when things don't turn out to your liking. In so doing you will not only purify your old memories and create beautiful new memories, but you will also make the fulfilling discovery that you have walked with your Master through pain and tribulation, thus creating precious memories.

Merciful God and Father, my future is in Your loving hands
and therefore I can live to Your glory in the present. Purify my
memories through Your great love, so that they may honor You.

JESUS UNDERSTANDS BECAUSE HE LOVES YOU

Jesus wept. Then the Jews said, "See how he loved him!" (Jn. 11:35-36).

There are people who are skeptical of any suggestion that Jesus understands human problems. Their conception of the Lord is that He is someone faraway and aloof, removed from our everyday life and only interested in matters of primary importance. Therefore it cannot be expected that He will concern Himself with the apparently inconsequential matters that relate to the personal lives of people.

Such an attitude manifests a complete misconception of God and His loving interest in the world that He created and the human beings for whom His Son died and was resurrected.

It is true that we worship a God who is King of kings and Lord of lords, but we must never lose sight of the fact that Jesus is not only your Master, but also your Friend. Because He lived, suffered, and died as a human being, He understands human problems and emotions, since He experienced them Himself. He endured suffering, as well as disappointment, sorrow, and joy. The Son of God laughed and cried just as you and I do.

The Savior is waiting for you to invite Him to share your life with Him. Open your heart to Him so that He may help you in whatever circumstances you may find yourself in. Never forget that He is a friend who loves you and understands you.

> *Lord Jesus, in You I have found a friend who is loving, faithful, and understanding. Grant that I will experience Your love under all circumstances in my life.*

MAKE JESUS' RESURRECTION A REALITY

"Do not be afraid, for I know that you are looking for Jesus, who was crucified. He is not here; he has risen, just as he said" (Mt. 28:5-6).

Without the resurrection of Jesus Christ, Christianity would have been a long-forgotten religion. His principles touch our hearts, stimulate our thoughts, and are an inspiration to innumerable charity organizations. But the same things may be said of other religious leaders.

What makes Christ unique is not only the inspiration that can be drawn from His doctrine, but He Himself. He courageously went forth to meet death, and conquered it. He came back from the dead and met His disciples under different circumstances and promised to be with them always.

It is the living Christ that reigns in the lives of a multitude of people in the new millennium. They have dedicated themselves to Christ and their worship of Him is a personal matter to them, not an organizational issue, a religious teaching, or a dogma. They meet Him daily in quiet seclusion and are always aware of His living presence.

These people may be unable to give a clearly defined explanation of their faith. In all likelihood they have no theological training, but deep down they know that Christ lives, that He loves them, and has made them His property. No one will undermine their faith that the risen and glorified Savior lives and reigns in their hearts and lives.

Risen Lord and Savior, I thank You that I may exult in Your resurrection and glorification. Help me never to live as if You are dead.

GOD WORKS IN EVERYDAY THINGS

In his heart a man plans his course,
but the LORD determines his steps (Prov. 16:9).

It is true that God often works in great and miraculous ways. We see His glory in the changing heavens; His handiwork in the beauty of creation. Despite appearances which seem to indicate otherwise, the earth still belongs to Him and He is still in control of it. When you ponder the greatness of creation, it is impossible to retain a narrow-minded conception of God.

However, you must not lose sight of the fact that God is also the Creator of the small and everyday things: the perfection of the rose; the frailty of the forget-me-not. All these things reflect a creative God who is also the Master of order and detail.

We so easily forget that God is interested in our well-being. If you doubt this, just consider how many times in the past He guided you through difficult circumstances. Looking back, you will realize that you should probably thank Him for prayers that remained unanswered. And sometimes He responded in such an everyday way to your prayers that you hardly recognized it as answers.

Be acutely aware of your circumstances when you pray, because you never know how God will answer. Many people continue praying for things long after God has answered their prayers. Others who see their prayers answered ascribe it to coincidence. God chooses His own way of working in your life and it is often through the everyday and familiar things in life that He chooses to do so.

Thank You, almighty God, that You never cease
working in my life and answering my prayers. You speak
with a thousand tongues; let me always hear Your voice.

ACCUMULATE SCRIPTURAL AMMUNITION

He will cover you with his feathers, and under his wings you will find refuge; his faithfulness will be your shield and rampart (Ps. 91:4).

The path of the Christian has its high as well as its low points. There are moments of victory when joy fills your spirit and thoughts, and your entire life appears to be full of the Spirit of the living Christ. Then there are times when life is filled with negativity and spiritual matters appear vague and unreal. In such times a heavy depression descends on your spirit and you may even feel that God has forsaken you.

One way to conquer spiritual dejection is to accumulate spiritual ammunition when you are spiritually strong. Don't read the Bible merely as part of a spiritual discipline, but learn to treasure certain Scripture verses that have a special meaning for you. Learn them by heart so that you can recall them in times of weakness and temptation. One thing is sure: a Christian who has knowledge of God's Word has a strong defense against the trickery of Satan. Anything that has been inspired by God to strengthen your faith is worth cherishing.

Knowing your Bible as a manual for the Christian life not only strengthens your faith but also helps you to become more sensitive to the ways in which God wishes to guide you. God often uses the Scriptures to manifest His will to His disciples. Always remember the words of 2 Timothy 3:16: "All Scripture is God-breathed and is useful for teaching, rebuking, correcting and training in righteousness."

Jesus my Lord, incarnate Word, through the Scriptures
I develop an ever-increasing love for You. Guide me
through Your Word, and strengthen my faith.

SPIRITUAL HUNGER

My soul yearns, even faints, for the courts of the LORD;
my heart and my flesh cry out for the living God (Ps. 84:2).

Spiritual hunger is not that easily recognizable and therefore many people deny its existence. They think that it is a religious term that has no bearing on everyday life. However, its symptoms are apparent to anyone who is willing to look.

Most people experience a profound longing for inner satisfaction. They feel that they would like to reach the point where they no longer have to strive after that which seems unattainable. If they do not experience such a feeling, they embark upon a restless quest for things that are of secondary importance.

This restlessness manifests itself in different ways. Life is lived at a pace and with a passion never intended by God. Time is devoted to and energy wasted on things that are of little or no significance. When this restlessness takes possession of your spirit, life becomes a cruel cycle of frustrated ideals and broken dreams.

A person who spends quality time with God is never spiritually hungry and is better able to live a balanced life and to avoid foolish mistakes. Spend time with your heavenly Father and note the effect that it has on your life. Spending time in His presence will fulfill all the desires of your heart and His peace will satisfy all your spiritual hunger.

Living Christ, through my communion with You
I experience the deep and peaceful fulfillment of all my needs.

EXTRACT THE MOST FROM YOUR FAITH

"Whoever has will be given more...Whoever does not have, even what he has will be taken from him" (Mt. 13:12).

There are many people who are deeply dissatisfied with their faith. They may not declare their disappointment openly, but their attitude towards the Christian faith is so apathetic that their faith in the living Christ has never inspired them to walk more intimately with Him. The inevitable result of this unhappy state of affairs is that their discipleship weakens and becomes ineffectual.

To receive everything that faith offers you, you should regard it as a full-time task and a dedicated way of life, and not as an addendum only to be used whenever convenient. A dedicated Christian must also be a scripturally bound Christian. Refusal to use the Scriptures as a code of moral conduct may cause your faith to become emotionally unbalanced. And then the message of the gospel becomes distorted to suit your own personal conviction and ideology. Eventually all the power of faith disappears in wishful thinking and unscriptural argumentation.

The church and the world currently have a serious need for disciplined Christianity that will affirm and proclaim the ideas of Jesus. The one truth that embraces all others is so simple that people have turned away from it and have called it impractical. Jesus said, "As I have loved you, so you must love one another" (Jn. 13:34).

The dedication that is required to live a life of Christian love demands a strength that can only be acquired from the Holy Spirit. This attitude is kept alive through prayer and contemplation and a constant yearning for a more profound experience with God.

I plead with You, O living Jesus, for the gift of Your Holy Spirit so that I may experience my faith to its fullest potential.

Read Matthew 5:43-48

BE AN INSPIRATION TO OTHERS

"If someone forces you to go one mile,
go with him two miles" (Mt. 5:41).

There are always two ways to carry out a task: you can either do it unwillingly and complainingly while trying to get away with doing as little as possible, or you can do it joyfully and diligently, thereby accomplishing more than what's expected of you.

If you work according to the first principle you will soon find yourself unpopular with your superiors and colleagues. Even more importantly, you will also be dissatisfied with yourself because you will know that you are not giving your best. To anyone worth his salt this will be an extremely unsatisfactory state of affairs.

However, if the second approach is your life philosophy, you will find that you not only hold the respect of your superiors and colleagues but also that your task—however humble it may be—has importance. It will provide you with a sense of satisfaction because you have set about a task and completed it joyfully and thoroughly.

You will run into problems if you try to do this on your own and in your own strength, but if you dedicate every aspect of your life to Christ and ask Him to guide everything you do, the strength of the Holy Spirit will soon enable you to undertake your task with a strength and enthusiasm that transcends human understanding.

Master and Savior, in Your strength I am capable of anything.
Help me to perform my duty joyfully and thoroughly.

LOVE IS THE KEY

Bless those who persecute you; bless and do not curse (Rom. 12:14).

There are those who find forgiveness extremely difficult. When you or someone that you love suffers as a result of someone else's behavior, you tend to harbor hatred in your heart towards the person responsible instead of granting complete forgiveness.

True forgiveness requires complete purification. You cannot pretend to forgive while still holding a grudge against the person concerned. Forgiveness demands that the slate be wiped clean so that you can start over without any anger in your heart.

This is humanly impossible, but with God the impossible becomes possible. The first step on the road to forgiveness is prayer. If someone has wronged you or someone you love, you must pray for the wrongdoer. Ask God to bless that person and to give you the grace to do so.

Pray that His love will take away all bitterness so that the healing balm of His peace may flow through your being. Once this has happened, you will find that the obstacle of bitterness has been removed, and the love of God will enable you to grant unconditional forgiveness.

The love of Jesus Christ has achieved victory over evil in its most barbaric forms. Why should you not allow this same love to cure you from your bitterness?

> *Jesus, my Redeemer, help me to forgive in love*
> *as You forgave me in love. You redeem me*
> *also from the bitterness of an unforgiving spirit.*

PROBLEMS CAN BE AN ASSET

We are hard pressed on every side, but not
crushed; perplexed, but not in despair (2 Cor. 4:8).

To be a disciple of Jesus in no way means that your life will be free of problems. Some of His noblest servants struggled with problems from the moment that they swore allegiance to Him. Even Jesus knew what problems His intimate relationship with God the Father would bring over Him.

The important fact is not the problem that confronts you, but the attitude with which you respond to it. Some people regard problems as obstacles or obstructions, while others see them as opportunities to grapple with a challenge or as ways to deepen their relationship with their heavenly Father.

It is possible to try and solve your problems in your own strength. Many people call this independent thinking, but if your thoughts fail, your problem remains just as insurmountable. It is at this point where those who have adopted Christ as their Lord and Master realize the value of His living presence. They take their problems to Him and in simple faith hand it over to Him.

The solution may appear immediately or it may be delayed, but no one who has ever sought His guidance has ever been disappointed. He guides those who place their faith in Him and turns their problems into an asset for life.

Grant me the faith, O Lord, to regard my problems as opportunities.

THE KINGDOM AND THE POWER AND THE GLORY!

The LORD has established his throne in heaven,
and his kingdom rules over all (Ps. 103:19).

In a world where so many people think that evil reigns over truth and justice, we must never lose sight of the fact that the power and the sovereignty and the majesty reside in God. It is this knowledge—and only this—that encourages and strengthens us even in our darkest hour.

History attests to many instances where it appeared as if everything was lost: when anarchy and lawlessness threatened to destroy all good order; when selfishness and lust dominated the thoughts of many people; when powerful nations attempted to destroy weak ones; when innocent people were oppressed and tortured.

Despite all these things history also manifests those times when truth and justice triumphed. There may have been a time of anxiety and concern when fear and suffering were rife, but ultimately the power of evil was destroyed and the righteous prevailed.

However hopeless circumstances may seem, never forget that God is almighty and great and that He is still in control. Place your trust in Jesus Christ your Redeemer and find encouragement and peace in the knowledge that our setbacks are merely temporary, because Christ has already conquered the world (see Jn. 16:33).

Almighty God, great wonders are performed by Your hand
and Your mighty deeds are borne out by the history
of mankind. From eternity until eternity You are God!

I IN HIM AND HE IN ME

*"Remain in me, and I will remain in you. No branch can
bear fruit by itself; it must remain in the vine" (Jn. 15:4).*

It is a sad truth that many people seek Jesus through inappropriate and
ineffective means. They take the inspiration that He offers them and use
it in different ways: they become ardent social reformers; they establish
political parties; they call themselves Christians and perform many
good deeds in His name.

It is possible to be active in Jesus' name and yet to forget the source that
inspired the service. Attempting to serve the Lord without the strength
that He alone can provide leads to frustration and disappointment.

The glorious truth that Jesus Christ is a living reality is a thought
pattern that every faithful person should cultivate until His presence
becomes a reality in our everyday lives. To be obsessed with the thought
of an immanent Christ does not turn a faithful person into a religious
fanatic, but simply creates a new awareness of the meaning of life. By
professing His presence you become aware of the problems, challenges,
joys, and sorrows of your existence as seen from His perspective. In this
way Jesus becomes an increasing reality in your life.

The pinnacle of your spiritual life is to know Him as a living reality.
This knowledge affects your practical and emotional life. Meeting Christ
in the silence of solitude and experiencing the touch of His Spirit upon
your spirit can have far-reaching consequences for your existence. It can
be a truly enriching experience for your soul, and to separate such an
experience from your everyday life may lead to great spiritual damage.

*O Hearer of prayers, grant me Your Holy Spirit,
so that I will persevere in prayer until I know your presence.*

WHAT GOD CAN ACCOMPLISH THROUGH YOU

"Remain in me, and I will remain in you. No branch
can bear fruit by itself; it must remain in the vine. Neither
can you bear fruit unless you remain in me" (Jn. 15:4).

You worship a God that performs miracles. In times of stress and tension you can call upon Him. Experience has proved that He will answer in His chosen way. With God you will always receive what you need, because He is the Giver of every perfect gift and you are the fortunate receiver.

Whenever you wish to respond to the benevolence of God, you usually start by looking around you for some or other good deed that you can perform to please the heart of God. You then start doing it with enthusiasm and dedication. But are you sure that this is what He wants you to do?

Discovering God's will for your life can be an exciting adventure. You may try out various directions before you finally discover the path upon which He wishes to lead you. But when you possess the inner conviction that you are within His holy will, you will discover that you are no longer working for Him, but that He is working through you.

When this happens the road ahead opens up miraculously. Problems suddenly become opportunities, and your faith becomes practical, alive, and dynamic. You realize that by working with God you become an effective instrument in His hand. You will never discover your full potential in the service of Christ until you realize what God can accomplish through you.

Holy Father, help me through Your guidance to become an instrument in Your hand so that I may work within Your will and to Your honor.

SHARE YOUR BURDENS WITH JESUS

"I have had enough, LORD," he said. "Take my life;
I am no better than my ancestors" (1 Kgs. 19:4).

How often have you felt, like Elijah, that perhaps it was time you gave up? Your plans go awry; your problems seem insurmountable; you have just managed to overcome one crisis when you have to face the next. Your good intentions are misinterpreted: you are misunderstood and blamed for things you are innocent of; you suffer injustice at the hands of others. When this happens you start wondering what precisely the sense and purpose of life is. You are tempted to stop trying to be the person that you intuitively know God expects you to be.

When you find yourself in this unbearable situation all you need to do is think back to the time when Jesus was alive. The Son of God—He who was born from God's love for the world and whose life exemplified the greatest love of all time—was despised and forsaken by people. He was crucified for our sins and to Him belonged the sorrow that brought us peace.

Despite injustice Jesus never hesitated or stumbled. He had a divine mission to complete. By placing His faith in God He completed His mission and as a result the world has learned to understand the meaning of the words "love" and "forgiveness."

When your spirit is at the low-water mark, turn your heart and mind to Christ who knows and understands your suffering better than you. Place your trust in Him and He will lead you from the darkness of your own despondency into His marvelous light.

Light of the world, bright and inextinguishable, dispel all darkness
from my life; banish all fear and lead me to Your wonderful light.

YOU HAVE RESPONSIBILITIES AS A CHRISTIAN

*"Now that you know these things, you will
be blessed if you do them" (Jn. 13:17).*

Where there is fear, there is mistrust, and this leads to confusion. This scenario is clearly evident in national and international state affairs, because fear and mistrust go hand in hand in many countries in the world, thus causing disorder and chaos.

What is happening globally is symptomatic of what is happening in the lives of many people. They become fearful of what other people think and how they act and then become defensive about their own faith and behavior. In this way the dismal cycle flourishes and spreads its destructive influence until all of humanity is possessed by fear.

It is no exaggeration to claim that a lack of faith in God and one another is what has forced human beings into this dangerous situation. A world that is controlled by fear is not a safe place to live in. How sad it is that people refuse to proclaim and use the antidote for fear. This antidote was set out by Jesus: "Love one another" (Jn. 13:34). And the apostle of love re-confirmed it: "There is no fear in love. But perfect love drives out fear" (1 Jn. 4:18).

Act positively and allow the Holy Spirit to fill you with so much love that you fear no more. Be a proclaimer and example of the peace that only Christ can give. You can influence a terror-stricken world, honor your Christian duties, and thereby become part of the solution and not the problem.

*Holy Spirit, grant me an infectious faith so that others
may share in the love and peace that You bestow upon me.*

A REASON TO LIVE

"Because I live, you also will live" (Jn. 14:19).

In these ominous times in which we live, there are many people who wonder whether living is worthwhile. They are possessed by a terrified doubt over an unknown future, and a spirit of pessimism and dejection prevails in their minds. However, life is extremely precious and even the most despairing person realizes this when his or her life comes under serious threat.

Despite how hopeless the future may appear, it is of the utmost importance to admit and accept the fact that both your life and the future are in the hands of God. The Christian's life is not ruled by blind fate. God is in control of every situation in which you may find yourself. He knows your needs and is always prepared to provide for you.

As your faith grows and you begin to trust Him more, you will also begin to realize the joy of a life in Christ and be comforted by the awareness of the unfailing and immutable God. He is the Rock upon which you can build your entire life and future.

Through His death and resurrection Jesus not only gave you life but also a reason to live. Through His Holy Spirit He also provides you with the ability to cope with life. Choose life and live it in the abundance of Jesus Christ, always honoring Him.

Faithful Leader, in the midst of the change and the corruption that I see around me daily, I am assured that Jesus lives and that He has also made it worthwhile for me to be alive.

FROM CONVERSION TO DISCIPLESHIP

*But grow in the grace and knowledge
of our Lord and Savior Jesus Christ (2 Pet. 3:18).*

There are people who can very clearly remember the moment when they accepted Jesus as the Lord and Redeemer of their lives. Others cannot remember a time when they did not love Him and did not acknowledge His sovereignty in their lives.

The crucial fact of your Christian life is not necessarily the moment of your conversion, but rather how far you have since progressed on the Christian path. Conversion is the beginning of your Christian pilgrimage, but discipleship implies growing trust, increasing love, and unconditional obedience to the Master. It is this dynamic discipleship that keeps your faith strong and meaningful.

Always rejoice in the truth that you believe in Christ as your Lord and Redeemer, and be assured that He will lead you in ever more wonderful ways on the path ahead. To begin a new life in Christ is like walking from the darkness into the light. The realization that Christ wants to live in you and wants to express Himself through you opens up an entirely new world. Discipleship means oneness with the Master, and as your love for Him inspires you to greater obedience, His immanent presence will become an ever greater reality to you.

Discipleship implies continuous growth in Christ, until He becomes the greatest motivating force in your life. Then you will discover that you can do nothing without Him, but that with Him you are able to accomplish all things. This is the pure joy of discipleship.

*Jesus, I place my love and trust in You and
rejoice in the knowledge that I can grow closer to
You every day, thus becoming more like Your image.*

CAN THE WORLD SEE THAT YOU ARE A CHRISTIAN?

They rested on the Sabbath in obedience
to the commandment (Lk. 23:56).

The cruel deed is done. The Son of God has fallen prey to man's inhumanity to his fellow man. The jeering, screaming, merciless crowds of Good Friday are now the pious people of the Sabbath. The evil deeds of the day are behind them and now they can return to their lives of devoutness and obedience to the law of Moses. They worship and rest as it behooves God-fearing people. It is the Sabbath.

There is a distinct quality of hypocrisy present in this situation, which should serve as a warning to all Christians. Just as you are shocked by the thought of these pious people parading through the temple with the blood of Jesus still on their hands, so you should realize that a Christian's surrender to the Master implies a life of complete obedience, not just an attitude that is displayed on a Sunday.

The authenticity of your faithfulness to Jesus will be judged according to the way you live your life at all times, and not only in the sphere of the church. Your faith and commitment to Christ's cause will be tested precisely when you are most susceptible to irritation, anger, jealousy, and pride. It is your responsibility to live every day of the week according to the instructions of Jesus—not only on Sundays. This is what your Lord trusts you to do to show His glory in this world.

Loving Master, I will prove to the world that I am a Christian through the consistency of my love. Enable me to do this through Your Spirit.

SPIRITUAL GROWTH
THROUGH PRAYER

After Job had prayed for his friends, the LORD made him prosperous again and gave him twice as much as he had before (Job 42:10).

It is by no means difficult to make enemies. You only have to say the wrong thing, or even do absolutely nothing, and you will find that you have somehow managed to make an enemy. Furthermore it isn't necessarily helpful to always hold a post-mortem over a dead friendship.

But some frank talking inspired by a sincere desire to revive a friendship can often be of great benefit. However, if this sincere desire is absent, the air will simply be contaminated even more by attempts of straightforward and candid conversation.

No one enjoys making enemies. Remember that it is possible to turn an enemy into a friend. Granted, this isn't always easy, because forgiveness requires true greatness. Trying to understand the false pride, secret fears, and plain foolishness of man is a beginning that may help in this process. Only those who have undergone meaningful spiritual growth can transform enmity into friendship. Those who are spiritually stunted keep the embers of bitterness burning in their words, deeds, and attitudes.

One sure and practical way of starting to turn enemies into friends is by praying for them. To many of us, this may sound absurd and excessively altruistic, but it is a truly wise act if you desire a constructive way of life. Prayer changes your attitude towards people and events, and when this happens, the battle is just about won. With God on your side, you are on the side of ultimate victory.

Dear Lord, help me to grow in You so that I may manifest a forgiving spirit. You have forgiven me through Your grace. Help me to follow Your example.

WE MUST LOVE ONE ANOTHER

Follow the way of love (1 Cor. 14:1).

All around the world people are seeking greater knowledge and aware-ness of our Lord, Jesus Christ. As the Holy Spirit awakens them, people are striving to meet the Master in prayer, worship, communion, and study. It is probably true to say that the enthusiasm which people have displayed in this quest is as great now as it has ever been.

While this diligent approach to one's faith is commendable and should be encouraged, one has to remember not to lose sight of the foun-dation of the Christian faith.

The birth, death, and resurrection of Jesus demonstrate God's un-fathomable love for His people. Through Jesus Christ He has made it abundantly clear that of all the things that He has commanded you to do, faith showing itself through love stands out from all other things.

Knowledge of the Master and the blessing of spiritual gifts are much sought after attributes among His modern disciples, but regardless of how scripturally knowledgeable you are or how much you know of God, there is nothing that manifests the glory of God more than the love of Jesus Christ.

Concentrate your pilgrimage on continually getting to know Him better. Don't merely learn about Him. Allow His love to fill your being so that you may reflect it in your everyday life.

Jesus, loving Master, let my daily life be an expression of Your love.

GOD IS WITH YOU

"The LORD your God is with you, he is mighty to save.
He will take great delight in you, he will quiet you with
his love, he will rejoice over you with singing" (Zeph. 3:17).

When things start going wrong in your life it is easy to throw in the towel. The battle in which you are involved just seems to be so unfair. There are many people who once seemed invincible, but who simply allowed themselves to be overwhelmed by a spirit of hopelessness.

If ever there was a situation when everything seemed hopeless it was on the day of Jesus' crucifixion. The hopes and dreams of those who thought that He would be the Savior of Israel were dashed when He died like a common criminal on the cross.

But then God interceded. The Lord God, who was Christ's hope and strength, miraculously turned defeat into victory. The sorrowful Good Friday was transformed into the triumphant resurrection of Easter Sunday when Christ rose in all majesty from death.

Whatever circumstances you find yourself in; however dismal the future may seem and despite all the problems that confront you, always remember that God is with you and that He is in control of your circumstances. Place your faith and trust in Him and He will grant you victory.

Redeemer and Friend, thank You that I may
be sure that God loves me and is always
with me. It makes my heart rejoice.

May

Loving triune God,
during this month we call to mind the descent of the Holy Spirit.
As always You have kept Your covenant:
You have sent us the other Comforter
to comfort us in our deepest sorrow;
to be our Leader when we are unsure of
the road that we must travel;
to be our Teacher who reveals Your will to us;
who teaches us how to love You truly and
how to serve our fellow human beings in love.
Send Your Spirit as a flame, to cleanse and purify me of all false
motives, all envy, all unforgiveness and hate,
all pride and self-exaltation.
Send Your Spirit as a wind, to rush through my life and bring
new life and growth.
Send Your Spirit as a dove, to confer on me the peace of God
that transcends all human understanding.
Send Your Spirit as water, to wash me whiter than snow
and to allow me to grow spiritually so that I may bear the fruit
that befits my conversion.
Send Your Spirit as the dew, to refresh me and nourish me
with heavenly strength.
Recreate, O Spirit, let live, O Spirit.
Let the kingdom come in glory.

Amen.

CONFIDENCE FOR THE FUTURE

The way of the LORD is a refuge for the righteous (Prov. 10:29).

To be forewarned should mean to be equipped to cope with every life situation. Unfortunately many people disregard warnings and then are surprised when they have to bear the consequences of their actions.

The Bible is full of warnings. Some have already been fulfilled, but others refer to prophecies that have not yet been fulfilled. It would seem as if current world events are inexorably moving towards a climax. The times in which we live are unparalleled in human history, and intelligent people justifiably wonder what the future holds.

People who live within God's will because they are faithful and who believe that mankind is not controlled by fate but by a loving Creator, draw comfort from the knowledge that, despite appearances to the contrary, there is a divine plan at work in man's life.

This faith creates trust and provides hope; it conquers fear and gives the Christian disciple the ability to step into the future with confidence and in the certain conviction that God is still in control. To possess this kind of faith, God must stand at the center of your life. If this is the case you will see world events in the light of the eternal design of God and you will be equipped to meet the future with confidence.

Almighty God, I believe with conviction that You are still completely in control of Your Creation as well as of the world events of our time. Once more I place my trust fully in You.

FAITH IS THE ANSWER

The mystery of godliness is great: He appeared in a body, was vindicated by the Spirit, was seen by angels, was preached among the nations, was believed on in the world, was taken up in glory (1 Tim. 3:16).

However contradictory this statement may appear to you, it remains an indisputable fact of the Christian faith, in all its simultaneous complexity and simplicity. Where else would you find God assuming a human form or a King living as a simple town carpenter? Kings live in palaces, and yet the Prince of peace had no place to rest His head. Jesus stood His ground against the scholars of His time and overwhelmed them with His knowledge and intellectual abilities. And yet simple people understood Him when He explained profound truths to them in the form of parables.

The circumstances of your life often confuse and trouble you, and sometimes you are simply unable to understand a particular situation. Your peace of mind can be disturbed by fear, illness, death, and so many other negative things. Your faith so easily becomes unsettled and then you start questioning God's love and the purpose of your faith.

This is the time for relying on God. He arranges everything for the benefit of those who love Him. For the faithful, good is born from evil. From the evil of Golgotha the victory of the resurrection emerged. God has a sacred purpose with everything that happens in your life, and when the time is right this purpose will be revealed to you.

I praise and thank You, Lord my God, that I may faithfully accept Your every act in my life because I know that everything works for the good of those who love You.

PONDER THE BENEVOLENCE OF GOD

"How I long for the months gone by, for the days when
God watched over me, when his lamp shone upon my head
and by his light I walked through darkness!" (Job 29:2-3).

There is nothing strange about people occasionally losing their spiritual way. It can easily happen after the ecstasy of a dramatic conversion has abated and you start living your life according to your accustomed ways again, with old temptations cropping up.

Or perhaps you are suffering from depression and despondency as a result of sorrow or illness, anxiety or fear, or setbacks and failures. It is in these circumstances that feelings of helplessness and despair may easily overwhelm you.

In times like these you need to hold on to your faith and to place your trust in Christ who has promised never to forsake or abandon you. Think of the goodness of God and constantly remind yourself of the path along which He has guided you up to now; how He has protected you and looked after you in the past.

Jesus never changes. As He has done in the past He now waits for you to turn to Him in your times of crises. Lay all your fears and worries before Him. True to His promises, His perfect love will drive away all fear and you will be enveloped in His love.

Be still my soul, the Lord is on your side. In this knowledge I will
struggle through all my disappointments, sorrow, and grief, because
You grant me the strength to do so. For this I praise and thank You.

SHARE YOUR PROBLEMS WITH JESUS

The troubles of my heart have multiplied;
free me from my anguish (Ps. 25:17).

There are few things that can have such a potentially negative effect on your spiritual, physical, and emotional well-being as problems and worries. They influence you subconsciously to such an extent that your mental abilities may be impaired. In many cases this results in people becoming spiritual and physical wrecks.

When Jesus called those who are weary and overburdened to Him, He did not guarantee them complete exemption from problems, nor did He promise that all their problems would disappear instantaneously. Instead, He offered to share their burden and also to teach them how to cope with it so that they may find peace of mind.

You can never predict when you will experience setbacks in life, nor can you foresee how serious these incidents will be. What is of crucial importance is that you prepare yourself to handle these problems when they crop up. To be unprepared for these eventualities may have devastating results.

To maintain a healthy balance and harmony in your mind, it is essential to develop a healthy personal relationship with the living Christ. Remain near to Jesus through faithful prayer and contemplation. If you do this, you will find that when problems strike, He will be with you to help you conquer them with peace in your heart.

Faithful Lord Jesus, thank You that I may come
to You with all my problems and worries in the
certainty that I will find peace and rest with You.

GOD'S WAY

Good and upright is the LORD; therefore
he instructs sinners in his ways (Ps. 25:8).

In today's world it is very easy to lose one's spiritual way. The pressure exerted by the sinful world is felt by young as much as old; temptations are countless and offered on a silver platter; the variety of detours make it extremely difficult to follow the right path. In an era that constantly questions standards and morality, there is always a fundamental danger that our principles may be compromised, however innocent and harmless the first step may seem at the time.

There is only one way to live your life and that is to keep to God's ways. In His commandments He set out the basic rules for a pious and devout life. In addition to this, Christ became a living example that demonstrated to us how such a life ought to be lived.

Even though centuries have passed, nothing has changed with regard to the way of life that is acceptable and pleasing to God. Christ is still the way, the truth, and the life, and the path of righteousness is still that of obedience to God in all things.

If you open your heart and life to the immanent Holy Spirit, you will become increasingly aware of His influence and suggestions. Follow His guidance and you will know that the path you are following is God's way.

Search me, O God, and know my heart;
test me and know my anxious thoughts.
See if there is any offensive way in me, and
lead me in the way everlasting (Ps. 139:23-24).

WHEN THINGS BECOME UNMANAGEABLE

And who is equal to such a task? (2 Cor. 2:16).

We all go through times when things threaten to overwhelm us and our faith appears to be an inadequate defense. It seems as if our circumstances are continually worsening, our relationships suffer grievous blows, and everything suddenly appears unmanageable.

What is actually happening is that you have allowed the challenges of the world to exceed your spiritual reserves. The demands of life have proved your faith to be insufficient. When you feel as if you have reached breaking point you need to return to the fundamentals of your faith and assure yourself of the presence of God in your life. This will help you to restore the balance in your life so that you can see people and events in the right perspective.

It is definitely not God's intention to place you under so much pressure that you reach breaking point and collapse under the strain. A living and positive faith is a stabilizing influence under the most confusing circumstances. Possessing such a faith is not a spiritual luxury, but an urgent necessity if you wish to deal with the demands of life successfully.

Realizing the necessity of faith is the first step to possessing it. If you are unaware of your need, how will you be able to fulfill it? When you tell the Lord that you need His help and trust Him unconditionally, you will know that He will carry you through, because you love and trust in Him.

Lord Jesus, through Your wisdom and strength I am able to cope with all the demands of life. Keep me close to Your heart at all times.

BOLSTER YOUR SELF-CONFIDENCE

The LORD is my light and my salvation—whom shall I fear? The LORD is the stronghold of my life—of whom shall I be afraid? (Ps. 27:1).

There are times when everything appears dismal and uncertain. Your thoughts are bewildered, with the result that your life loses its sense of direction. Your confidence in yourself starts fading until it is almost nonexistent. When this happens you inevitably become unsure of God, your faith falters, and your life starts losing meaning and significance.

A tried and proven way of restoring your faith in life so that you can live a life free from feelings of inferiority is to be absolutely sure that God is all-sufficient for you. This all-sufficiency is not something that is forced upon you from an almighty being, but is rather the effect of the merciful Spirit of God in your own spirit. It is the knowledge that God lives and works in you daily. This tremendous truth gives you the self-confidence to face the demands of every day.

When you invite the Spirit of God into your life all detrimental fear is defeated and eventually vanishes because you know that God is busy actualizing His plan with your life. Because His presence is a reality to you, the future will unfold before you in all its joy, peace, and self-confidence.

Thank You, almighty God, that destructive fear is removed from my life by the ministry of the Holy Spirit and instead replaced with quiet confidence.

AN EXERCISE IN PRAYER

Be joyful in hope, patient in affliction, faithful in prayer (Rom. 12:12).

Is your prayer life everything that you would like it to be? And everything that Christ would like it to be? You may regard this as a rather presumptuous question, but you are the only one who needs to know the answer. However, your answer can make the difference between an ineffective prayer life or one that is filled with an awareness of the presence of God.

While you are praying you undoubtedly think of your family and friends. They probably form part of your normal prayer pattern, and it is possible that you seldom think beyond them. And yet the whole world is pleading for prayer. If you doubt this statement, all you need to do is take a look at your newspaper. Every newspaper is a prayer manual in itself. You can pray for the editors and those who are responsible for forming public opinion; you can pray for those who grieve; who are the victims of violence, and if your soul is noble enough, even for those who committed the acts of violence. If you search for it, you may even be able to find something for which to thank God.

When you move out of your everyday world, you will find innumerable opportunities for prayer. Give some thought in prayer to those who seem tired and disillusioned or to all the irritable people you encounter. Rejoice together with those who are happy and thank God for their happiness. You never have to search for a reason to pray.

The great advantage of expanding your prayer base is the fact that it intensifies your own quiet time with God. While you are praying for others, you will find a more intimate communion with the living Christ.

Lord Jesus, with Your disciples I want to plead: Teach me to pray!

BEWARE! PITFALLS AHEAD!

They mingled with the nations and adopted their customs. They worshiped their idols, which became a snare to them (Ps. 106:35-36).

It is an overly familiar fact that people attach much value to material things and the pleasures that life offers. This often becomes the dominating factor of everyday life and eventually life in its totality begins to revolve around materialism and pleasure, so that people become completely dependent on it. This dependence may be work or leisure; it may even include some kind of addiction. Whatever it may be, it becomes the controlling factor in the life of the particular person and has preference over everything else.

Regardless of what it may be, when it relegates God to a lesser position in your life, it becomes an idol. And whether people like it or not, or whether they are willing to admit it or not, he who makes himself guilty of this becomes an idolater.

Any form of addiction, be it work, pleasure, or habit, leads to a road that is riddled with pitfalls. Obsession, addiction, and uncontrolled desires are but a few forms of fixation that, if left unchecked, will inevitably lead to disastrous and grim consequences for those involved, as well as their loved ones.

Beware of anything in your life that runs counter to your relationship with Jesus. If it clashes with His life, example, and principles, abandon it. Follow the living Christ and enjoy a life of peace and fulfillment.

I know, my Redeemer and Savior, that I will only be happy and prosperous in this world if I follow Your example meticulously. Please let Your Holy Spirit assist and help me in this.

SPIRITUAL MATURITY

You are controlled not by the sinful
nature but by the Spirit (Rom. 8:9).

To appreciate the greatness of God and to rejoice in the majesty of His creation elevates the human spirit above the pettiness that is the product of a limited view of life.

When you cannot rise above the pain inflicted upon you by the thoughtless tongue of a flippant person; when it seems as if your life is restricted by a lack of opportunities and undesirable circumstances; when you have fallen into a rut from which you just can't escape—these are the times when you should start questioning the basic reason for your existence.

The direction in which you are traveling clearly manifests where you have chosen to place the emphasis in your life. If you seek financial success or social prestige to the exclusion of more important things in life, you may reach your destination but also lose much.

Because God has created you to be a spiritual being, your spiritual life can never be satisfied by purely material matters. You need a dynamic relationship with the Holy Spirit, which is the only thing that will provide you with permanent satisfaction. This personal relationship with God can be achieved only through a steadfast faith in Jesus Christ. This faith is more than an emotional experience. It encompasses your acceptance of Jesus in your life as well as your willingness to allow His Spirit to manifest Himself through you. Together with this acceptance comes spiritual growth that will give your life new meaning.

Holy Father, grant me a profound awareness of
the importance of spiritual growth, so that
I may possess a meaningful and sensitive spirit.

PROVE TO GOD
THAT YOU LOVE HIM

If anyone obeys his word, God's love is
truly made complete in him (1 Jn. 2:5).

There is often a kind of sentimentality present in our spiritual lives that detracts from the force and strength of the Christian faith. To resist this, many disciples of the Master refrain completely from any sentiment and bring forward an unfeeling faith that is often also aggressive.

Telling God how much you love Him may create an impression of cheap sentimentality, and yet it is one of the most inspiring things that you can do. It fortifies your inner spirit, focuses your thoughts on eternal realities, and confirms the convictions that you have always held but seldom expressed.

To tell God you love Him is much more than a noble sentiment, because love without constructive action is useless. Love demands deeds that uplift and inspire. James asks, "What good is it if a man claims to have faith but has no deeds?" (see Jas. 2:14). How genuine can your love for God truly be if you are aware of a serious need and do nothing to alleviate it?

When you tell God that you love Him without any intellectual or spiritual reservations, you are offering your very best to Him and expressing your willingness to serve Him in any sphere where He wishes to use you. Love that does not practically manifest itself becomes an emotional gimmick that lacks the essence of dynamic spirituality.

Beloved Father, I want to tell You repeatedly and with
complete conviction: I love You with all my heart, O Lord!

DO YOUR THOUGHTS BETRAY THE MASTER?

"I tell you the truth, one of you is going to betray me" (Jn. 13:21).

The name of Judas Iscariot has a place in the annals of history that will never be erased. His betrayal is known to everyone who has ever heard the name of Jesus Christ. The world has never given the name of Judas the opportunity to disappear into obscurity.

Nonetheless, is he really the only person to have betrayed Jesus? Whatever the motive for his betrayal, it must already have been developing in his mind while he enjoyed the intimate companionship of Jesus and his fellow disciples. He was one of the chosen twelve. However, the motives that drive people are known only to themselves and God. Judas was probably frequently excited when Jesus spoke of the kingdom of God. Unfortunately his idea of the kingdom of God differed radically from that of Christ. Judas tried to force Jesus' principles into his own thought patterns, with disastrous results.

We must guard against trying to force Christ and His powerful principles into our own preconceived ideas and doctrines. If you are trying to force Christ into your thought patterns you are betraying Him because you are attempting to limit Him. What is of fundamental importance in your relationship with Christ is not what you try to do with Him, but rather what you are willing to allow Him to do with you. Allow Christ to control your thoughts and to expand your spirit.

Pull me ever closer to You, dear Lord, so that I may better understand Your purpose with my life and never betray You for the sake of things that are of lesser importance.

SOMETHING TO LIVE FOR

*"Before long, the world will not see me anymore, but you
will see me. Because I live, you also will live" (Jn. 14:19).*

In these ominous times there are many people who wonder whether it is
worthwhile to be alive. They harbor doubt over an unknown future, and
as a result they lapse into a mood of pessimism and dejection. Regardless of this we have to remember that life is extremely precious, and even
the most despairing person realizes this when his or her life is threatened.

Despite how hopeless the future may appear, it is of the utmost
importance to admit and accept the fact that both your life and your
future are in the hands of God. The Christian's life is not ruled by a blind
fate. God is in control of every situation in which you find yourself. He
knows your needs and is prepared to provide for you through the wealth
and abundance of Jesus Christ.

As your faith grows and becomes stronger and as you start trusting
Him continually more, you will also begin to realize how great the joy
of a life in Christ is and how trustworthy God is. He is the Rock upon
which you can build your entire life and future, knowing that His grace
is enough to get you through each day.

Through His death and resurrection Jesus not only gave you life but
also a reason to live. Through His Holy Spirit He provides you with the
ability to live life to the fullest. Seize this life and live it in the abundance
of Jesus Christ your Lord.

*Throughout all the changing circumstances of life, beloved
Lord, in joy as well as sorrow, my heart will sing Your praise.
Thank You for the abundant life that You have made possible for me.*

A PART OF GOD'S FAMILY

You are all sons of God through faith in Christ Jesus (Gal. 3:26).

No one is alone in this world. This is the gospel of God. There are many people who feel that they have no one to turn to, and there are others who claim that they have no family. Neither they nor you are alone in this world, because through Jesus you are part of the most privileged family on earth: the family of God.

Your surrender to the Lord Jesus opened the door to the love and concern of the almighty God who is also your heavenly Father. In the coming of Christ, the love of God was manifested to the world.

Through Christ you too are invited to become a child of God, and as such to enjoy the ultimate loving relationship that exists between Father and child. This is a constant relationship, because the Lord has undertaken to be with you always and to never forsake you (see Heb. 23:5).

If you remember to turn to Jesus in all circumstances and place your trust in Him completely, you will experience the protective love of God that will grant you the peace that transcends all understanding. And then you will never again feel as if you are alone in life.

> *Great and holy God, it is beyond my understanding how You can condescend to be my Father and Friend. My life is too brief to thank You sufficiently for this.*

WORSHIP GOD

My message and my preaching were not with wise and persuasive words, but with a demonstration of the Spirit's power (1 Cor. 2:4).

There is a great danger present in our churches today, namely, the number of people who attend services to hear the speaker rather than the Word. This kind of attitude may easily lead to church attendance for the sake of entertainment rather than for the sake of worshiping God and sharing communion with the faithful.

In the establishment of the first church, Christ predominantly used simple and uneducated people. Throughout the ages many of the great pillars of the church possessed little or no learning, and yet hundreds of thousands were converted by their preaching. God has often chosen people who would by conventional standards fail a preaching test to be His instruments.

This serves to prove that it is the Holy Spirit, and not people's competence, which moves people to surrender their lives to Jesus and trust in Him. In all preaching the emphasis should be on the glory of God, and Christ should be its main content.

In your worship you should always seek the guidance of the Holy Spirit. If the message impels you to dedicate your life to Jesus Christ, you will know for sure that you worship God in spirit and in truth.

Help me, O Lord, to worship only You as the triune God: Father, Son, and Holy Spirit.

YOUR INVISIBLE SUPPORT

For who among men knows the thoughts of a man except the man's spirit within him? In the same way no one knows the thoughts of God except the Spirit of God (1 Cor. 2:11).

Homeless people have no social support structure. These unfortunate people have no money and are dependent on the generosity and charity of their fellow human beings. They live in truly dismal circumstances.

Spiritually, many people live in similar circumstances. These are the people who manage their pilgrimage towards eternity only by being carried along by the faith of their parents or by a religious tradition. They pride themselves on a religious inheritance, but when tension and pressure start taking their toll and life becomes harsh and merciless, the inadequacy of their faith is revealed and their entire lives collapse. They too have no apparent support structure.

As a Christian the inner support of your spirit cannot be calculated in terms that the world would understand. Paul writes, "God has revealed it to us by His Spirit. The Spirit searches all things, even the deep things of God" (1 Cor. 2:10). Only when you have surrendered yourself to the living Christ and have felt His love and strength course through you can you know the force that supports your inner spirit.

Without a personal experience of Jesus, the qualities that are necessary for a living faith are absent from your inner life. It is Christ in your spirit that is your invisible support structure.

Holy Lord Jesus, I praise and thank You for giving me inner power and strength and sustaining me through Your Spirit that is in me.

ASPIRE TO THAT WHICH IS NOBLE

Finally, brothers, whatever is true, whatever is noble, whatever is right, whatever is pure, whatever is lovely, whatever is admirable—if anything is excellent or praiseworthy—think about such things (Phil. 4:8).

Life can be an unpleasant or an exquisite experience, depending on your attitude towards it. It is unfortunately true that when you are confronted with the cruelty of life it is all too easy to allow it to become ingrained in your nature and personality. Because we live in a world where the accepted norms are not the standards of God, it is dangerously easy to set your spiritual goals lower in order to conform to popular opinion. When this happens life loses its beauty and you no longer experience the joy and strength of the immanent Christ.

It requires spiritual sensitivity to appreciate the beauty of life. To believe in God as the origin and Creator of all things that are beautiful and noble, you should start by seeing Him in unexpected places: in the smile of a friend, the innocence of a child, the unobtrusive deed of love, the ultimate success of someone who has struggled for a long time. In ways that are too many to mention, you will begin to see the wonder and beauty of life.

However, the greatest gift of all is when through the grace of God you develop the ability to distinguish between that which is base and offensive, and that which is noble and beautiful, and to accept the responsibility for making the right choice. In choosing Christ you open your life to beauty, nobility, and truth.

I bring You my humble thanks, O Savior, that through the awareness of Your immanent Spirit I have the ability to appreciate the beauty and grandeur of life.

CONQUER BOREDOM

His commands are not burdensome, for everyone
born of God overcomes the world (1 Jn. 5:3-4).

It is astounding to see how many people are bored with life. Boredom is also not limited to a particular group or class of society. Young people who ought to be enjoying life complain that they have nothing to do and show little or no interest in the world around them.

Many of the elderly who are no longer active find life tedious because they have lost all interest in it. Boredom deprives life of its beauty and creativity. However, those who find life boring have no one to blame but themselves.

God has placed you in a wonderful world filled with fascinating people. If you are bored, you have simply become detached from the wonders of God's creation. It is also an indication that your faith is insufficient to satisfy your spiritual needs and therefore you experience a serious deficiency within yourself.

If you are filled with the love of God, it will be manifested in your love for people, your appreciation of life, and your enthusiasm for everything happening around you. True love creates interest and involvement.

When you begin a new day, believe that it will be the best day ever, and live it to the fullest. Resolve to be enthusiastic and joyful. Allow God's purpose with your life to unfold while you live purposefully for Him. Your enthusiasm and joy will flow to others and life will prosper. There will be no time to be bored.

Heavenly Father, because Your Holy Spirit is my inspiration and guide,
I can never be bored with life. I stand before You in grateful awe.

TRUE RELIGION

Now to each one the manifestation of the
Spirit is given for the common good (1 Cor. 12:7).

There are many people who refuse to identify themselves with any form of religion. They point out the failings of religion and the hypocritical behavior of religious people or the apparent conflict between science and religion.

Arguments such as these have existed from the earliest days of Christianity and are still with us today. The main objection is not against the Christian faith as such, but against what its followers have made of it and the way in which it is presented. The quality of many of these followers' lives seldom achieves the high standard set by Christ. Theirpronouncements and confessions of their faith are not confirmed by their lives, and this causes disappointment and even aggression.

God is closely connected with people. He created us and He supports us with His strength. To those who have broken through the barrier of religious formalism, He is a dynamic personality. Because Jesus was the consummate revelation of God to man, and because He still lives today, He manifests Himself in the lives of those disciples who love Him and who discipline themselves to live according to His will.

Innumerable numbers of people have reacted to His summons to become vessels that His Holy Spirit may fill and use. True religion is God at work through your life as a dedicated disciple.

Holy Spirit of God, teach me to be a willing instrument
in Your hands, so that I may reflect Your image in the world.

LET CHRIST REMAIN CENTRAL

*They were furious and began to discuss with one
another what they might do to Jesus (Lk. 6:11).*

It is so easy to allow your values to become jumbled. When this happens unimportant things become extremely important and essential matters are treated as trifling. This confusion of priorities happens in all spheres of life, but when it occurs on the spiritual level, the consequences can be disastrous.

Confessions and dogmas are important because they strive to express the deepest feelings of a group of dedicated people. But if these take the place of Christ, the result is pettiness, bitterness, and hate. Whatever your Christian convictions may be—and there are many—nothing should detract from the sovereignty of Christ in your life. Christ is the center of your religion; He is your inspiration and the strength that enables you to live and act in the awareness of His presence.

These spiritual privileges are not your due because of your personal moral or spiritual achievements, but rather because of the grace and mercy of Christ. If His Spirit takes possession of your spirit and you experience a sense of unity with Him, all pettiness, bitterness, and hate will disappear from your life and spirit. If Christ's life fills your entire being, all disparaging and disobedient characteristics are eliminated from your personality and replaced by a constructive attitude towards life and a desire for God's will to be done in your life.

*Come and fill my life with Your Spirit,
Lord Jesus, so that there will be no room in
my life for bitterness, jealousy, and hate.*

GOD IS WITH YOU EVERYWHERE

When Jacob awoke from his sleep, he thought, "Surely the
LORD is in this place, and I was not aware of it" (Gen. 28:16).

Through the ages the practice or convention of worship services was
developed to help God's people enter into communion with God. It
is true that many search for Him in their quiet time through private
prayer, Bible study, and contemplation. But in many cases there is still
the feeling that you can only really encounter God during the communal worship of a church service.

However, God is omnipresent. While it is undoubtedly true that you
are uniquely in the presence of God during church worship, you should
remember that He is present in every situation in life.

When you stand in awe before the beauty of a sunset or are astonished
by the wonder of a sunrise; when birdsong fills you with excitement or
the laughter of playing children gladdens your heart; when you look
with reverence at the grandeur of the mountains or the splendor of the
restless ocean; when you admire nature's wealth of flowers: be assured
of God's presence!

When you enter a sick-room or provide help to an aged person; when
you assist someone in need or offer loving sympathy to someone who
is grieving; when you rejoice with someone who is happy or help carry
someone else's burden: then too will you become aware of the presence
of God. Look around you and you will see God everywhere.

Omnipresent God, when I put myself in Your service, I realize
once again the wonder of Your love and I know that You are with me.

PREPARE YOURSELF
FOR ETERNITY

"Do not work for food that spoils, but for food that endures
to eternal life, which the Son of Man will give you" (Jn. 6:27).

It is amazing how many people have limited patterns of thought. Some live from day to day without any thought of tomorrow. Others, who carry certain responsibilities, plan their financial matters carefully, but refuse to think about the certainty of death.

It is astonishing that intelligent people seriously consider the development of their earthly plans, but pay no attention to the time when they will leave this world and step into eternity. Only a fool ignores this certainty. To plan for greater profits and to neglect planning for death is to be spiritually short-sighted; it is to avoid something that you have to face at some point or another.

To say that one cannot plan for something that you cannot know or determine is also not an appropriate response, because the Scriptures teach us the truth about the spiritual world. Jesus spoke of the life after death in realistic terms and His words ought to be sufficient for anyone thinking seriously about the matter.

To survey life with a sense of eternity is to give new perspective to your daily life. You ought to perform your daily task to the honor of God and should live your entire life so that it is acceptable to Him. To stand in the doorway of the spiritual life and place your hands with love in the hands of God is the soul-enriching culmination of this life.

Risen Savior, I place my life and welfare in Your faithful
care and step into the unknown future with confidence.

JESUS: TRULY HUMAN

Many deceivers, who do not acknowledge Jesus Christ
as coming in the flesh, have gone out into the world.
Any such person is the deceiver and the antichrist (2 Jn. 1:7).

It is fundamental to the Christian faith that Jesus Christ was born as a human being and lived, died, and was buried as such, and that He was resurrected from death and ascended into heaven.

Throughout all of history, God pursues people even when they disobey and reject Him. Even as our sin created a barrier between us and God, He pursued us in love by sending His Son, Jesus. Jesus became human so that He could die the death we deserve and give us a righteousness we can't earn.

Jesus is Immanuel, God with us. Since there is no aspect of humanity that Jesus did not adopt, He personally experienced the burdens of living on earth as a human. He shared in our joy and sorrow and suffered the same pain and emotions as we do. Therefore, this Jesus understands people and life—the good as well as the bad. This places an extremely strong emphasis on the importance of Christian love. If God had not assumed human form, we would never have known the dynamic impact of Jesus Christ on mankind, and man would still be walking in darkness.

It is now your duty as a disciple to show Jesus to the world in the way that you live your life. His Holy Spirit enables you to be a follower of Jesus, and your task is made easier by the knowledge that Jesus understands because He has walked along this path as you are doing now.

Lord Jesus, You left the glory of heaven and laid down
Your royal crown to come to this world for the sake
of people like me. For this I thank and praise You.

THE DANGER OF SPIRITUAL LETHARGY

*"Wake up, O sleeper, rise from the dead,
and Christ will shine on you" (Eph. 5:14).*

Abnormal sleepiness is also called lethargy. The dictionary defines this word as "apathy; lack of interest and energy." This drowsiness can sneak up on you unexpectedly and when it takes hold of your spiritual life it spells disaster for you as well as your church.

No one deliberately wishes to be a lukewarm or weak Christian, but when your Christian standards are compromised, your spiritual life will inevitably be adversely affected. It is simply a matter of time before these second-class standards drive out the dynamic principles of the Master. And then they become a pleasant, gentle-sounding philosophy that no longer challenges you to a life of quality and excellence.

To keep your faith alive you need to work at it constantly. It is fatal to rest on your spiritual laurels, because in the love to which God has called you, there can be no vanity. How does one then sustain a living and dynamic faith? A continually deeper prayer life, an inspired and intelligent study of the Bible, and participation in the fellowship of the faithful are essential factors for spiritual growth. You know all these things; the question is whether you apply them.

If every believer would wake up spiritually, the world would be on fire for Christ. It would mean the end of violence, racial tension, bitterness, and materialism, and Jesus Christ would reign as King.

*Holy Master, through the inspiration of Your immanent Holy Spirit,
I plan to be a resolute and alert Christian, all to Your honor.*

CAN PEOPLE SEE JESUS IN YOU?

If Timothy comes, see to it that he has nothing to fear while he is with you, for he is carrying on the work of the Lord (1 Cor. 16:10).

So many of people's problems originate from their inability to communicate. Interpersonal relationships are of the utmost importance for our social well-being, and yet it is a sad fact that we often pay little attention to this important aspect of our behavior.

This is especially true of the relationship between employer and employee, because it is a relationship in which social status and rank play an important role. In the same way, someone who asks a favor of us may become the victim of a curt refusal, and this can wound deeply and inflict severe emotional scars.

Jesus commanded us to love one another, and Christian love may be basically defined as doing good. It follows necessarily that when we do something for someone else we should do it in such a way that the presence of Jesus is evident. Treating someone with contempt or creating the impression that they are a nuisance is in direct conflict with everything that the Master taught and did, and everything that He expects of you and me.

In order to create good relationships among people, it is essential to follow Jesus' example. Seek the help of the Holy Spirit and ask Him to take control of your life so that you may act with love, peace, joy, patience, benevolence, compassion, faithfulness, gentleness, and self-control. This will be your contribution to making the world a better place.

Holy Spirit, please help me to act towards all people in the example of Jesus Christ.

IN THE SERVICE OF GOD

Do your best to present yourself to God as one approved,
a workman who does not need to be ashamed and
who correctly handles the word of truth (2 Tim. 2:15).

God has many workers who are active in His service. Their involvement becomes apparent in various ways. They often attend church meetings, persevere in doing good deeds, and seldom have idle time on their hands. Some of them tend to move in a clique that forbids interaction with anyone whose feelings and beliefs are different from theirs. The sad result is that their mental and spiritual views are very limited.

This can have dismal consequences. You can become so involved in God's work that you lose your vision of what God wants you to do. Then you are diligently working for God without working with Him. You may nevertheless be industriously busy and other Christians may be impressed with what you are doing for the kingdom of God. You may even delude yourself into thinking that you are doing extremely important work.

And one day, when it is too late, something suddenly just dries up in your soul, you become tense, and you simply snap. You cease your Christian activities because of a nervous breakdown, and a life that may have been of great importance to God is lost.

The most important duty of any Christian worker is to maintain and strengthen his relationship with God every day. If you are too busy to spend time with Him in daily prayer, you are simply too busy to be an effective servant to Him.

Loving Master, I humbly ask that You will inspire and strengthen me
for the service that I offer to You in gratitude for my redemption.

LIGHT IN THE DARKNESS

To those who have been called, who are loved
by God the Father and kept by Jesus Christ:
Mercy, peace and love be yours in abundance (Jude 1-2).

For as long as one can recall, it has seemed as if the world were in a state of chaos. Apart from dozens of lesser confrontations between nations and people, humanity has also experienced two world wars in the past century. Lawlessness and violence have lately been increasing steadily. The cost of living continues to climb, and people live lives of fear and insecurity. What is the solution to this sad state of affairs?

There can be only one answer and this is to fearlessly place your faith and trust in Jesus Christ. He has conquered a dark and hostile world and replaced fear with love. He has restored hope where circumstances appeared to be hopeless. To those who believe in Him, He has given the blessing of His peace that transcends all understanding.

This is your answer to the dismal confusion and fear of our time. Believe in Jesus Christ and His promises, place your trust in Him unconditionally, and He will lead you from the darkness into the light of His unfathomable love for mankind. If you do this you will no longer worry about the future because you will always be protected by the peace of God.

Thank You, Lord my God, that You grant perfect peace to
Your children in this dark world. Thank You that I may
experience this inner peace because I trust in You.

WHAT DO WE
OWE ONE ANOTHER?

Bear with each other and forgive whatever grievances you may have...Forgive as the Lord forgave you. And over all these virtues put on love, which binds them all together (Col. 3:13-14).

Courtesy is not so much an outward act as the expression of an inner spiritual experience. If Christ lives in you, you will be kind and patient towards your neighbor. This is what courtesy is all about: to take others and their feelings into consideration.

In some social circles courtesy is cultivated only to impress those gullible people who are easily deceived by appearances. A person who is truly courteous is humble and never tries to impress others. His attitude is the same regardless of whether he is talking to his equals or his subordinates. He treats everyone alike, regardless of race, color, or religious creed. He rejoices in making his neighbor's path easier to travel. This attitude is the consequence of regular contact with God.

It is impossible to say that you love and serve God while at the same time treating your neighbor with contempt and disrespect. If you choose the people you want to treat with respect, you expose the superficiality of your spiritual experience. Courtesy is not something that you can switch on and off. It is either an inherent part of you or an act of hypocrisy that is despised by your fellow human beings.

When the Holy Spirit lives in you, you reflect the qualities of Christ in your life. Love and courtesy are basic characteristics of the Christian life, and good manners are the product of true Christianity.

Favor me, Lord Jesus, with the gift of courtesy that springs from a heart that is in harmony with You.

THE SCOURGE
OF DISCOURAGEMENT

*Though he stumble, he will not fall, for the
LORD upholds him with his hand (Ps. 37:24).*

Feeling discouraged is an experience that is all too familiar to most people. It usually occurs when disappointment or failure destroys a long-cherished dream or when lofty ideals and plans collapse like a house of cards. If discouragement takes hold of your spirit, your life becomes bitter and you may find it difficult to recover your vision or ideals.

If you are discouraged by the rejection of an idea of yours, carefully scrutinize the idea in its relation to your discouragement. If you are convinced that the idea is bigger, you can reject the discouragement as the nonsense that it really is. Always keep the vision of what you are trying to attain clearly in your mind, and do not allow it to be suppressed by thoughts of failure.

Apart from always focusing on positive thoughts, it is also important to retain an inner strength that enables you to control those thoughts. When your spirit is sound and healthy, it will be able to limit negative thoughts. Therefore it is important to cultivate a positive spirit.

The application of Christ's teachings and the guidance of His immanent Spirit form the foundation upon which your decision rests to fight discouragement as something fleeting, so that you may achieve the goal that burns brightly in your heart.

*I praise You, Lord my God and Father, that I am able
to combat discouragement successfully with Your help.*

GOD CALLS EACH OF US INDIVIDUALLY

Let us examine our ways and test them,
and let us return to the LORD (Lam. 3:40).

One of the wonderful facts of the Christian life is that the Lord knows our backgrounds and personalities, and yet still loves us. Sometimes His challenges to us are so direct that we want to avoid them if we can, but at other times He calls us to Him with a tenderness from which we cannot turn away, because we know of His eternal love for us.

No one can say how God will work within a particular person or in which way He will choose to call someone to His service. He has His own methods of doing this, and a wise disciple will never try to enforce his own will on another person. Instead, he will always be sensitive to how the Master directs other people's lives.

To know that the living Christ works in different ways with different people deepens our understanding, expands our view, improves our sympathy, and enriches our communion with the Master. If your heart is filled with love towards your neighbor, there can be no space for the meanness that embitters your spirit and deprives it of the wealth and beauty of God's grace. By realizing that God uses different methods for different people, you will intensify your understanding of the Master and add to your love for Him in a marvelous manner.

Be continually mindful of the way in which the Lord handles people. This will not only strengthen your faith but also make life interesting and exciting.

Lord Jesus, grant me an immeasurable love for my neighbors and their unique personalities so that I may serve them more effectively.

THE JOY OF OBEDIENCE

Moses did as the Lord commanded him. He took Joshua
and had him stand before Eleazar the priest and the whole
assembly. Then he laid his hands on him and commissioned
him, as the Lord instructed through Moses (Num. 27:22-23).

Faith and obedience are essential ingredients of a Christian life of
maturity and fulfillment. When a Christian complains that his life is at
a spiritual low-water mark, or that it seems as if the spark that used to
bring him so much joy has lost its radiance, you may be sure that he is
trying to live his life in his own strength or in his own way. When this
happens and you refuse to place your trust in God or obey His will for
your life, you are on your way to a dismal spiritual existence that will
cause your life to become without purpose and direction.

Among the heroes of faith that we encounter in the Old Testament,
Moses stands out as one who placed his faith in God despite the
opposition of both the Egyptians and the Israelites. He obeyed the Word
of God, and as a result he played a leading role in the establishment of
the Jewish nation, acting as mediator between them and the Almighty.

You too have an important role to play in your modern life. You must
guide others towards a deeper and more meaningful relationship with
the living Christ. The only way in which you can hope to achieve success
is to trust that He will give you the ability to accomplish your goal, and—
just as importantly—to obey His will unconditionally. Do this and He
will use you for great deeds among the people of your time.

Loving Father, through the strength of the
Holy Spirit I will try to remain within Your will
and to trust and obey You without any protest.

June

Holy God and through Jesus Christ my heavenly Father,
You are the God who created the universe.
I thank You for Your grace that I may believe the invisible
and may be sure of the things that I hope for.
I believe that You sent Your Son, Jesus Christ, to the world
to reconcile mankind to You
and also to become my Redeemer and Savior.
I believe that He lived, died, and was resurrected
to be the guarantee that through faith I too will live eternally.
I believe that through His Spirit He lives in His children
and that I too can be a dwelling of the Holy Spirit.
I worship You, Lord Jesus, as my Redeemer, Friend, and Savior.
I worship You, O Holy Spirit, as Immanuel, God with me.
I thank You that death is merely the luminous portal through which
we will walk into the brightly lit glory of God
that we call heaven.
I thank You for the example of thousands of believers from all ages
who light the path before my feet.
Help me to serve Your church on earth faithfully, thereby contributing
to the advent of Your Kingdom.
I pray this in the name of Jesus Christ,
the name before which every knee will bend
and every tongue confess that "Jesus is Lord."

Amen.

WHEN YOU PRAY

One of them...came back, praising God in a loud voice (Lk. 17:15).

It is probably accurate to state that a large percentage of people's prayers consist of requests. We are always asking things of God: we pray for healing, for guidance, for deliverance from our distress, for peace, and for God to provide in our needs.

Prayer encompasses matters as diverse as journeys, the weather, family life, and business ventures. We seek God's help in matters pertaining to the church as well as the state. Ponder this matter for a moment, analyze your own prayers, and you may find that the above description is fairly accurate.

There is nothing wrong with this, because our Lord Himself invited us to come to Him with our needs. However, what is our response when God answers our prayers? How do we react when He, in His infinite wisdom, does not give us what we ask for? Or when He gives us something different from what we asked?

Paul encourages us to present our requests to God in thanksgiving, so that we may experience the peace that surpasses understanding (see Phil. 4:6). This is the key to true prayer and a life of fulfillment.

When you lay your prayers before the Lord, leave it to Him and His will. Be grateful that He hears and understands you. Know that in His own perfect time and in His own unique way He will answer in a way that is best for you. Gratefully accept everything that God bestows upon you from His house of treasures and be content with His will.

> *I praise and thank You, O God, for all the gifts of grace that I receive undeservedly from Your hand. Even when You say no to me, I know that it is for my own good.*

CAN YOU COPE
WITH CHANGE?

*Since you are my rock and my fortress, for the sake
of your name lead and guide me (Ps. 31:3).*

As you grow older you become increasingly aware of the changes that
are taking place around you. "Things are not what they used to be," is
a phrase that escapes our lips all too easily. This constant change can
become a problem if you have fallen into a rut. If you are constantly
criticizing new ideas and innovative actions, it is time to reassess your
approach to life.

Although it is true that God has existed for all eternity, He is also just as
modern as this precise moment, and what is more, He also encompasses
the future. There is nothing old-fashioned about the eternal God, and
even though theories and ideas about Him come and go, He remains
the eternal God. His everlastingness is the foundation upon which those
who love and serve Him build their lives.

As a child of God you will be confronted with change in every sphere
of life. Some changes you will reject and others you will accept. Some
will threaten your faith, but if you hold on to the scriptural promise
of Malachi 3:6 ("I the Lord do not change") and judge everything by
Scripture, you will survive and even be enriched by new ideas.

In the steadfast knowledge of the unfailing truth that the eternal God
is also eternally present in your life, you can scrutinize and evaluate
every change in light of the knowledge that He gives to you. Then you
can be assured that He will guide you on the path of truth in the midst
of an ever-changing world.

O Lord that never changes, stay with me!

SLOW DOWN

I trust in you, O LORD; I say, "You are my God."
My times are in your hands (Ps. 31:14-15).

There are people who are so busy that they have no time to really live. Every minute of every day is jam-packed, and the mere thought of slowing down fills them with aversion. However, these people do not always achieve more than people who have learned to live at a slower pace and with greater balance.

It is really a question of determining your values. That which some people regard as a waste of time others gratefully view as a time of rest and rejuvenation. There are people who believe with conviction that they have no time to develop a meaningful prayer life. They are so busy working—even working for God—that they regard it as unimportant to spend quiet time in His holy presence.

Only a spiritually immature person will write off time spent in prayer, Bible study, contemplation with God, spiritual relaxation, and other spiritual disciplines as time wasted or lost. If you use your quiet time with God to plan your life, the world may speed on, but you will achieve more in eternal value than those who anxiously drive themselves on from minute to minute.

Never make the mistake of regarding the time you spend with God as squandered time. To be still in His presence can be the most constructive and productive moments of your life.

Holy Spirit of God, make me aware that the most precious
moments of my life are those that I spend in Your presence.

THE REDUCTION
OF GOD'S WORD

The law was added so that the trespass might increase.
But where sin increased, grace increased all the more (Rom. 5:20).

Many new Christians tend to disregard the principles of the Old Testament in their zeal to get to know Jesus better. As a result they limit their study of the Bible to the Gospels and the letters of the New Testament. While any form of Bible study is commendable, it needs to be pointed out that knowledge of the New Testament only is insufficient, because it lacks the foundation of the Old Testament.

Many claim that the love of Jesus Christ is all-absorbing, and this may blind you to the basic duties of the true Christian. While it is completely true that Jesus came to bring the love of God to His people, Christ never intended that we should do away with the law of God. Indeed, Jesus said that He came to fulfill the law.

If you scrutinize the Ten Commandments, you will discover that they provide an infallible blueprint for the one all-encompassing commandment: love.

The importance of the commandments of the Old Testament live in the fact that they leave little space for speculation or interpretation by the human mind. They are distinct and clear, and indispensable if you wish to live a truly Christian life.

In my zeal to get to know You better, Lord Jesus, let me never lose sight of the fact that You are the Word of God made flesh.

LOOK AROUND YOU

*Then the disciple whom Jesus loved
said to Peter, "It is the Lord!" (Jn. 21:7).*

There are numerous people who yearn for a personal relationship with Jesus Christ. Some are new converts to the Christian faith while others have been Christians for many years but have lost their way and are struggling through a spiritual desert. Whatever the reason, these people are constantly seeking something, and in some cases they risk becoming discouraged and damaging their faith. This is especially true when they see other Christians who rejoice in an intimate and personal relationship with the living Christ.

One of the mistakes made by people who seek the Lord is to limit their search to the time that they spend in a place of worship, or the hours spent in prayer and contemplation. While these things are essential to your Christian conduct and while God will certainly manifest Himself to you in these circumstances, prayer and Bible study should equip you to move out into the world so that you can serve God among His people.

The Scriptures show how Jesus manifested Himself to people in their everyday lives. He asks a publican to follow Him; in a crowd He sees Zacchaeus sitting in a fig tree; He asks a Samaritan woman for water to drink. He breaks through the ranks of status, and through these deeds gives new hope and life to people.

Seek the Lord in the everyday, simple things of life, because even here you can find Him, too.

*Teach me, Lord my God, to see You in all things,
and to do everything I do for others as if for You.*

BE PATIENT AND SYMPATHETIC

Be merciful to those who doubt (Jude 22).

The story of the torment in the mind of Thomas the Doubter is well known to all Christians. While the other disciples rejoiced in the knowledge that Jesus rose from death and was alive, Thomas flatly refused to believe it before having sufficient proof. Ultimately it was Jesus Himself who proved to Thomas beyond all doubt that He is the living Christ, and the Bible confirms Thomas' poignant acceptance of this fact (see Jn. 20:26-31).

There are many people today whose thoughts are filled with doubt about their Christian pilgrimage. The most general and destructive doubt is caused by a feeling of unworthiness or rejection, or the inability to find God regardless of how hard they try. Some people are constantly filled with doubt and it seems to be an impossible task to try and help them because they reject every suggestion you make. They live in a state of self-inflicted despondency.

However difficult and appealing the temptation to abandon your efforts to help them, you must persevere in the name of Christ. Try to understand the torment in their minds and hearts, and show them patience, understanding, and above all, the love of Jesus. When you finally notice the signs of their acceptance of Jesus into their lives, it will be more than sufficient reward for your perseverance.

Loving and patient Lord Jesus, grant me the patience, love, and understanding to assist those who are doubting through Your strength, and to bring them to You to be healed.

MANAGE ANGER CAREFULLY

Do not let the sun go down while you are still angry (Eph. 4:26).

There are times in life when anger can correct social and moral evils. And our society would be all the poorer if those who were moved to indignation did not act according to the instructions of their hearts. This kind of anger can be creative if the person experiencing it always keeps his ultimate goal in sight.

One of the disastrous consequences of unchanneled anger is that it easily rages out of control. When this happens, reason is supplanted by panic and planning by confusion. The vision of the greatness of life is reduced to the meanness and pettiness of the moment. The greatest tragedy of self-centered anger is that it separates you from God. If you feel insulted and hurt, or if you have allowed anger to saturate your spirit, it is certain that God will feel far away from you.

The answer to this sad state of affairs is to restore God to His rightful position at the center of your life. It is surprising how easily anger abates and balance returns to your life if He is at the center of your life. If anger erupts once again, it will not be over a personal matter, but rather because God's name has been dishonored or because a fellow human being has been wronged.

Uncontrolled anger can destroy your life, but the force of anger can become a righteous power if it is controlled by the Holy Spirit.

Holy Father, allow all the energy aroused by emotion in my life to be controlled by the Holy Spirit.

LIVE IN THE FATHER'S LOVE

For you did not receive a spirit that makes you a slave
again to fear, but you received the Spirit of sonship.
And by Him we cry, "Abba, Father" (Rom. 8:15).

One of the fundamental differences between the Christian faith and paganism is that the pagans' idols are feared, while we as Christians know that God is love. The pagan is focused on pleasing his gods because he fears that they will be angered and that he will become the object of their terrible wrath. The Christian desires to please God because of his love for the One that he calls Father.

Nevertheless, the spiritual growth of many Christians is stunted because fear penetrates their hearts. This may sound somewhat paradoxical, but even in the life of a Christian there is a great temptation to yield to feelings of guilt, shame, and worthlessness. The Devil uses all his cunning to discourage the disciples of Christ and lure them away from the path upon which Christ wishes to lead them.

While we do not for a moment allege that Christians cannot commit sin or be overwhelmed by feelings of guilt, the important thing is the way in which we handle such situations. Be fully aware of the love that God has for you, confess your shortcomings in prayer to Him, be sincerely repentant, and gratefully accept the assurance of His loving forgiveness. And then continue with your life: victorious and with complete trust in the love of your heavenly Father.

Heavenly Father, I rejoice in the fact that
You have called me to be Your child.

TALK THINGS THROUGH
WITH THE MASTER

Be joyful always; pray continually (1 Thes. 5:16-17).

There are many ways to pray. Some people find liturgical prayers digni-
fied and valuable. Prayers that are spoken in deep distress possess an
urgency that does not take style and composition into consideration.
The silence of contemplative prayer is another way to move into the presence of God. Prayer in whatever form is a way of reaching out to a God
that cares. The steadfast belief that God does answer your prayers is of
cardinal importance, regardless of the form of prayer that you use.

In prayer the attitude of the heart and mind is of essential importance. No fixed and predetermined method should have preference over
the cry of the yearning heart that craves communication with God.
At any given time or place this cry has priority over all other forms of
prayer. When you are confronted with overwhelming temptation; when
the heavy burdens of life threaten to crush you; when life is comfortable
and attractive—these are all occasions that may be shared with Him.
Whatever your circumstances or your needs, learn to turn to God and
share them with Him.

As you talk things through with God, you will discover that you
become sensitive to His guidance and leadership. You will also become
aware of a newly found strength that inwardly fortifies you. Eventually
everything that you think or do will come under the influence of your
conversation with God. And then your prayers become meaningful
and significant.

*Loving Master, I entreat You to fill me with the gift of Your Holy Spirit
so that I can pray meaningfully in any place and in all circumstances.*

FAITH REQUIRES TRUST

"Master, we've worked hard all night and haven't caught anything. But because you say so, I will let down the nets" (Lk. 5:5).

To many people true faith is nothing more than an unattainable dream. They will sometimes admit with reservation that other people's faith is rewarded, but they seriously doubt whether faith will work in their own lives.

The Bible provides us with ample proof of the reality and the rewards of faith in the lives of ordinary people. One of the great misconceptions about true faith is that you can simply ask what you want from God and then sit back and wait for it to realize.

The disciples once worked hard throughout the night without catching any fish. They were experienced fishermen and knew that under the circumstances that prevailed there would be no fish to catch. Regardless of this, as well as the risk of appearing foolish in front of their colleagues, they let down the nets once more.

According to the Scriptures they caught so much fish that the nets almost tore. In this way their faith was rewarded.

When you lay a matter before God, you should trust Him so much that you will be willing to accept His will and be obedient to the suggestions of His Spirit. Forget about what others will think or say. Trust God unconditionally and He will reward your faith.

I place my trust in You completely, Lord Jesus,
in the knowledge that You will never disappoint me.
Help me not to disappoint You through my disbelief.

THE SIMPLICITY
OF JESUS CHRIST

*Yet I am writing you a new command; its truth is
seen in him and you, because the darkness is passing
and the true light is already shining (1 Jn. 2:8).*

Religion has always been a controversial subject. Since the beginning
of time people have argued about doctrinal issues, and much blood has
been shed in the name of the Prince of Peace. The thought of this is
distressing and confusing to ordinary people whose only desire is to
experience the reality and the abundance of Christ in their lives.

Too many dedicated Christians are dogmatically oriented instead of
being Christ-centered. They argue so seriously about a dogmatic detail
that they become isolated from their fellow Christians. Their love for
Christ is not big enough to include someone who differs from them
theologically. Unknowingly they become trapped in a haze of religious
narrow-mindedness.

If you are experiencing a phase of mental and spiritual confusion
and feel inclined to abandon all faith, briefly take a step back from all
your doubts and uncertainties and again experience a vision of the holy
simplicity of the living Savior.

Despite His greatness and uniqueness Jesus lived a simple life. He was
at home among people, and they were able to identify with Him. Christ's
message of love is that all who would trust in Him will be received by
God and washed clean of all sin. His commandment of love for God and
for one's neighbor was all-important. Let this command be the motivating force for a more effective faith.

*Beloved Savior and Redeemer, my faith in You is
strong and simple because it is focused on You alone.*

USE TRIBULATIONS
TO YOUR ADVANTAGE

Consider it pure joy, my brothers, whenever
you face trials of many kinds, because you know that
the testing of your faith develops perseverance (Jas. 1:2-3).

We are easily inclined to become discouraged when problems and trials come across our way. Depending on the circumstances there is always the danger that you may lose all hope and surrender to despair. Anyone who has experienced prolonged illness or who has had to carry heavy financial burdens will know the destructive effect that these things can have on your life perspective.

If you tend to become discouraged, try to accept the situation as a challenge and a discipline of your faith. Try to take the best from the circumstances of your tribulation. Instead of giving up, earnestly try to understand the reason for it and decide how to best limit its damage.

If you persistently maintain an intimate relationship with the Master and remain open and sensitive to the influence of His Holy Spirit, you will find that you possess the strength and wisdom to look beyond the present moment. Then you will realize that God is in control of your life. Despite your immediate problems and tribulations, He will enable you to surrender all of them to Him in the joyful knowledge that He desires only the best for His children.

Master of love and grace, I will continue to trust You
unconditionally and so continue on the path to spiritual maturity.

GOD IS IN CONTROL

He is before all things, and in him all things hold together (Col. 1:17).

Whether in matters pertaining to the state or the world of commerce or your personal life, there are always times when it seems as if everything is going wrong. The future appears dark and uncertain, and the present is unstable and leaves much to be desired. It is in these circumstances that we tend to look back with a feeling of nostalgia and yearn for "the good old days."

Whatever problems you may experience in the world, why don't you for once look back to the very beginning? If you do this you will find that people and nations have lived through dismal times that are comparable to our own situation. In the past people have experienced disaster, suffering, and danger. They had to struggle with sorrow, adversity, and pain equal to what we experience today. Regardless of this, they managed to survive and remain faithful.

Before you yield to a mood of intense despondency, acknowledge the greatness and glory of God. He who created the world and mankind will not simply let go of the work of His hands. He has watched over us for centuries and has kept us from all evil.

In His unfathomable love He gave His Son to the world so that those who believe in Him will not be lost, but will be redeemed for all eternity. Through Him we will be able to overcome every tribulation. God is in control!

Almighty God, You are my powerful Redeemer, and therefore I will not fear. In the darkest night You are my light and my strength. Therefore I will not despair.

CULTIVATE TIME FOR WAITING

Those who hope in the Lord will renew their strength.
They will soar on wings like eagles; they will run and not
grow weary, they will walk and not be faint (Is. 40:31).

The results of waiting for the Lord are truly astounding. You find strength to sustain you in days of frailty and an enthusiasm that never wanes.

You may rejoice in the truth of this wonderful promise, but the problem is to know how to wait for the Lord. There is a world of difference between knowing the truth and practically applying it. The average disciple does not find it easy to trust in the Lord and wait for Him. Impatience, lack of time, thoughts that wander, an unforgiving spirit, and the desire to satisfy yourself instead of God are all contributing factors that make the art of waiting for the Lord a difficult one.

You must first realize that the heart inside of you governs your mind. If you convince yourself that you cannot control your wandering thoughts, you will never manage to control them. But Christ's Spirit inside you can help to subdue your thoughts. It may require patience and perseverance, but if you allow the Spirit of God to control your spirit and mind, your quiet wait for the Lord will not be a time of tribulation, but a blessing filled with hope and expectation.

When you have developed the art of waiting for the Lord, a sacred quality will fill your life and be reflected in everything that you do, because then you have discovered the secret of allowing the Lord to work through you.

Empowering Master, under the guidance of Your Spirit
and in Your strength, I will develop a patiently waiting spirit.

WITH WHOM DO YOU IDENTIFY?

Does not he who guards your life know it? Will he not repay each person according to what he has done? (Prov. 24:12).

You cannot go through life without certain influences having an effect on you. If you were born in circumstances dominated by hate, your character and your perspective on life will constantly be threatened by hatred. If you grew up in a family where every penny had to be counted, you will feel its influence in some way or another. These are influences over which you have little or no control.

While growing up you also willingly identified yourself with certain forces that had a formational influence on your life. Many of these influences would have been positive and progressive, while others would have had a destructive effect on your character and life.

It is unquestionably true that you eventually become like the company you keep. There are many young Christians who try to maintain connections with their former friends after their conversion and then find that the influence of the past is too strong.

Consequently they start straying from their faith. They should rather start by cultivating strong Christian friendships. It is true that the love in your heart is that which you identify with.

If you identify yourself with the living Christ, His influence will rapidly become visible in your life. Your perspective, attitude, hope, and ambition all fall under His control and you continually grow in His image. Then your life will assume a purposeful course.

Come live in my heart, Lord Jesus, and make me what You are.

RESIST THE TEMPTATION

"Bad company corrupts good character" (1 Cor. 15:33).

There are those unhappy individuals who find it immensely difficult to follow Jesus. They want to receive Jesus into their lives, but they find it difficult to break with old habits. They want to be His disciples, but on their own conditions. This is simply impossible, because Jesus Himself said, "He who is not with Me is against Me" (Mt. 12:30).

If you are sincere in your desire to be a follower of Jesus, you should be prepared to make sacrifices. Habits or a way of life that is contrary to His will must be discarded. If the company you keep is dubious, you will have to avoid it, unless the persons involved are willing to accept your dedication to the Master. There is simply no space to compromise your Christian principles or to allow anything that could possibly negatively influence your commitment to the Master.

It requires great strength of character and faith to be able to resist these temptations, because the temptation to compromise is great.

However, Jesus Himself was no stranger to the subtle tactics of Satan, and He is prepared and willing to give you His strength to resist temptation. Place your trust in Jesus and faithfully walk the path that He has mapped out for you. He will not disappoint you, and you will certainly experience success.

Help me, almighty God, to resolutely resist
temptations that will impede my Christian pilgrimage.

AVOID LIMITED KNOWLEDGE

The peace of God, which transcends all understanding, will
guard your hearts and your minds in Christ Jesus (Phil. 4:7).

If you have trust in your Christian faith, thank God for the certainty that you have about the reality of the living Christ. In this fortunate state of being, you should just be wary of your steadfast conviction degenerating into fanaticism. It is easy to convince yourself that you know everything and then to walk with hobnailed boots right over things that were of great help to other pilgrims on their journey.

Many dedicated disciples speak proudly of the number of times that they have read right through the Bible from Genesis to Revelation, as if this is a qualification for a superior species of Christian. Yet others declare that they read only the Bible and no other reading matter, without realizing that in this way they isolate themselves from an understanding of the historical and social background and customs of biblical times. By refusing to study the accounts of the struggles, sorrows, victories, and tribulations of those people God used in generations past, you are denying yourself a source of immense encouragement and inspiration.

When your heart is filled with Christ and the Holy Spirit, and your mind is focused on seeking God's will in your life, you will not hesitate to explore other channels of truth that have enriched the lives of fellow disciples, even though they might have been of a different Christian conviction. A prideful mind is no tribute to God.

Beloved Lord Jesus, as I grow in Your grace, grant that
I will gather knowledge to develop my spiritual perspective.

THROUGH THE SCRIPTURES

Christ is all, and is in all (Col. 3:11).

Christianity is divided into innumerable factions. Many claim to be the sole possessors of the Christian truth and regard those who differ from them as being outside of God's plan of redemption.

The vast majority of churches and sects base their faith on their tradition's exegesis of the Scriptures. Unfortunately there are as many interpretations of the Scriptures as there are organizations that claim to be inspired by the Scriptures. What should one believe and accept?

The purpose of the Word of God is to lead people towards an understanding of the merciful God and to manifest His will to them. Unless your Bible study leads you to a personal experience with Jesus, your studies are worthless. Jesus Himself said, "You diligently study the Scriptures because you think that by them you possess eternal life. These are the Scriptures that testify about Me, yet you refuse to come to Me to have life" (Jn. 5:39-40).

It is sad that so many people know their Bible but do not know Him of whom the Bible speaks. If every student of the Bible possessed the Spirit of Christ, there would still be dogmatic differences, but a spirit of love and compassion would transcend all intellectual differences, and love for Christ would be the unifying force.

You get to know Jesus in the Bible through an act of surrender and dedication. Then you will also be able to love those who differ from you in the interpretation of God's Word.

O Holy Spirit, lead me through the Scriptures
to know more deeply the living Christ.

BE PRODUCTIVE

The LORD said to Satan, "Where have you come from?"
Satan answered the LORD, "From roaming through
the earth and going back and forth in it" (Job 1:7).

There are people who are exceptionally active and yet seem to achieve little. They seldom have time to become still and ponder the beauty and love of God. They live at such an accelerated pace that they have no time for the bonds of friendship or any of the ordinary small pleasures of life. Their lives are busy but unproductive.

To live a constructive and therefore productive life it is essential to plan wisely. A life without a plan is like a ship without a map or compass. The plan doesn't have to be fully detailed, but it is crucial to know your purpose and aspiration. Without a sense of direction your life will become meaningless and frustrating.

How is it possible to plan your life? It depends on the stage of life in which you find yourself. Young people will have different goals from a more mature person, but in all cases judicious planning is required. It is God who guides us. To understand and execute God's plan for your life requires faith, patience, and courage. Faith to believe that God has a plan for your life; patience to wait until He unfolds His plan to you; courage to obey His commands.

If you carry out God's will in your life, you will be constructively busy, and as you work with God, you will get to know Him more intimately and deeply.

Heavenly Father, when I am busy,
may it be to carry out Your holy will for my life.

SELF-RESPECT
THROUGH DEDICATION

*Who will rescue me from this body of death? Thanks be
to God—through Jesus Christ our Lord! (Rom. 7:24-25).*

If we could see ourselves as others see us, we would probably hold an entirely different opinion of ourselves. In our own estimation we are virtuous people with a few flaws (we hesitate to call them sins).

All in all we are able to maintain completely normal and average relationships with the people we live and work with. True goodness should not leave anyone without hope. Jesus, who was the personification of virtue, attracted large crowds of ordinary people to Him and they liked to listen to Him.

Maybe it is because we know ourselves so well that we hold such a low opinion of ourselves. Hidden in our minds are thoughts and deeds that we would rather forget. Our spirits have often been damaged by narrow-mindedness, fanaticism, and laziness. We realize what we ought to be and know what we are, and therefore we become discouraged.

The strength that Jesus grants to all people who trust in Him for the forgiveness of their sins and the receiving of His Holy Spirit enables ordinary people to live extraordinary lives. A life that was morally weak is strengthened; through His redeeming grace and love, a life is liberated from guilty feelings, and a broken life is made new and strong.

Although the experience of renewal is often a moving one, it also surpasses all emotion. It is the dedication of every aspect of your life to the service of the risen Christ.

*I praise and thank You, my Lord and my God, that through
dedication I may achieve spiritual and mental maturity.*

GOD AND HIS MESSENGERS

In the sixth month, God sent the angel Gabriel
to Nazareth, a town in Galilee, to a virgin (Lk. 1:26-27).

From Genesis right through to Revelation references to angels are common. Some appear in their heavenly glory while others show themselves as ordinary people. All of them, except for the rebellious ones, are in the service of God. Because God's messengers often appear in ordinary, human guise, the writer of the book of Hebrews admonishes us: "Do not forget to entertain strangers, for by so doing some people have entertained angels without knowing it" (Heb. 13:2).

Perhaps there have been occasions in your life when someone, whom you would never have classified as an angel, brought God's comfort to you in times of sorrow. Sometimes the message was conveyed to you through an ordinary conversation or maybe through an act that reminded you of Jesus' life. Some of God's messengers wear ordinary clothes or the apron of a housewife or even a servant. But they have one thing in common with the angel Gabriel: they have encountered the one true God and declared themselves willing to be His servants.

Let us thank God for these people, for our lives are enriched because they move among us. Let our gratitude also lead us to commit and dedicate ourselves sincerely to the service of God, so that we too may become messengers of God, conveying the message of His will and His love to others.

Holy Father, may I be Your dedicated messenger
in whatever place You choose to use me.

DEATH BRINGS HOPE

*Brothers, we do not want you to be ignorant about those
who fall asleep, or to grieve like the rest of men (1 Thes. 4:13).*

Up until fairly recently the color black has always been associated with death: black clothes, black drapery, black armbands, black-bordered writing paper. This somber and morbid color contributed to the sorrow that hung like a dark cloud over those touched directly by death and added to the sadness and grief they experienced.

While it is both natural and understandable that we should feel sorrowful when we are separated from a loved one, the death and resurrection of Christ should bring an end to inconsolable grief.

Jesus Christ has conquered death and has taken our sins upon Himself through His crucifixion. He has given us the assurance of redemption, and His triumphant resurrection offers us the certainty of eternal life and His Kingdom. The brightly lit gateway to this kingdom is death.

Eternal life in Jesus Christ is offered to anyone who dies as a believer in Christ. In addition we have the steadfast knowledge that we will also be reunited with our loved ones. Death should be accepted as an unlikely servant, because through death we inherit the ultimate glory of eternal life.

Risen Lord Jesus, when the darkness recedes and the new day dawns, we welcome the luminous rays of sunlight because they illuminate everything. Let us perceive death in the same way.

SO MUCH DEPENDS ON YOU

*In the same way, faith by itself, if it is not
accompanied by action, is dead (Jas. 2:17).*

To be a Christian means to accept responsibility for your own life. You may argue that, because you belong to God, He is in control and therefore everything depends on Him. Nevertheless, if God is to do anything with your life, He needs to have your cooperation.

The Creator has equipped you with a mind, not only to enable you to excel academically but also so that you will manifest the right attitude towards Him and towards life. A sound and positive mentality is the product of a life lived in harmony with God

The vast majority of people yearn for happiness. They work and strive to achieve it. They often pray to God to make them happy, but in spite of their prayers, they still maintain unhealthy patterns of thought.

If you lead a self-centered life and only live for the things that concern you personally—if you are blind to the distress of your neighbor—you are ignoring the great truth that helping others is a prerequisite for happiness. You cannot be truly happy without trying to alleviate the unhappiness of others. This is done by prayer and creative deeds.

Whatever your prayer requests may be, offer yourself to the Father so that He may work through you. In that way your works can collaborate with God's works. Become an active partner with God, and experience how He works in your life and expands your spiritual understanding.

*Heavenly Father, grant me the earnest desire
to become Your working partner in my daily life.*

BE POSITIVE

*Do everything without complaining or arguing, so that
you may become blameless and pure, children of God without
fault in a crooked and depraved generation (Phil. 2:14-15).*

Circumstances in large parts of the world leave much to be desired.
There are wars, bitterness, poverty, famine, disasters, corruption, and
scandals. If one takes stock of the situation, one can't help but feel that the
world has veered far from what God meant for it to be and that humans
are abusing that which God has entrusted to their care. Consequently
mankind has become unhappy, discontented, and unsafe. People have
developed the tendency to assume a critical and pessimistic attitude
towards life in general.

Even if we accept that there is much that is wrong with the world, the
fact remains that we as Christians are Christ's ambassadors, with the
duty and the privilege to preserve the Christian faith in even the most
negative and difficult circumstances.

If you open your life to the influence of the Holy Spirit and allow
Him to strengthen your faith so that your life may bear witness to the
power and glory of God's love, you cannot be anything but positive. In
so doing you will uplift the spirits of those around you and once again
find meaning and significance in life.

*Lord, You have always been the mighty Redeemer.
Use me through Your Holy Spirit to be Your witness in the world.*

ARE YOU A CHRISTIAN?

Follow my example, as I follow the example of Christ (1 Cor. 11:1).

How do you recognize a Christian? More to the point: how can others recognize Christianity in you? There is much to ponder in these questions, and we should consider them thoughtfully. If we try to answer these questions in all honesty and sincerity, it will invariably lead to deep and earnest self-scrutiny.

If you profess to being a Christian, it is your responsibility to manifest the characteristics of Christ in your life. No amount of biblical knowledge or church attendance can ever substitute for the reflection of the Master in your life. However laudable good works may be, unless they are based on and performed to the honor and glory of Jesus Christ, they lose their impact and meaning.

Your entire life will have to reflect the sacrificing love, grace, and forgiveness of Jesus so that people may know that you are a true Christian. You should be tolerant and understanding; without being overly pious you should lead a life of integrity that in no way compromises your Christian standards.

When you manifest Christlike qualities in your life, nothing more will be required to confirm that you are a Christian.

O Holy Spirit, I plead that You will grant me the ability to live like Christ more and more each day.

DO NOT RESIST AUTHORITY

We ask you, brothers, to respect those who work hard among you,
who are over you in the Lord and who admonish you. Hold them
in the highest regard in love because of their work (1 Thes. 5:12).

Throughout the ages the Christian church has suffered as a result of internal strife and arguments. You will find examples of this even in the letters of the apostles. In some cases the differences were about important theological matters. However, in most cases they were of a more personal nature, originating from conflicting personalities, antagonism between people, and other similar causes of quarrels.

Healthy leadership is essential if a community is to function successfully and in an orderly manner. This is evident even in the animal world. Someone has to be given the authority to make decisions for the good of others, so that the entire group may lead an orderly and peaceful life as far as possible.

In this respect the church is no different from any other group, except that the responsibility that rests upon church leaders and members is much greater, because they are working for the kingdom of God. To ensure that a harmonious and effective testimony exists in your denomination, church leaders should be elected in strict accordance with the will of God as revealed through Scripture.

If it is certain that they have been chosen according to this principle, you should continuously pray for them, so that the heavy burden of their responsibilities may be eased by Jesus. His will and pleasure should be the principal matter at all times.

Holy God, and in Jesus my heavenly Father, help me to rise above
pettiness and personality differences so that I can praise Your name.

THE VALUE OF MEMORIES

I remember the days of long ago; I meditate on all your
works and consider what your hands have done (Ps. 143:5).

Every one of us has memories. Depending on their nature, they may cause either joy or intense sorrow. It is a wise person who realizes that today creates tomorrow's memories and that their future happiness is therefore in their own hands.

Memories of the past play an important role in your everyday life. If you have clung to an unhappy incident for more than twenty years so that it ultimately became a hidden obsession, you will find that all your thoughts are tinged with bitterness and negativity. The grace of forgiveness is essential, and so is the blessing of being able to forget.

Recalling happy memories is a source of inspiration and joy and can often provide guidance for future behavior. Such memories are strengthened and ennobled by sincere deeds of gratitude. To say to the Father, "I thank You for happy memories and the ability to recall them," is in itself a way to enrich your relationship with Him. Consequently life will possess a deeper meaning and happiness for you.

Because you have a choice regarding the memories that you create, you should be extremely careful. Look ahead and try to imagine how they will appear in the distant future.

Merciful God and Father, let nothing that I do today
cause me sorrow and remorse when I look back on it.

WHAT MAKES A CHRISTIAN DIFFERENT?

Therefore, as God's chosen people, holy and dearly loved,
clothe yourselves with compassion, kindness,
humility, gentleness and patience (Col. 3:12).

Because you are a Christian, people expect an honorable code of conduct of you. This is a challenge, and yet also a disturbing thought. It is a challenge in that it calls you to be Christlike, but also disturbing because it invariably brings with it the realization that you have failed to achieve the spiritual goals that Christ has set for you.

Whatever your reaction to the world's expectations of you, the fact remains that you have to be different because you are a Christian. Your value system is determined by the Master; your code of conduct gives precedence to others above yourself; you have a constructive approach to life and therefore you are slow to judge and quick to forgive.

When you are confronted with destructive antagonism, you have the ability to demonstrate love in the face of hatred. Above all, because you are a disciple of Jesus Christ, you possess His Spirit. Make no mistake: you are different and it is his immanent Spirit that makes you different.

If this truth overwhelms you and causes you to feel inadequate in your spiritual experience, thank God that His Word gives you this guarantee: "My grace is sufficient for you, for My power is made perfect in weakness" (2 Cor. 12:9). It is precisely your inadequacy that may be transformed into constructive purposefulness if you relinquish it to the Master. As a Christian you possess something very special, because the Spirit of Christ lives in you.

In Your strength, Master, I can become what You meant for me to be.

GOD WILL SHOW YOU THE WAY

After the death of Joshua, the Israelites asked the Lord (Judg. 1:1).

Joshua was well known as a loyal and dedicated servant of God and also as a wise and respected leader of his people. The Israelites relied very heavily on this man who has been described as a soldier-saint. He became the leader who safely led them to take possession of the long-awaited Promised Land.

It then follows as a matter of course that with the death of Joshua his people would feel confused and lost. This is what happens when we have to bid farewell to someone in whom we have placed a considerable amount of trust. Usually the first question that we ask is: "What are we to do now? To whom can we turn? Whom can we trust?"

A similar situation can crop up in basically any of life's circumstances. Few people can say that they have never experienced something like it and that they have always been in control of all circumstances.

If you find yourself in such a situation, do not suffer through the frustrations, sadness, and anxiety of trying to continue in your own strength. Follow the example of the Israelites and seek the help and guidance of the Savior.

He alone wants to and can lead you in His path of righteousness, and as He leads you, He will grant you the ability to handle every situation so that you may have the peace of mind that banishes all fear and anxiety.

*Mighty Redeemer, in all the circumstances of my life
I will seek comfort and guidance from You alone.*

THE FRIENDSHIP OF JESUS

"You are my friends if you do what I command" (Jn. 15:1).

The risen Christ gives abundant blessings to those who love and serve Him: liberation from the bondage of sin; a new life in Christ; a deeper and richer communion with the heavenly Father; the awareness of the practical feasibility of His precepts. For these and many other gifts we praise and love Him.

One gift that is highly valued by Christian disciples is the gift of friendship that Jesus offers to everyone who acknowledges His sovereignty. It is a gift of grace, because it is one that you can never earn, but only accept. Christ very simply says, "I am your Friend. Will you accept this and treat Me as a friend that you love?"

If you accept this invitation, you submit yourself to His loving discipline, because it is only in doing so that you can grow in the generous friendship that He offers you. True friendship with Jesus can be strengthened only by persevering in communion with Him and by a continually purer understanding of His love. Such a communion and understanding is the result of a meaningful prayer life that is developed through complete obedience to your Lord.

The friendship that Jesus offers you can only become a reality if you submit yourself to His will. He knows what is best for you, and only by obeying Him, will you realize that your Friend is your Guide through life.

Thank You, loving Lord Jesus, for the merciful gift of Your love, which I accept in thanksgiving together with the demands associated with it.

July

Eternal God, You who hold our times and fortunes in Your hand,
thank You for giving us life, our most precious possession.
We ask that You would bring about an awakening
of Your presence as never seen before.
We pray that You would unify Your people for the glory of Your name,
and that all who call themselves Christians would rise up,
believing Your great truth.
Remind us to live aware, to redeem the time, to listen to Your words,
and to be willing to make a difference.
Shine Your face on us, dear God.
We need You now, more than ever before. Our times are in Your hands.
Thank You that You are rich in mercy and full of grace.
Thank You that You are forgiving and merciful.
Make us salt for the earth and light for the world.
We pray this in the powerful name of Jesus Christ, our Savior.

Amen.

KNOW GOD AND LIVE IN ABUNDANCE

This is what the Lord says to the house of Israel:
"Seek me and live" (Amos 5:4).

However dismal it may sound, there are innumerable people in today's world who have little or no desire to live. Perhaps death has taken a loved one from them; maybe illness or tribulation has drained the dynamism from their lives.

Loneliness may have deprived them of their will to live, or scandal and financial disaster may have caused them to lose their ability to face life. Whatever the reason, to them life has lost its meaning and in their sorry state they can find no reason to live.

If you are seeking a reason to live in your own life or in the circumstances in which you find yourself, you will be disappointed. The only true life comes from Jesus Christ alone, who came to the world so that you could have life in all its abundance (see Jn. 10:10). This is what the Son of God, who is the true source of life, is offering you. He is the bread of life and He invites everyone who is hungry to come to Him.

When you are experiencing those human emotions that spring from the misfortune in which you find yourself, turn to the living Christ. Seek Him in prayer and contemplation, hold on to His promises, and, however dark the road ahead may seem, cling to Him. He will grant you life in all its abundance!

In You alone, Lord Jesus, do I find true life and a reason to live.

THE POWER OF PRAYER

"I tell you, whatever you ask for in prayer, believe that you have received it, and it will be yours" (Mk. 11:24).

Many things are grounded in our thoughts. Our snap judgments reveal what we believe about situations, coworkers, and loved ones. Our day-dreams are a window into what we secretly desire most in our hearts. And what we set our minds on can set the trajectory of our lives, for good or harm.

This fact means that you are responsible for the thoughts you voice in prayer to God. Before choosing what to pray for, search the thoughts of your heart with great circumspection. Because you love God, your requests should be related to what you believe His will is for your life.

You should accept the assistance of the Holy Spirit in the development of your thought patterns. This is the only way to have prayers that can inspire, heal, empower, and guide your step on a path of no regrets. Begin by learning the Spirit's voice in Scripture; He authored the Word and will only lead you in line with what He has already written in the Bible. Practice by praying your favorite Bible verses, making them your own. Learn to listen to the Spirit's guidance in prayer and be patient.

My example in prayer, Lord Jesus, help my thoughts be inspired by your Holy Spirit as I pray to you.

GRACE INDESCRIBABLY VAST

"My grace is sufficient for you, for my power
is made perfect in weakness" (2 Cor. 12:9).

People often find themselves in situations that make them feel incompetent and inadequate. You may have a mission to carry out, a task to perform, or a decision to make, but you feel that you are simply not up to it. The immense magnitude of the situation, the responsibility attached to it, its possible consequences in your own life or in the lives of others—all these factors weigh heavily upon you and so you tend to avoid the responsibility as much as possible.

When you find yourself in such circumstances and are required to take action, you should never rely on your own abilities. Jesus made it very clear that we are capable of doing nothing without Him, but that with Him we can accomplish anything. In this truth lies the answer to all your fears, doubts, and feelings of inadequacy.

Whatever you undertake in your life, first take it to God in prayer and confess all your expectations, fears, and worries to Him. Jesus is your Friend, and in the same way that you would consult with another person, first seek Christ's help in prayer and in the serenity of contemplation.

His Holy Spirit will stimulate you to move forward in faith. By allowing Him to work through you, you will achieve the kind of success that would be unattainable in your own strength. His grace is sufficient to sustain you in all circumstances.

Loving Father, I praise and thank You for the joyous assurance that
I can achieve anything through Christ who gives me the strength.

YOUR RESPONSIBILITY AS A CHRISTIAN

Instead, speaking the truth in love, we will in all things
grow up into him who is the Head, that is, Christ (Eph. 4:15).

The moment you accept Christ as the Lord of your life, you also accept certain responsibilities. Refusing these responsibilities creates a weak spot in your dedication and commitment, which leads to your spiritual life becoming crippled and your relationship with the Master, weakened.

When you become a Christian you step into a new life with new values and fresh goals. You no longer live to please yourself, but your goal is Christ, and therefore you attempt to forget yourself in your service to others. The good works that you do for others are the expression of your faith. However, it is not faith itself, because a person who does not believe in Christ can also do good works. Your good works will earn you nothing, but are proof of your gratitude for your redemption.

The new life in Christ has certain requirements if you wish to grow spiritually. It is your responsibility to stimulate this growth. As a disciple of Christ you have the responsibility of honoring your Lord and pleasing Him. You dare not live only to please yourself. You must be completely obedient to God's will for your life. You are responsible for confessing your sins before God.

Paul continually urges us to be filled with the fullness of God. Christ should become visible in you, and it is the sacred responsibility of every Christian to constantly grow spiritually, so as to reach maturity in faith.

Help me, Lord Jesus, to strengthen my bond with You
so that I will never fail to walk with your Holy Spirit.

ACHIEVE YOUR GOALS THROUGH THE STRENGTH OF CHRIST

Be on your guard; stand firm in the faith; be men of courage; be strong. Do everything in love (1 Cor. 16:13-14).

As the years pass it seems as if life is becoming more and more rushed. There is so much to be done that we often complain of not having enough time to do everything. In addition there are so many distractions and diversions that we easily neglect the things we know we should do.

There is really only one way to achieve those truly worthwhile objectives, and that is through the strength of the living Christ. If this sounds like too much of a simplistic approach to you—especially considering the busy life that you lead—just think of everything that Jesus achieved in the three short years of His ministry on earth. Think of all the achievements that He accomplished regardless of the strenuous demands placed upon Him and the threats that He had to endure.

Jesus now offers you His Holy Spirit to enable you to meet the demands of modern life—and to do so with love. Trust Him to lead you on the paths of service in His name. He will grant you the ability to accomplish everything that you undertake in His strength and love.

Keep me, O Holy Spirit, from becoming so involved in my personal goals that I fail to see God's great goal for my life.

THE GIFT OF GRACE: TO GIVE YOURSELF

They gave themselves first to the Lord and
then to us in keeping with God's will (2 Cor. 8:5).

You can only lead a rich and satisfying existence if you are willing to give yourself completely to a life lived God's way. You have a personal contribution to make to ensure a life that will be happy and beneficial to yourself as well as to other people. You may initially question the truth of this statement, possibly because you think that you have nothing worthwhile to contribute. If your idea of giving is limited only to money, prestige, and social status, this may be the case, but the old saying that the best things in life are free still holds true.

When someone has to endure fierce opposition for the sake of a just cause and you make it clear that you support them, they will be very encouraged. Maybe some of your family members feel that you are taking them for granted, and if you display some love and affection towards them, you will bring joy and inspiration to their lives. It is within your ability to freely share true love, profound understanding, faithful friendship, and other forces of healing and blessing with other people.

The glorious truth is that when you give these precious things to others, your own life is enriched far beyond comprehension, because it is impossible to be a source of blessings for others without receiving blessings yourself. Your own life will begin to flourish and bear fruit because you give yourself joyfully to the Lord, to life, and to your fellow human beings.

Lord Jesus, You who have given Yourself
for me, make my life a blessing to others.

WHEN FEAR OVERWHELMS YOU

Jesus immediately said to them, "Take courage!
It is I. Don't be afraid" (Mt. 14:27).

Fear is an ugly reality of contemporary society. It dominates the council chambers of the world. It destroys the peace and harmony of innumerable lives. The vast majority of people live in the shadow of fear from morning to night; even when they are asleep fear still remains active in their subconscious.

The fruits of fear emerge in all spheres of human life. For example, irritation easily leads to strained and broken human relationships. When you are afraid, you are not open to reason and consequently you become aggressive. Fear also manifests in illness or a desire to avoid life's responsibilities.

Fear has a thousand faces. However, Jesus knows all of them, and He still tells you not to be afraid. Remember that He commands His disciples to banish all destructive fear, regardless of external circumstances and pressures, and to be happy in the surroundings of their lives.

You and this world still belong to God, even though it might not always seem so. Your heavenly Father has not abandoned or forsaken you or His world. He promised the Holy Spirit to those who love Him. If this Spirit takes possession of your life, destructive fears will no longer have any hold on you. And then you will begin to know the joy of a fearless life.

When Your Holy Spirit fills my life,
Lord my God, there is no space for destructive fear.

GOD IS WITH YOU
WHEREVER YOU GO

"You are the God who sees me," for she said,
"I have now seen the One who sees me" (Gen 16:13).

The question on everybody's lips is: "Who is God? What is He really like?" In their imaginations people conjure up images of Him in an attempt to visualize the Almighty. Some people claim to have seen Him in visions. However, others feel that they are unable to see Him and consequently start to doubt or even deny His existence.

Jesus Christ told His followers that no one has seen the Father except for the Son. On another occasion He told them that no one will come to the Father except through the Son, who is the way to God. It therefore follows as a matter of course that you cannot know the Father except through faith in His Son who died to wash your sins away.

In your search you will quickly realize that your relationship with Jesus requires you to fully surrender and commit your life to Him. And as you become more and more involved in His service, you will become increasingly aware of His presence. When you visit ill, lonely, and sorrowful people, you will find Him there. In your acts of compassion you will experience the living Christ. Through your ministry of love to those in need, you will be serving the Creator of every person you help.

Because Jesus is in the Father and the Father is in Him, you ought to remember that in every act of grace, every little bit of compassion and every fraction of love that you show to others in the name of Jesus, you will meet God in Jesus Christ.

Holy God and Father, I rejoice in the knowledge that
I encounter You in every deed that I perform in Your name.

HUMILITY IS
NOT A WEAKNESS

Be completely humble and gentle; be patient,
bearing with one another in love (Eph. 4:2).

In the demanding world in which we live there are many people—especially in the business world—who look upon humility, patience, and a loving, caring spirit as signs of weakness. They tend to regard people with these traits as ineffectual failures in the business world, and as such they are supposedly not worthy of respect. When it comes to promotions, people who have this attitude and who occupy positions of power often overlook many competent people for the sake of others who are more aggressive or even reckless. Ultimately the business world is all the poorer for this view point.

The greatest leader ever known to mankind is Jesus. His entire being reflected humility, meekness, patience, and love. People paid attention to what He said and did. They obeyed and followed Him. Even His enemies respected and admired Him.

To achieve success in life you don't always have to prove that you are better than others are. You don't continually have to try to outdo your adversaries or assume a domineering and aggressive attitude. Be firm, definitely; be sincere in all your negotiations; but temper everything that you do with the Spirit of the Master. Then you will undoubtedly gain the respect of those with whom you interact.

Lord Jesus, help me to reflect Your love and compassion
in all my interactions. Protect me from the monster of pride.

IT'S IMPOSSIBLE!

Where can I go from your Spirit?
Where can I flee from your presence? (Ps. 139:7).

It is a comforting and encouraging thought that however far away you may feel from God, God is never far away from you. The feeling of isolation lies within you; it is of your own making, not His. It is worthwhile to remember this fact when your spirits are low and you feel powerless, or when your love for the Master is not as ardent as it used to be.

If your faith has lost its spark and you are feeling that it no longer benefits, but rather obstructs, your attainment of a creative life, it is definitely time to take stock of your life and to discover what exactly it is that has replaced your burning love for the Father.

When your faith starts to degenerate, it is inevitably because you are trying to eliminate God from your mind and life. You are deluding yourself if you claim that it is because you have outgrown religious superstition. You will not get rid of God that easily. Even though you are dishonoring Him by refusing to acknowledge His presence in your life, He will still be with you always. It is impossible to escape from God and His unfathomable love for you.

Because He only desires what is best for you, it is wise to accept His love and grace, and to enjoy the life that He wants to give to you.

I have surrendered myself to Your love, O God,
and therefore I enjoy the goodness and grace that
flow from Your throne. For this I thank You, O Father.

GROW TO MATURITY

When I was a child, I talked like a child, I thought like
a child, I reasoned like a child. When I became a man,
I put childish ways behind me (1 Cor. 13:11).

Sadly, there are some people who never become spiritually mature. With every passing year their bodies grow older, but they continue to cling to childish and immature thought patterns. The hurts of their past are consistently transferred into the present, poisoning their spirits and ruining their future plans.

You should forgive and forget the injuries and insults that you have nursed over the years. To say that an injury was so serious that it could never be forgiven or forgotten is to allow its effect to continue and become even worse. Harboring such an attitude can cause you irreparable harm.

The quality of your Christian experience should enable you to unequivocally overcome all injuries and irritations that are impeding your spiritual growth. Now is the time to grow in grace.

God has granted us the gift of the Holy Spirit to be our Leader to spiritual maturity. If you open your spirit to the grace of His Spirit and allow Him to reveal Himself through you, a new phase will open up in your life. One aspect of this new life is that it enables you to forgive and forget and to commit yourself to everything that is good, loving, and noble.

Holy Spirit of God, please grant me a fervent
desire to grow towards spiritual maturity every day.

PLACE YOURSELF IN THE OTHER PERSON'S POSITION

"Do not judge, or you too will be judged" (Mt. 7:1).

It is easy to criticize others, and therefore it happens all too often. Businessmen criticize each other's behavior and plans; sportsmen and referees endure criticism; neighbors are critical of each other's houses and gardens; parents find fault with other people's children; professional colleagues are highly critical of each other's work. The fact of the matter is that criticism is the order of the day, and it is truly refreshing to meet someone who reveals a measure of tolerance.

Constructive criticism that is a sincere attempt to help someone is commendable and should always be accepted in the spirit in which it is offered. Unfortunately most criticism is negative and is aimed at ridiculing and humiliating its victim. It is sad that the majority of people are only too eager to listen to this kind of criticism, while few are interested in hearing the positive attributes of the person in question.

Before you add your voice to the crowd of critics, become still for a moment and place yourself in the other person's position. Try to understand the reason for his behavior. There may be worthy and honorable reasons for the behavior. We don't always understand the tension and stress in other people's lives so look at your neighbor through Jesus' eyes. Then you will not only be reluctant to criticize, but by following His example you will compel the critic to silence.

Loving heavenly Father, make me ever tolerant, sympathetic, and understanding in my interaction with other people.

IN PARTNERSHIP WITH GOD

"Now let the fear of the LORD be upon you. Judge
carefully, for with the LORD our God there is no
injustice or partiality or bribery" (2 Chr. 19:7).

There are those who believe that religion and business should be kept separate. Some people accept this idea on the basis that the two matters simply do not mix, while others become uncomfortable when they consider their business practices in the light of Christian principles.

There is no doubt that there is a place for God in your business practices and in your social life, for you cannot eliminate Him from one of these spheres without inflicting damage on yourself. Your entire life is ruled by Christian principles, and you should bear witness to your Christianity, regardless of the sphere of life that you are moving in—both in your worship and in your activities outside of the church.

Integrity is one of the most important qualities in this respect. The surest way to reflect integrity in all your interactions is to make the living Christ your business partner. Whatever you do, scrutinize it through the eyes of Jesus; ask yourself how He would have reacted and what He would have done in your circumstances.

Follow Christ's example and you will be assured of a virtuous life that will earn you the respect of everyone you interact with.

Lord Jesus, I am not ashamed to acknowledge You as the Lord
of my life or to profess Your name under any circumstances.

BE CONTINUALLY GRATEFUL

Continue to live in him, rooted and built up in him, strengthened in the faith as you were taught, and overflowing with thankfulness (Col. 2:7).

It is extremely easy to be unhappy and ungrateful. This is especially true in these ominous times in which we live, where there are so many people who restlessly pursue empty dreams of a better world and a better life. It so often causes a negative perspective on life as well as a limited and purposeless lifestyle that finds fault with everything. People focus so much on the flaws and faults around them that they fail to see the wonders of God and His grace.

Every detail of your life, from the cradle to the grave, is known to God. In His design for eternity He plans what is best for you. It is true that things sometimes go wrong, but you can't always attribute it to God. However, He can, at any given moment, change your life situation to such an extent that light radiates from the darkness and hope is born from despair.

If you feel dejected, maybe it is time to think back on all the good things that have happened in your life. Recall those times when Christ's presence was an undeniable reality to you and His love filled your entire being.

Thank the Lord for His grace and blessings. Then the Holy Spirit will start His healing work in your life, and you will once again see life in a positive light. Praise and gratitude uplift the heart and honor God who is the giver of all that is good.

We praise and thank You, O Lord, with our hearts, our mouths, and our hands for all the wonders that You have done.

THE REWARDS OF PATIENCE

I waited patiently for the LORD; he turned
to me and heard my cry (Ps. 40:1).

We often feel like our prayers are ineffectual; that our cries of distress go unheard and that He takes no heed of them. We pray earnestly and sincerely, but it seems as if there is no answer. When this happens we begin to doubt our faith, or even worse, we begin to question the purpose and value of prayer. As a result, many people end up in a spiritual wilderness.

We have to realize that God is all-knowing, and consequently He views life from the perspective of eternity. You, on the other hand, cannot see beyond the present with any measure of certainty. He knows everything that awaits you, today as well as in the distant future. Consequently God's answers to your prayers take into consideration what will be best for you—today, tomorrow, and all the days after. Therefore God also sometimes needs to lay a restraining hand on your impulsive spirit.

He often does this by withholding the answers to your prayers until the time is right. Never become impatient with God or try to anticipate His answers. Seek His presence in prayer and contemplation and become still before Him. In His own perfect time He will reveal Himself to you. He will answer your yearning cries for Him.

O Hearer of prayers, everyone has to draw near to You.
As our help in troubled times You are tried to the extreme,
and yet You have always proved Yourself to be faithful.

UNITED IN JESUS CHRIST

Make every effort to keep the unity of the
Spirit through the bond of peace (Eph. 4:3).

Since the time of its inception, the church of Jesus Christ has been subject to the onslaught of the forces of evil, which have threatened to undermine Jesus' work. This is just as much the case today as it has been throughout the ages, as is evident in all spheres of life.

Unfortunately, it is true that at a time when all churches ought to stand united in keeping the core beliefs and practices of the faith, conflict and intolerance seem to be the order of the day. Denominations devour each other regarding minor issues of dogma, theology, and the interpretation of the Bible. All too often these differences escalate into bitterness and anger, which are in contradiction with the principles of the love of Christ upon which the church is founded. Churches should always oppose heresy, but in all other areas, they should always show charity.

No one has the right to deny anyone else his own opinion, and your Christian testimony should be founded on the kind of tolerant love that is evident in all your interactions and deeds. It may be true that you disagree with others' approach to the Christian faith or their understanding and interpretation of the Holy Scriptures, but you should be able to exercise restraint so that you will not allow anger to cloud your judgment or to alienate you from your fellow believers.

When you surrender yourself to the living Christ and open yourself to the influence of His Holy Spirit, you will find that He grants you the ability to cope with all situations in the love of Christ.

Holy Lord Jesus, as Your body on earth we dare not
be divided against ourselves. Make us one in mind,
spirit, and love through the strength of the Holy Spirit.

HOW TO LIVE

How can a young man keep his way pure?
By living according to your word (Ps. 119:9).

One of the most prevalent questions of our time is: "How is it possible to live a virtuous life in today's world?" When one considers all the temptations and enticements that are associated with contemporary life—the pressure under which people live and work as well as the high expectations that young people are required to meet in their studies—you simply cannot help having sympathy for those in such situations. You sense a feeling of helplessness in those asking this question.

There are no instant solutions to the problem. Our Savior made this abundantly clear during his earthly ministry. Obedience to His commandments is essential, and this means that you should submit yourself to His dominion in every sphere of your life.

Many people feel that they simply cannot satisfy all the demands that Jesus places on them. Consequently they turn away from Him. This reveals their lack of faith, because they are not willing to trust Jesus in their surrender.

Jesus Christ will never expect something of you without assisting and supporting you. Christ died to wash away every failure, reconcile you to God, and fill you with His Spirit. Therefore walk the path of the Lord in this assurance, and enjoy the peace and fulfillment that is experienced only by those who serve Him with sincerity.

Lord my God, let Your will and not mine be done in
all spheres of my life. Help me through the Holy Spirit
to live according to the instructions of Your Word.

EXCESSIVE EMOTION IN SPIRITUAL MATTERS

From the ends of the earth I call to you, I call as my heart grows faint; lead me to the rock that is higher than I (Ps. 61:2).

Emotion plays an important role in the Christian faith. When the mind is tranquil and the spirit repentant, the awareness of God's presence is an acute reality. His Spirit draws near to your heart and fills you with the love of God. These moments may be laden with nourishing emotion that refreshes and invigorates your entire life.

Ecstatic religious emotion may provide you with a sense of contentment, but if it is not founded on and controlled by the infrastructure of reality; it will never lead to effective service to the Master.

The pure Christian experience is a combination of emotions inspired by the Holy Spirit and their daily practical application. If you found your faith purely on emotion, it is only a matter of time before it collapses under the pressure of ever-changing moods. On the other hand, if you advocate a "practical" religion and try to avoid all forms of religious emotion, you deny yourself a spiritual power that should be an inspiration to you.

To be a well-balanced Christian you need to be empowered by the Holy Spirit, to be spiritually enthusiastic, and to manifest your deepest spiritual experience in a practical way in your everyday life.

Master and Leader, I continually seek the inspiration of the Holy Spirit to temper my emotions, so that I may lead a practical Christian life.

LOOK FOR THE
GOODNESS IN OTHERS

Finally, brothers, whatever is true, whatever is noble, whatever is right, whatever is pure, whatever is lovely, whatever is admirable—if anything is excellent or praiseworthy—think about such things (Phil. 4:8).

There are Christians who unconsciously usurp the functions of the Holy Spirit for themselves. They are constantly busy trying to convince others of their sinful nature and therefore continually point out others' mistakes. Although we should help our fellow Christians by gently helping them see where sin remains in their lives, it is the prerogative of the Holy Spirit to convince people of their sinfulness and to guide them to a real experience of the living Christ. When a Christian constantly condemns other people, he becomes blind to an important dynamic element of the Christian gospel: that all believers are new creations in Jesus Christ.

Someone who has been renewed in Christ has been forgiven, and though he is still prey to temptation, he is able to deal with it through the strength of Christ, his Savior. A true Christian sees the newly born-again disciple in a new light. He no longer only sees the weakness, impatience, and sin of the human personality, but starts to comprehend the hidden potential for good that is always present. He sees good even in those who are unfaithful to Christ, and he appreciates everything that is true, noble, just, beautiful, and praiseworthy.

When a Christian expects to find virtue in people, he will observe that people gradually start reacting in a way similar to what is expected of them. It may take time, but if you use the intuition granted to you by the Holy Spirit to seek only the best in others, you will often find that people accept the challenge of Christ.

Loving Master, through the enlightenment granted to me by the Holy Spirit, I always see the good in my neighbor.

THE STRENGTH OF THE HOLY SPIRIT

So I say, live by the Spirit, and you will not
gratify the desires of the sinful nature (Gal. 5:16).

Much has been said and written about the necessity of putting Christ first in your life. The call to submit yourself to His will and to be obedient to His commands is often emphasized. Christians are urged to turn away from the demands of society so that they may joyfully follow Christ. Countless sincere believers have tried to measure up to the demands imposed on Christians. However, if they were to be honest, they would have to confess that it is much easier said than done.

If we take into account all the temptations and enticements that come across our paths, it is understandable why it is so difficult to live a life that complies with the demands of Jesus Christ. It requires a measure of willpower and a strength of character that are far beyond the capacity of the average person. The pace and tension of contemporary life places you under enormous pressure. This pressure only increases when you are called to testify for Him in circumstances that are in direct contradiction to a Christian lifestyle.

It is precisely in these circumstances that you have to open your life to the influence of the Holy Spirit. Invite Him to take control of your entire being, and you will experience the power of Jesus that enables you to overcome all obstacles while you live for, through, and in Him.

Come, O Holy Spirit, and permeate my life so
that the strength of Jesus may be revealed in my life
and I may become a powerful witness for You.

TO IDENTIFY
WITH CHRIST

The life I live in the body, I live by faith in the Son of God,
who loved me and gave himself for me (Gal. 2:20).

This is one of the most inspiring and yet also challenging texts in the entire New Testament. It transcends theological argument and penetrates into the sphere of true spiritual experience, where the fullness of God saturates one's life as far as it is allowed to. The love, peace, strength, and other attributes of the living Christ become a glorious reality to those who accept Him and who are obedient to His will.

However, no human being can, in himself, accomplish such an intimate identification with the living Christ. It is only through God's goodness and grace that we can experience the reality of Christ's Spirit. Union with Christ happens by trusting Jesus for the full forgiveness of your sins and accepting that He died your death.

This privilege also encompasses weighty responsibilities. To be one with Christ implies an involvement with His redeeming purpose for the world. It means experiencing some of the pain that He suffers as a result of the depravity of mankind. It means to be compassionate and generous, and to love others in His Spirit and His love.

To identify with Christ you need to surrender and commit yourself completely to Him. You need to have the same disposition as Jesus Christ did. Your attitudes, behavior, motives, and lifestyle should be the expression of the Spirit of Christ in you. Identification with Christ means to grow towards being increasingly more like the Master.

Thank You, heavenly Teacher, that I may grow in the grace and
wisdom of my Redeemer, Jesus Christ. For this I thank and praise You.

JEALOUSY AND CHRISTIAN SERVICE

Let us consider how we may spur one another
on toward love and good deeds (Heb. 10:24).

Unfortunately jealousy is a common sin among Christian workers. It is often concealed in religious semantics and clever phrasings, but where competition exists in a church or Christian organization, the results quickly become evident. And once these results become apparent in church organizations, the testimony of the body of Christ is weakened and undermined.

Jealousy is the consequence of self-centeredness. When you are interested solely in your own little world of service, while simultaneously envying the success of others, your vision becomes limited and restricted. Your service is no longer a source of satisfaction to you. And if you persist in your jealousy, it eventually weakens your spiritual life until you no longer experience God as a reality.

The most basic way of conquering jealousy in your Christian service is to allow the Holy Spirit to take possession of your life. The practical manifestation of this experience will encourage you to serve others in sincerity. To overcome jealousy you should take control of your thoughts and allow the Holy Spirit to renew your mind. Be sincere in your delight over the successes and achievements of others.

It may not be easy initially, and you may even feel like a hypocrite, but as your awareness of the presence of the Holy Spirit in your life increases, you will experience a wonderful feeling of liberation. Then you will be able to inspire others to achieve their full potential in Christ.

Holy Jesus, through Your immanent Holy Spirit I am gloriously
liberated from all forms of jealousy. For this I sincerely thank You.

SIN WILL COST YOU DEARLY

"The soul who sins is the one who will die" (Ezek. 18:4).

In contemporary society sin has lost its sting. It is undermined with psychological terms and referred to as weaknesses or illnesses. But the consequences of sin still remain the same. Sin separates us from God, creates feelings of guilt, inferiority and frustration, and deprives the sinner of an inner calm and peace of mind.

You cannot sin without eventually being caught. This is a fact that many people try to ignore with all their might. They believe that they are the exception to the divine law that you reap what you sow—with interest. People commit sin without giving any thought to the consequences. Sin has its own price, and it can be extremely costly if we calculate how much sadness, scandal, and sorrow is inflicted upon loved ones when sins are revealed.

God does not tempt anyone; you commit a sin through your own free choice. You isolate yourself from Him by walking your own path and deviating from God's path. To deliberately continue sinning is to commit spiritual suicide.

To accept Jesus Christ as the Redeemer and Savior of your life and to consciously live in the presence of God are the only ways to preserve yourself from sin. In doing so you will experience freedom and be liberated from your sense of guilt. The Holy Spirit grants you the strength to live victoriously.

Through Your immanent Spirit, holy Lord Jesus,
I obtain the strength to live in triumph over sin.

CHRISTIAN FANATICISM

Some of the Pharisees said, "This man is not from God,
for he does not keep the Sabbath" (Jn. 9:16).

The dictionary defines a fanatic or zealot as someone who admires and worships something in an excessive manner, or someone who is stubborn and intolerant. Unfortunately these traits are often found in religious people. Their misplaced values cause unimportant things to become crucially important.

Jesus restores a blind man's sight on the Sabbath, yet the Pharisees fail to notice the miracle because they are unable to see beyond the violation of the law of the Sabbath. They couldn't share in the man's joy at being able to see, because they classified his cure as "work." They condemn both the man and his Healer.

In your Christian life it is easy to become so entangled in matters of lesser importance that you start confining the living Christ to your intellectual limits. Because you cannot understand how the Master did some of His miracles, you refuse to accept that they were done at all. You ignore the fact that there are depths that are as yet unexplored by your intellect.

No disciple of Christ should be so unwise as to close his mind to new ideas about his faith. There are many facets to the life, teachings, and values of our Lord Jesus, but the common factor among all His disciples is faith in His redeeming death and an overwhelming love for the Master and for one another. Love is the death-knell of fanaticism and the origin of understanding. Fanaticism will prevent the love of Christ from flowing through you.

Beloved Master, Your love for me and my love for You rescues me
from blind fanaticism. For this I praise and exalt Your holy name.

RECEIVE GOD'S FORGIVENESS

I prayed to the Lord my God and confessed (Dan. 9:4).

It is one of the great privileges and joys of the Christian faith that, regardless of what you have done, God is always waiting for you to come to Him in prayer. His love for you is so vast that you are assured of His forgiveness even before you enter into His presence. This assurance was given once and for all on Golgotha. All that you have to do is turn in repentance to Christ and confess all your sins to Him.

Maybe it is precisely because it seems so simple and easy that so many people do not make use of this glorious offer of grace from Christ. Or maybe they are too ashamed to confess their failures. However, one thing is sure: the longer you postpone matters and bottle up your guilt, the more difficult it will become to make your confession, and the more unhappy you will become.

There are two important matters that you need to consider. One is that God knows everything about you, including your weaknesses and shortcomings. The other is that despite this He still loves you and always will. He gave His life in Christ to prove it.

Why would you continue to torture yourself and deny yourself the inner calm and peace of mind that Jesus offers you? Open your heart to Him and lay your guilt and fear before His throne of grace. Here you will experience the purifying balm of His unfathomable love.

> *By confessing my sins to You, gracious God, I experience Your merciful forgiveness and can therefore live in joyful abundance.*

GOD CHOOSES
HIS WORKERS

*Being confident of this, that he who began a good work in you will
carry it on to completion until the day of Christ Jesus (Phil. 1:6).*

In every generation God has had followers to proclaim His truth and do
His will. Sometimes they have been held in high esteem by the community. Others have remained unknown and have modestly performed the
task that He assigned them to the best of their ability. Regardless of their
status, all of them loved God with a fervor that inspired and challenged
their fellow human beings.

The spiritual giants of the Christian faith have always had a uniquely
personal experience of the living Christ. Paul never forgot his meeting
with the Master on the road to Damascus; Brother Lawrence met Christ
in his kitchen; John Wesley felt his heart becoming strangely warm in a
room in Aldersgate Street in London; many other disciples experienced
the reality of the Lord in a unique way.

Every child of the Lord should realize that Christ comes to each of us
in a personal and unique way, meeting us on our own level. The ordinary
disciple will not necessarily have a Damascus road experience, because
the Savior will prepare a special experience that is uniquely suited to
every individual person.

As your experience of Jesus deepens and expands into constructive
service, you will become aware of a divine plan that is in the process of
unfolding in your life. This plan may not be particularly dramatic or
impressive by the standards of the world, but it will be God's plan for
your life. In living it you will experience immense joy and satisfaction.

*Leader and Redeemer, I pray that I will be a faithful worker in Your
service and that I will never be ashamed when You judge my work.*

THE IMPORTANT ROLE OF WOMEN

Early on the first day of the week, while it was still dark,
Mary Magdalene went to the tomb (Jn. 20:1).

Throughout the Scriptures women play an important role, and their influence on the Christendom should never be underestimated. Women were the last ones present at Jesus' cross and the first at His tomb; they were the first to announce His resurrection and they were undoubtedly present at the first domestic devotions. While Jesus ministered to the crowds of Galilee, He was served by a group of women who used their own possessions to support Him and His disciples. When the apostles first arrived in Europe, they were welcomed by women.

The church is greatly indebted to devout women who love Christ with so much dedication that they are willing to sacrifice anything. When cynical people declare that most congregations consist almost entirely of women, they are merely confirming a scriptural pattern of godly women who faithfully love their Master and Lord, Jesus. Some men would have been much wiser and richer if they had followed the advice of a devout mother or a dedicated spouse. Others are where they are today only because of the prayers and support of a loving woman.

Paul tells us that there are no differences between men and women, Jews and Gentiles, slaves and free people: in Jesus Christ we are all one. This unity in Christ makes Christians dependent on each other, and men and women draw their inspiration from the same source. Therefore we should show respect and appreciation for the service every person offers.

Thank You, heavenly Father, for the noble and enriching service
that devout women have offered to You and Your church.

GUARD AGAINST
DOUBLE STANDARDS

But you—who are you to judge your neighbor? (Jas. 4:12).

It is inevitable that you will form opinions about things that you approve of and things that you condemn. However, we have to ensure that our condemnation is always tempered with forgiveness, because we must also be perpetually aware of our own weaknesses and the failures in our pasts.

Many people have a condemnatory attitude towards their fellow human beings. They scrutinize every deed as if under a magnifying glass and are quick to emphasize others' mistakes. In addition, they also like to insinuate that they would never be associated with such deviant behavior. People who are constantly passing judgment on others usually have a limited spiritual outlook and inevitably only manage to make life miserable for themselves as well as others.

People with a condemnatory attitude seldom use the same standards to judge themselves as they do others. They expect a high standard of behavior from others, but not of themselves, and what is more, they are quick to make excuses when their behavior falls short of this standard.

In the Christian life there is only one standard that applies to everyone. What is applicable to one is applicable to all. Therefore, if you see someone doing something that contravenes God's laws, you should ensure that you are also not guilty of transgressing a law before you pass judgment. The law that you are violating may not be as blatant as the one you are condemning, but the awareness of your own sin should humble you and make you more careful in your judgments.

Merciful Lord Jesus, because I am so aware of my own weaknesses,
I should be slow to condemn others and quick to forgive them.

PRAY FOR YOUR NEEDS, NOT YOUR WANTS

"Every word of God is flawless; he is a shield to those who take refuge in him" (Prov. 30:5).

We often hear people complaining that God has disappointed them by not answering their prayers. All too often these are also the people who blame God for their circumstances. When misfortune or disappointment strikes, God is blamed for the predicament.

In order to find an answer to these accusations, it is necessary to ask this question: how many of these people have entrusted their requests in prayer to the throne of grace and have completely submitted themselves to the will of God?

Jesus invited us to ask anything of the Father in His name and promised that we would receive it. However, this by no means implies that God will give you everything you ask for. What it does mean is that He will provide for all your needs through Jesus Christ. You should pray for God's guidance before making your requests, so as to ensure that what you are asking for are truly needs and not just things you desire.

God never disappoints, but you have to completely surrender yourself and your will to Him and open yourself to the influence of the Holy Spirit, who will guide your thoughts and deeds. In this way you will live in harmony with God's will and experience the abundance of true life.

O Holy Spirit, help me to grow in faith through enthusiastic prayer. I know that my heavenly Father will provide for every legitimate need that I have.

YOUR REPUTATION IS OF INESTIMABLE WORTH

They loved praise from men more than praise from God (Jn. 12:43).

Your good reputation is of inestimable worth. Your good name depends on society's opinion of you. It cannot be gained overnight, nor can it be bought by favors with hidden agendas. It can only be earned by living a noble life.

Standards that are founded on essential values should not be influenced by the opinions of other people. Your standards should not be of the world, but rather of God. If you allow your reputation to be shaped by other people's opinions and expectations of you, your life will be governed by ever-changing values. People have differing value systems, and you cannot comply with all of them.

When you live to please God alone, you accept principles that create a strong character and a good reputation. Your word becomes your bond; your candor is tempered with love; honesty becomes an integral part of your being; and, because you are aware of your own vulnerability, you refrain from harsh criticism.

Living to please God has a powerful formative influence on your life. If you honor God and allow Him to govern your life, you will have the respect of those who maintain God's standards.

Holy Lord Jesus, help me to live to please You alone.
May Your values always be manifested in my life.

THE SECOND COMING
OF CHRIST

The end of all things is near. Therefore be clear minded
and self-controlled so that you can pray (1 Pet. 4:7).

For centuries people have been trying to determine the exact date on which the world will end. Despite the fact that Jesus expressly told us that it is not for us to know the time and that God alone knows it, the prophecies just seem to continue.

The actual date of the end is of little importance if you are equipped and ready to meet it. The most important aspect of the second coming of Christ is not when it will take place, but rather whether you will be prepared to meet your Lord and to account for your life and deeds.

People go to much trouble to prepare themselves for special occasions; they make ample provision for their retirement; they ensure that their affairs are in order should they suddenly pass away. When a storm looms, the doors and windows are locked; farmers protect their livestock from the cold of winter; insurance is taken out to provide in the event of theft, loss, and accidents.

How much more important is it then to prepare yourself spiritually and mentally so that you may joyfully anticipate the second coming of Christ? Discipline yourself to spend time in prayer and contemplation in the presence of the Master; surrender yourself to the influence of the Holy Spirit so that you will be ready whenever He comes.

Come, Lord Jesus, come soon!

August

Heavenly Guide, I so much want to begin this month with
faith, hope, and love in my heart.
I so much want to believe unconditionally:
like Abraham and Enoch and Moses and all those in the
gallery of heroes in Hebrews 11.
But so often I am more like Thomas; I first want to feel and see;
my faith is often limited to my senses.
I so much want to believe the unseen and quietly profess:
"My Lord and my God!"
I so much want to experience perfect hope,
hope that all the ardent and noble ideals of my heart
will be realized;
that my spiritual life will grow in knowledge, love, and truth,
so that I will be able to distinguish what is truly important.
Keep the spirit of optimism burning in my heart.
I so much want to love, God of love.
I want to say to You with the honesty of dying words:
"Lord, You know everything. You know that I love You!"
I want to love my neighbor with a sincere, unselfish love
that breaks down all the walls that divide us
and make reconciliation a glorious reality.
In this month, guide me to a true understanding of
faith and hope and love!
In the glorious name of Jesus.

Amen.

RESPECT THE SCRIPTURES

All Scripture is God-breathed and is useful for teaching,
rebuking, correcting and training in righteousness (2 Tim. 3:16).

The Bible is an essential manual for the Christian. From it you draw guidance, admonition, hope, and everything else that is necessary for your spiritual development. However, it is also often abused, not only by its enemies but also by those who acknowledge it as the Word of God. This happens especially when texts are used out of context to construct religious theories. Inevitably, these theories are divested of any true meaning. For many dedicated Christians the letter of the Scriptures is much more important than the spirit behind the words. It is disturbing to hear the Word of God loudly quoted without the presence of the Spirit of God.

For centuries people have explained the prophecies of the Scriptures in the light of their own times, forgetting that the Master expressly told His followers that it is not for us to know these things. Many believe that the times in which we are now living are the "last days." This knowledge belongs to God alone. Never try to answer divine questions in human terms. You are not expected to strive after the possession of knowledge about matters that God keeps secret. Rather, you are expected to trust the Master to bring all things to their God-determined end, while living in harmony with Him.

The Bible encompasses the whole world, but it also speaks deeply to the individual human soul. It is especially for the latter purpose that the Scriptures may be most useful to you.

Incarnate Word, I thank You for revealing Yourself in the
Word that God has made available to us in our own language.

JESUS ILLUMINATES
THE DARKNESS

*Let him who walks in the dark, who has no light, trust
in the name of the LORD and rely on his God (Is. 50:10).*

There comes a time in everyone's life when the path ahead seems dark;
when difficulties overwhelm you and you become despondent because
of the darkness and despair that seem to surround you. Often your circumstances are so desperate that you feel completely helpless and simply
cannot free yourself. In these circumstances you are at your most vulnerable and pressurized.

Despite how far from God you feel in times like these, you must
remember the glorious truth that He is actually closer to you than ever
before. Your heavenly Father has assured you that He will never abandon
or forsake you. He is constantly at your side, waiting for you to turn to
Him for help, which He is always ready and willing to provide.

Regardless of what is happening in your life, yes, even when you are
unable to pray, never neglect turning to Christ and laying your fears and
concerns before Him. Because He lived among people He is all too aware
of the difficulties and problems that you experience. Allow Him to lead
you and you will experience the blessing and joy of His love and peace.

*O Lord, please send Your light and Your truth to me; let it guide me to
Your holy mountain so that I may enter and go to the altar of God.*

HOW GREAT THOU ART!

Since ancient times no one has heard, no ear has perceived,
no eye has seen any God besides you, who acts
on behalf of those who wait for him (Is. 64:4).

Throughout history Christianity has come under fire from all quarters. The validity of our faith and even the existence of God have been challenged and questioned. Many have suffered torment and persecution for the sake of their faith, and thousands have chosen death rather than to deny their God. This surely indicates the greatness and strength of God's love for the Christian and the Christian's love for God.

As you live your life faithfully in Jesus Christ, you will become more and more aware of His presence with you. When you place your trust in God and dedicate your life to Him, you become increasingly aware of the fact that His hand rests upon you and guides you through the maze of life. The healthier your relationship with the Master, the more aware you will be of the Holy Spirit who speaks to you and leads you through each day.

A life that is lived in, with, and for the living Christ will strengthen your faith and allow you to seize each day joyfully. Nothing else can provide you with this joy and peace. And then you can do nothing but whisper in grateful prayer, "How great Thou art!"

Savior and Redeemer, I kneel in helpless wonder
before Your greatness and majesty. I truly love You, O Lord!

THE INSPIRATION
OF THE HOLY SPIRIT

*"And I will ask the Father, and he will give you another
Counselor to be with you forever—the Spirit of truth" (Jn. 14:16).*

If one considers all the demands and expectations of modern life, it is
not surprising that there are so many people who collapse under the
pressure and fail to comply with the standards expected of them. Sadly,
this often causes people to turn away from the Christian faith in despair,
and consequently they experience the torment of wandering around in
the wilderness of uncertainty.

Jesus knows human fallibility and fragility all too well. That is why
He prepared His disciples for a life without His physical presence. He
granted them the gift of the Holy Spirit to enable them to cope with the
demands of life. And they undoubtedly needed it, because they experienced such intense opposition to their preaching of the gospel.

The gift of the Spirit is yours too, because God has said, "I will pour
out My Spirit on all people" (Joel 2:28). Jesus confirms this in the words
of today's Scripture verse.

To enable you to cope with life in all its many facets in accordance with
the instructions of the Master, it is essential to allow the living Jesus into
your life. Trust Jesus, the One who baptizes with the Spirit, and allow His
Spirit to direct you according to the will of God. Then you will be able to
handle any situation, however difficult.

*O Holy Spirit, come and fill my life. Inspire me to live according to the
will and instructions of God the Father and my Savior, Jesus Christ.*

CHOOSE GOD'S WAY

Surely the arm of the Lord is not too short to save,
nor his ear too dull to hear (Is. 59:1).

Often we live as though God does not exist. We make our own plans and work hard to accomplish them. We create goals and devise plans without any thought of what God expects of us.

And usually, when we decide to follow our own way instead of God's way, things start going awry. We run into the proverbial brick wall and start thinking that we are being pursued by bad luck. We become despondent and feel that it is useless to attempt anything, because it will just be a failure anyway.

The truth of the matter is that our problem is not bad luck, but rather our deliberate disobedience to God's call to live a nobler life. If things seem to be going wrong for you all the time, pause and consider why this is so. Are you choosing your own way instead of God's way? However desperate your circumstances may appear, it can always be reversed if you abandon your own selfish way and choose God's perfect way. But this is a demanding process, and few people are willing to pay the price exacted by it. However, it remains a fact that being obedient to God and walking in His way will bring deliverance from even the most wretched circumstances.

Holy Master, Your way for my life may seem demanding
and difficult, but it is the only and the best way
for my life. I want to follow You every day of my life.

TOGETHER WITH GOD

I can do everything through him who gives me strength (Phil. 4:13).

When you think of God in all His divine glory and of yourself as an insignificant little speck on earth, it becomes incredibly difficult to identify yourself with Him. Despite this, the Holy Spirit of God, who inhabits God's entire creation, can also inhabit your spirit through faith in Christ. Accepting this truth releases a previously unknown force in your life. It is God's will that you should have a vigorous and living relationship with Him.

When you think of yourself as a part of God's revelation of Himself, you share an empathy with Him that will bring strength, balance, and dynamism into your life. It will also provide you with a strong sense of responsibility. If you realize that you have been created by God and that you are sealed by His Spirit, you also realize that your life should live up to His expectations. You no longer live to please yourself, but rather to do His will. Through the grace of God you can attain this kind of life in the strength of the Lord Jesus Christ.

Before our Savior ascended to heaven, He promised that the Holy Spirit would be with those who have accepted Him as Savior and Lord. It is the Holy Spirit who makes God a reality in the life of the Christian and who enables him to live in harmony with and in the strength of God.

Merciful Lord Jesus, I accept the gift of the Holy Spirit and therefore enjoy intimate communion with You, my Lord and my God.

THE WILL OF GOD ALONE

*"By myself I can do nothing; I judge only as I hear, and my judgment is
just, for I seek not to please myself but him who sent me" (Jn. 5:30).*

There are few people who have not at some point experienced the frustration of plans that go awry or expectations that are disappointed. In many cases it goes much further than mere disappointment because of failure; the consequences of failure can take on immeasurable proportions. When this happens, many people ascribe it to fate, economic circumstances beyond their control, chance, bad luck, or any of a host of other reasons. Few people will admit that the fault lies within themselves, because they refuse to live according to the will of God.

God's sacred plan for your life is one of perfection. Because you are His child and He loves you, He wishes only the very best for you. For this reason everything that happens in your life is intended to ultimately give you the very best, even though it may not appear so to you at the time.

To achieve this goal with as little trouble as possible, it is your responsibility to live and work within God's will. Submit your ideas and plans to Him and faithfully seek His guidance. The closer you live to your Master, the easier it will be to discover His will for your life. Never embark on any endeavor that falls outside the will of God, and you will experience peace of mind and tranquility, as well as the assurance that Jesus will be with you in all your endeavors.

*Eternal and loving God, I surrender myself to You completely.
Lead me according to Your will from day to day.*

INTEGRITY BEFORE GOD

I know, my God, that you test the heart and
are pleased with integrity (1 Chr. 29:17).

If you sincerely try to cultivate a positive and meaningful prayer life, you will at some time or another have experienced the problem of wandering thoughts. In the time you have set aside to be alone with your heavenly Father, you may read a passage from the Bible or from an inspirational spiritual book. Then you start praying, only to discover that instead of being focused on God, your thoughts run amok and start focusing on the most irrelevant things.

If this has happened to you, take comfort in the thought that it happens to everyone who takes prayer time seriously. However, those who have persevered have ultimately succeeded in making their prayers a delightful reality and a powerful force in their lives.

When your thoughts wander, don't become upset or frustrated, because then you are playing right into the hands of the Evil One. Gently turn your thoughts back towards God, and ask the Holy Spirit to take control of your mind. You may rest assured that the problem of your wandering thoughts can be conquered, so don't allow it to spoil your relationship with the living Christ.

The wonder of Christian prayer is that when you turn to Jesus you will find that He is already awaiting you. Prayer is not a one-way communication; Jesus is just as eager to meet you, His child, as you are to meet Him.

Thank You, heavenly Master, that I may experience the reality of
Your living presence through prayer. For this I praise Your name.

DOES YOUR RELIGION LEAD YOU TO GOD?

Taste and see that the Lord is good (Ps. 34:8).

It is commendable to accept the doctrine of your church, because it provides you with a foundation upon which to build your faith. In a traditional church environment you may become familiar with certain liturgical forms of worship from which you can draw hope, courage, and strength. Or perhaps you are profoundly touched by the warmth, enthusiasm, and spiritual intensity of the charismatic movement. Whether slow and methodical or energetic and enthusiastic, churches can be filled with lukewarm Christians who fail to know a living faith.

The litmus test of your worship is whether it is Christ-centered, God honoring, and leads you into the presence of God. If the living Christ is at the center of your faith, you will know the deep hunger of the soul that yearns to know Him more intimately. You will discipline your prayer life and organize your reading of the Scriptures to facilitate a more profound understanding of the Master and His way of life.

Whatever your theological position or church affiliation, the crucial aspect of your spiritual pilgrimage ultimately remains your personal relationship with Christ Jesus. Knowing Him through faith, prayer, and Scripture will transform your dogma from something memorized to something felt. It will create in you a love for all people and transcend all differences. When this happens, you will be overwhelmed by the greatness and benevolence of your living Lord.

Merciful Lord, grant me a spiritual temper
that will enable me to transcend denominational
differences, so that I may meet You in all Your glory.

LISTEN TO GOD

Listen to what the LORD says (Mic. 6:1).

Most people have an opinion on virtually every matter under the sun. Should you pose some or other abstract question to them, their response would probably be, "I don't really know because I haven't considered the matter, but I think that…" If a great number of people start enthusiastically expressing immature and rash thoughts, the situation can easily become chaotic.

However, if you are sensible you will remember that behind this Babel of tongues the proven truths of God stand steadfastly. In the heat of the argument, these truths are seldom evident.

God reveals His truths to those who invite Him to share in their lives; who gladly give up time to be with Him; who ponder His Word so that they can understand His will more thoroughly. Make sure that you always spend more time in the awareness of God's presence than in argumentation—regardless of how interesting the argument may be.

The art of listening to God is an enriching and inspirational experience. It imparts tranquility and balance to your spirit and mind in the midst of disquiet and endless arguments. The art of listening to God is usually practiced in a private, sacred place, but this discipline yields its abundant results when you have to venture into our tumultuous world.

Holy God, in listening to You I receive wisdom,
peace, balance, and stability in my daily life.

ESTABLISH TRUST THROUGH PARTNERSHIP

So we say with confidence, "The Lord is my helper;
I will not be afraid. What can man do to me?" (Heb. 13:6).

If you are trying to take on life's difficulties and problems in your own strength and wisdom, it is likely that you are fighting a losing battle. This does not necessarily mean that you are grumbling or complaining, or that you are constantly asking for the sympathy of others, but if you were honest with yourself and others, you would have to admit that there are moments when you long for your burden to be lifted by some positive guidance.

In such moments it is advisable to grow quiet before God and to realize that He is closer to you than your breathing or your hands and your feet. The only reason why He did not come to your rescue was because you did not ask Him to. You cannot take God's help for granted. When you seek His help, you place what you are and what you have at His disposal.

You become God's partner in your everyday life. This partnership means that you should constantly do the will of your heavenly Partner, and do it in such a devoted and enthusiastic manner that destructive fear will have no place in your life.

When you have conquered fear through constructive service, you can face anyone with a peaceful confidence that is the direct consequence of your union with God. Because God is your Helper, and because you serve Him joyfully, you can step fearlessly and confidently into the future.

Good Shepherd, because You are my Helper
and I serve You with sincerity, my life is filled with
trust that is born from my relationship with You.

JESUS WILL LEAD YOU SAFELY

"When you pass through the waters, I will be with you; and when you pass through the rivers, they will not sweep over you" (Is. 43:2).

Anyone who is a poor swimmer will know the fear of finding themselves in a pool, a river, or the sea, and realizing that they are out of their depth. It causes a feeling of uncertainty, danger, and anxiety, because they have nothing to hold on to and no fixed foundation to stand on. The thought of sinking and drowning only contributes to the fear and can easily change into panic.

Your pilgrimage through life can be a similar experience. There are so many situations in which you feel incompetent, vulnerable, and uncertain. In the business world, you are constantly expected to act quickly and decisively, but a wrong decision or move can mean the difference between success and dismal failure. In your personal life you constantly have to make decisions, and these decisions often have far-reaching consequences for yourself and for others.

The question is how are you supposed to act logically and calmly in these circumstances? There is only one way, and that is to cultivate an awareness of the living Christ in your life. Let Him be the deciding factor in all your ventures and first seek His will before you make any decisions or take any steps. Do so in faith and in the knowledge that He is the only way to success.

> *Lord Jesus, I worship You as the Way, the Truth, and the Life. Not my will, Lord, and not my way, but Your will and Your way for me.*

IS YOUR CONCEPT OF GOD BROAD ENOUGH?

"How great is God—beyond our understanding!" (Job 36:26).

One of the obstacles to our spiritual development is our limited concept of God. You may believe that God loves and cares for you. You freely accept that He is all-powerful, all-knowing, and omnipresent. But as soon as disaster starts to threaten, you relegate God to the back seat. You fail to use the wisdom, calmness, and strength that He has placed at your disposal. In these trying moments you find that you do not live up to that which is expected of you. Your problems appear to be bigger than your concept of God.

You ought to broaden your vision of God while things are going well. This may be accomplished by intensifying your quiet time with Him and expanding your interest in the world around you. Be determined to increase your awareness of the greatness of God and use all the agents of His grace that He puts at your disposal to get to know Him more intimately. When the inevitable storms start looming, you will find that you possess spiritual reserves that will enable you to be strong; regardless of how difficult your circumstances are.

The greater God becomes to you, the more strength you will draw from Him in moments of temptation. Your faith will no longer be an emotional matter, but rather a lasting experience of God Himself. He will give you the assurance of His presence at all times. Know that your God is great, and you will possess a lasting faith!

Great and wonderful God, grant me a spirit and attitude of appreciation for Your greatness, so that my spirit and perspective may be broadened.

THE REALITY OF
THE LIVING CHRIST

*The Spirit himself testifies with our spirit
that we are God's children (Rom. 8:16).*

Whichever Christian dogma you ascribe to or whichever church you belong to, your ultimate goal should be to know and experience the living Christ in your life. Without Him your faith may maintain a high moral standard, but it will lack the spiritual dynamism and force that are essential elements of a living faith.

Jesus Christ is much more than a historical figure who can be conceptualized in religious terms. He is the inspiration and driving force of innumerable lives in our modern age. It is insufficient to recognize only the Christ of history: what you really need is the living Christ working in your life today.

The yearning for this awareness should be the first priority in your life. It will never become a reality before you have been possessed by a passionate longing to make Him your own. A half-hearted desire will simply not be spiritually good enough.

When your greatest passion is to experience the immanent presence of Christ, you should act as if you are always in His presence—which you are, in reality. Speak to Him from the silence of your heart; share with Him the things that are happening to you; and if there have been moments when you excluded Him from your life, don't waste time in self-reproach. Tell Him that you are sorry, and you will find that His grace enables you to renew your relationship with Him. Then He will become an ever greater reality in your life.

*Merciful and loving Master, I praise and
thank You for Your presence at all times in my life.*

BE PATIENT WITH OTHERS

When he saw the crowds, he went up
on a mountainside and sat down (Mt. 5:1).

The wonder of Jesus' ministry lies in the fact that He had time for everyone. Despite the immense pressure that heavily burdened Him, He was able to accomplish more in three short years than what we accomplish in a lifetime. And yet He was never hurried, impatient, or tense. When reading the Gospels you can share in that feeling of peace and calm that He radiated to everyone who came into contact with Him.

There are many occasions when we are required to provide some advice, support, or companionship, and so often we respond only by showing our impatience. We are pressed for time; we have very busy schedules; we are working to beat the clock. We show it in the hurried way in which we try to get rid of people in distress, so that we can rush on to whatever else is demanding our attention. This inevitably leaves the other person with the feeling that he is nothing more than an annoying intruder who has to be pushed aside.

If you are faithful to your calling as a follower of Jesus, you should never show impatience or irritation when you are dealing with the problems of other people. Despite your busy life, Christ will always give you the time to do His work. Trust Him unconditionally and you too will be able to treat people with the same patience, compassion, and empathy that He did. In this way you will become a source of encouragement, calmness, and peace for others.

Lord Jesus, I open myself to Your Spirit of peace, patience,
and encouragement in my interaction with other people.

LASTING GLORY

And if what was fading away came with glory, how much greater is the glory of that which lasts! (2 Cor. 3:11).

Some things are made to last, while others are created only to fulfill a passing need. Both kinds of things may appear attractive and enduring. Only time and use will show how one differs from the other. This is true of every aspect of life, and our spiritual life is no exception.

There are many forms of the Christian faith that appeal to people because they emphasize material assets, which people usually desire. Prosperity, luxury, and happiness are falsely promised and guaranteed to those who follow Christ's precepts. Unfortunately many people are drawn to following Jesus because of what they can get from Him, rather than for the sake of Jesus Himself. If their expectations do not materialize, the glory of their faith fades along with their expectations.

The true glory of the Christian faith intensifies as the years pass. A young disciple may be extremely enthusiastic about his faith and his zeal for the Lord may be a joy to see. But all the beauty of youth cannot compare with the fullness of character that is part of someone who has followed Christ through decades.

The eternal Christ brings lasting glory and enrichment to every person who trusts in Him. This glory develops slowly, like an oak tree rather than like a mushroom, but it always reflects the lasting glory of the living Christ.

I pray, Lord my God, that my life will reflect Your lasting glory, for the sake of Your exaltation and my spiritual growth.

THE BIG MYSTERY

I present to you the word of God in its fullness—the mystery that has been kept hidden for ages and generations, but is now disclosed to the saints. To them God has chosen to make known…the glorious riches of this mystery, which is Christ in you, the hope of glory (Col. 1:25-27).

There is a certain quality of mysticism that is inherent to all religions, and Christianity is no exception. Since the early days of the church there have been schools of mysticism whose doctrine was known only to the initiated. This exclusivity often creates the false impression that God only reveals His mysteries to a select group of individuals.

The Scriptures reveal the amazing truth that God has no favorites and that He is willing to share His truths with everyone who is willing to live up to His demands. Paul tells us that God wants to reveal His mysteries to His people, and that this secret is the fact that Christ is united to us. This secret is the basis of a dynamic Christian lifestyle. If you accept the principle that Christ can live in you, you have discovered the greatest mystery ever to have been revealed to mankind.

If you trust Christ is with your thoughts and emotions, and believe that He seeks to manifest Himself in your deeds, you will be carried to new spiritual heights. The things you used to fear attempting now become possible, and the things you used to shy away from no longer scare you. If you possess God's secret of the immanent Christ, you are able to face life with self-confidence and expectation.

Holy Jesus, open my life to Your immanent presence. I humbly plead that You will make me a channel of Your love to the world.

SOURCE OF INEXHAUSTIBLE POWER

Those who hope in the LORD will renew their strength. They will soar on wings like eagles; they will run and not grow weary, they will walk and not grow faint (Is. 40:31).

Familiarity is a great threat to our spiritual lives. It is possible to become so familiar with religious clichés and phrases that they lose their deeper meaning. The spiritual discipline that once fortified your faith may have become an obstacle that prevents you from growing spiritually. You may have addressed God as "Father" for so long that you have come to think of Him as a grey old Lord who closes His eyes to your sins, thus forgetting that He is also a God who punishes sin. If you have lost your sense of wonder and awe for the greatness of God, you have lost something for which there is no substitute.

To regard God with respect and awe moves you to true worship. It once again creates a moral and spiritual basis for your worship. It is unlikely that you will spend time contemplating the wonder of God and His truths revealed through Jesus Christ and still remain spiritually weak and ineffectual. There is an essential power in praising and worshiping Him.

To praise God not only means that you become involved in an act of communal worship. It implies an attitude towards life that is constantly on the lookout for opportunities to praise and thank God. Let the thought of praising Him dominate your thoughts, and you will feel the power of the almighty God flowing through your life.

Through praise and worship, heavenly Father, my strength is renewed so that I can grow spiritually to be more like Your Son, Jesus my Lord!

FREEDOM COMES WITH RESPONSIBILITIES

Live as free men, but do not use your freedom as
a cover-up for evil; live as servants of God (1 Pet. 2:16).

The word freedom is a much-abused word. It is used to muster rebellious people together, and heinous crimes are committed in the name of freedom. Those who follow false leaders promising freedom usually find themselves trapped in a new form of slavery.

True freedom can only be experienced if the human spirit is liberated from hate, cruelty, and envy, because true freedom possesses a spiritual quality that is known and experienced by everyone who loves and serves God.

The vast majority of people live in slavery. However, they may be unaware of the bindings that constrain them because they have grown so accustomed to them that they have simply become habits. Their preconceived ideas and false thought patterns are reflected in their negative attitudes. Their tempers, their hate, and their bitterness all reveal the slavery that constrains them.

The message of the Christian gospel brings freedom for everyone who is held captive by the destructive influences that control their inner being. The living Christ forgives our sins and frees us from the shackles of the Evil One. This is a gift, part of God's perfect love, if it is accepted in faith. As you experience the blessing of God's deliverance, you will be transformed into a new, free being who lives in harmony, peace, and love with God and your fellow human beings.

Perfect Jesus, through Your Spirit I am freed of all sin and
unacceptable habits. Because I know You, I have become truly free.

LOVE IS THE ANSWER

*This is my prayer: that your love may abound more
and more in knowledge and depth of insight, so that you
may be able to discern what is best (Phil. 1:9-10).*

Decision-making is a process that is often the source of much perplexity. It may influence your future well-being or that of those whose interests you take care of. It may have a bearing on your business, your personal life, or your career. Whatever the circumstances, the fact remains that, unless you have a stable and level-headed approach to the problem, you run the risk of being overwhelmed by the anxiety of uncertainty and indecisiveness, and your fear of the consequences fogs your decisions.

There is no doubt that you need the guidance and wisdom of the Holy Spirit to provide you with clarity of thought and vision. He views matters from the perspective of eternity, while you can only observe the here and now. For this reason, and also so that you can obtain peace of mind, it is essential to pray constantly for the guidance of the Holy Spirit.

To prepare yourself for this you need to have an intimate personal relationship with the living Christ, so that your thoughts can be focused on His will. The more you love Jesus, the closer you will live to Him, thus enabling Him to speak to you through the promptings of His Holy Spirit.

*I thank You, Redeemer and Savior, for the assurance that he
who loves You is Your child and can know the God of love.*

Read James 4:1-10

IT IS YOUR RESPONSIBILITY

Come near to God and he will come near to you (Jas. 4:8).

The depth and quality of your spiritual life is your responsibility. It may be that you yearn for more faith and plead with God to give it to you, but if you don't practice the faith that you already possess, you cannot expect God to give you more. You may crave a deeper and more realistic prayer life, but only you can silently wait upon God and cultivate an awareness of His holy presence. God planted a yearning for Him in your deepest being. This hunger to know Him better is one of His greatest gifts to you. He is constantly calling: "Come to Me!" and it is in your answer to this call that your Christian perseverance is truly revealed.

To accept your Christian responsibility is a solemn undertaking, and if you accept it in a half-hearted way you are insulting God and depriving yourself of true communion with Him. God demands a devotion that encompasses your entire life, and it is this devotion that many people shy away from. They are unwilling to meet the demands of total commitment, and the unfortunate result is that they end up living in the twilight of an insufficient faith.

God will never require you to give up something without giving you something better in its place. When He asks for your devout life, He gives you more grace in return, and you step into deeper maturity you would never have thought you could experience. By accepting the responsibility for your own spiritual growth, you continually move closer to your Master and Redeemer.

*Holy Father, in Your strength I accept the responsibility
for my own spiritual development. I want to make use of
all the instruments of Your grace that You put at my disposal.*

YOUR DIVINE COMPANION

The righteous cry out, and the LORD *hears them;*
he delivers them from all their troubles (Ps. 34:17).

The dreadful feeling of loneliness is a devastating experience. Many people struggle with loneliness caused by a variety of circumstances: the loss of a loved one; the fear caused by serious illness; struggling with problems all by yourself when it seems as if no one can help you. These are but a few of the situations in which people despair in their loneliness, often with disastrous consequences.

It is precisely when you find yourself in these circumstances that you are most vulnerable. It is also then that Satan sows his seeds of doubt, discouragement, and despair in your heart. Those who succumb to it feel that there is no future and no hope, and it is not long before they slump into the depths of self-pity and despair.

In the Scriptures, as well as in secular history, it has been proven time and again that you are never alone, because the hand of God rests upon you. All that you have to do is hold on to His assurance that He is always with you.

When it seems as if life is treating you unfairly, don't give up hope, but rather lay your fears and worries before the living Christ. Open your heart and life to the influence of the Holy Spirit and He will fan the flame of hope yet again, so that the tiny flame that threatened to die out will become a bright light to illuminate your path.

Powerful Redeemer, grant me the strength to keep my hand
firmly in Yours even under the most difficult circumstances.
Lead me from the darkness into Your wonderful light.

WHEN LIFE GETS COMPLICATED

In all your ways acknowledge him, and
he will make your paths straight (Prov. 3:6).

Sometimes life becomes complicated in very covert and subtle ways. Small and apparently inconsequential things are neglected because other things demand your urgent attention. Eventually you are confronted with a whole array of unfinished tasks, irritations, and confusions.

To simplify your life and create a blueprint for success, you need a goal towards which you can work. A life with a multitude of goals achieves little, because you waste all your energy without accomplishing anything. Therefore, focus on a positive goal and bring order to your life.

A sure way of complicating your life is to take on a task for which you lack both the time and the energy. There are people who cannot refuse a request, with the result that they leave many tasks unfinished. Determining your priorities is crucial if you want your life to run smoothly and productively.

Creating such a list of priorities should have preference in the planning of your life, and it should be determined in the presence of your heavenly Father. Under the guidance of the Holy Spirit, you should consider the demands placed on you and ask for them to be prioritized in the right order. If you accomplish this, you will live an organized life. Don't forget God when your life becomes complicated.

Heavenly Master, I ask that You will grant me an uncomplicated
and inspired life under the guidance of the Holy Spirit.

FAITH OR WORRY?
THE CHOICE IS YOURS

Cast your cares on the LORD and he will sustain you (Ps. 55:22).

It isn't hard work that causes mental, spiritual, and ultimately physical breakdown—it's worry. Work that is free of worry is stimulating and enjoyable. It gives substance to your daily life and also confers a feeling of belonging to the human family and contributing to the well-being of the human race.

It is worry that exhausts you, and if you are worried, you cannot achieve anything constructive. Worry alienates the willing worker from his rightful inheritance and true purpose and satisfaction of life. However, the greatest tragedy of worry is that it estranges you from God. Faith and worry cannot cohabit in the same life. If your faith is a living reality, there will be no space for worry, but if worry is the dominant force, faith will wither and die.

Worrying can so easily become an indulgent habit. Only a radical adjustment of your thought patterns can free you from worry. Having a practical faith in the omnipotence of God and His purpose for your life is essential. The conviction that all things work together for the good of those who love God should be the dominant thought in your mind. Then you will experience the renewing power of a living faith, which is the death-knell of all worry.

Merciful Lord, from today onwards I am determined not to allow worry to spoil the beauty of my life or to destroy my faith in You.

WHEN YOUR BURDEN BECOMES TOO HEAVY

"Come to me, all you who are weary and burdened,
and I will give you rest" (Mt. 11:28).

In these times so many people live under incredible pressure. Tension and stress take their toll on young as well as old. Children and young people are under immense pressure to excel in their studies and their sporting activities.

Business people struggle to keep their heads above water in an extremely competitive environment. The elderly experience an increasingly uncertain future and constantly worry about their security. People of all ages are exposed to all kinds of temptations that promise only disaster for them and their loved ones.

Professional counseling, medical treatment, and medication have become common remedies for people suffering from tension. In most cases these are only temporary measures that are merely a crutch to help people stumble through life. And still the tension keeps increasing.

There is only one infallible way of coping with tension and stress, and this is Christ's way. He, who also lived and worked under immense pressure, offers you the peace of God that surpasses all understanding. It is a peace that banishes all anxiety and fear and gives you the ability to cope with life in the strength of the Master. Accept His gift of peace and rest.

I praise and thank You, Lord my God, that the peace and quiet
of Jesus fills my life even amidst life's greatest tensions and pressures.

DISCIPLE AND DISCIPLINE
ARE SYNONYMOUS

Therefore, if anyone is in Christ, he is a new creation (2 Cor. 5:17).

There are people who desire to have a religion that suits their personal lifestyle. They seek a church that is broad-minded and liberal, and that places few demands on them. Unfortunately, these people never experience the impact of a living faith.

If the challenge to discipleship is to be truly effective, it must have an impact on your life. A positive and constructive spirituality should influence every facet of your life. This means that you have to admit the weaknesses in your character to yourself, confess the sins and failures of your past, and realize your dependency on God. It is this realization of your own inadequacy and frustration that brings about the turning point in your pilgrimage.

When you feel that you can't meet the demands of the Master and it seems as if your spiritual life is falling apart, you ought to share your unhappy circumstances with God and plead for His help. No one's request for Jesus' help has ever been in vain.

When you accept Christ's assistance, you also accept the responsibility of willing discipleship and discipline. Your mind and spirit should be brought under the dominion of the Holy Spirit. In this way your thoughts become constructive and your character strong so that you can do the will of God and become a disciple who is worthy of your calling.

I thank You, merciful Master, for the strength
that You give me through Your Holy Spirit so that
I can live my life in the way that You expect of me.

YOUR SAVIOR IS ALWAYS THERE FOR YOU

Because of the LORD's great love we are not consumed,
for his compassions never fail (Lam. 3:22).

In our lives there are often times when everything seems hopeless and lost. We succumb to illness; adversity descends upon us; fear overwhelms us; or we experience the pain of death's ultimate separation. These things leave us with a feeling of loneliness that borders on despair. What does one do in such circumstances, and how do you cope with life?

Some people are extremely fortunate in experiencing the support of their family and friends in such times. Others who are less fortunate are not as blessed. And even though you may have people who stand supportively around you, there are still times when even that support falls away, because at some point they have to return to their own lives and their own families.

When life plunges you into some or other crisis, you should never forget the goodness and faithfulness of God. You are His child, whom He has chosen, and in His Word He time and again reassures you of His constant presence. The living Christ is at your side at all times and under all circumstances. He will guide you from the darkness of despair into His wonderful light of hope and peace. Walk with Him and be filled with His love and peace.

Heavenly Companion, even though I sometimes feel lonely,
I know that I am never alone, because You have
promised never to forsake or abandon me.

YOUR LIFE IS
SECURED IN CHRIST

*There is now no condemnation for those who are in
Christ Jesus, because through Christ Jesus the law of the Spirit
of life set me free from the law of sin and death (Rom. 8:1-2).*

When the strength of your Christian faith threatens to wane, you start
looking for all kinds of excuses for the apparent deterioration. Such
excuses are not difficult to find, but it seldom happens that you turn
the spotlight of truth upon your own inner being. Only if you have
the courage to allow the Holy Spirit to reveal yourself to you will you
discover the causes of your spiritual deterioration.

You will discover that your faith is inadequate because you have
allowed something or someone to take Jesus Christ's place in the center
of your life. When your awareness of the presence of Christ starts to
fade and your intellectual approach becomes confused, your awareness
of Jesus starts disappearing.

If you wish to be united with Christ, He has to be the focal point of
your faith. Then your faith will once again become a dynamic reality and
you will unequivocally know that sin can no longer control you, because
you are controlled by Christ. Freedom from sin and the awareness of
Jesus' presence will impart a special quality to your life, which cannot
be obtained from any other source. This freedom and this special quality
constitute more than just an emotional experience. Your entire life
changes because Jesus works through you and you are secure in Him.

*Savior and Master, I humbly plead that my life
will channel Your life into the world in which I live.*

MORE CHRISTLIKE EVERY DAY

*Instead, speaking the truth in love, we will in all things
grow up into him who is the Head, that is, Christ (Eph. 4:15).*

It is a glorious truth that believing in Jesus Christ as your Redeemer and Savior redeems you from your sins. This is the foundation of the Christian gospel. But you should never forget that after you have accepted Jesus Christ as the Lord of your life, the process of growth should continue. If you ignore the necessity of growth, your spiritual life will start to flounder in the ocean of disappointment and despair. There must be growth and development.

In His mercy, God has put many resources for spiritual growth at our disposal, but we should be careful not to let these resources become an end in themselves. Communion with fellow believers is essential, but communion that is not centered on Christ serves no spiritual purpose.

Studying the Scriptures is a source of inestimable inspiration and guidance, but you must remember that the purpose of the Scriptures is to point the disciple to Christ. Good works and helping those less fortunate than yourself are undoubtedly agreeable to God, but these things are only the fruits that spring from knowing Christ. In themselves they do not necessarily lead to Christ.

Spiritual growth can occur only when your ideal is to be more like Jesus. This should be the yearning of every disciple. Spiritual growth transcends emotion and demands your everything in the service of Christ.

*Fill me so completely through Your Holy Spirit,
O Master, that my life will reflect Your glory.*

AVOID UNNECESSARY WORRY

Out of the depths I cry to you, O Lord; O Lord, hear my voice.
Let your ears be attentive to my cry for mercy (Ps. 130:1-2).

Have you ever taken a moment to ponder how patient God is? He continually offers His children love, forgiveness, comfort, encouragement, assistance, and an array of other gifts that allow us to live a life of comfort and certainty.

He promised to be with us always. He has even offered to live in us. Despite all of this, however, how often do we only ask for His help after we have exhausted all other sources? How often do we, like the psalmist, only call to Him from the depths?

The wonder of it is that God—unlike people—never tires of us. He is never impatient and His love remains constant. However difficult our circumstances are, He is always at hand to hear our cries for help and come to our rescue.

People could spare themselves a great deal of worry and fear if they would immediately turn to Christ for help when a problem crops up. There is no point in being secretive or hesitant, because Jesus has invited all those who are tired and overwhelmed to come to Him so that He may give them rest. Do it, and worry will no longer reign supreme in your life.

Beloved Savior, whether I find myself in a stormy crisis
or in the peaceful sunshine, I bring all my worries to You.
You have proved that You have the solutions for all of them.

THE LIVING WORD

*Then he opened their minds so that they
could understand the Scriptures (Lk. 24:45).*

There are many people who regard Bible study as a bit of a nuisance. They have been taught that it is a duty, and consequently they struggle through the pages and breathe a sigh of relief when they have read the prescribed passage.

Others find that they don't understand what they are reading, or that their daily problems destroy their inclination to read the Bible. Many people read the Bible only in the evening after a day's work when they are tired and cannot possibly take in what they are reading.

If you are having problems with your Bible study because of these or other reasons, it might be worthwhile to consider that perhaps you are spending more time reading about God than spending time with God.

It is necessary to know the incarnate Word personally so that you can live the life of spiritual abundance that He offers you. In order to know Him it is necessary to reach out to Him in the silence of your inner room through meditating on Scripture and prayer. And to validate this activity you should serve Him among your fellow human beings.

If you draw near unto God in this manner, you will find that the Word starts to assume new life and meaning, because you are no longer merely reading a book. Instead you are living the Word together with its Author!

*Incarnate Word of God, I open myself to You, so that You can
fill me with Your Spirit and Your Word, and truly live in me.*

September

It's fall, Lord and God of creation,
fall with its mellowness and abundance of opulent color.
Thank You for spiritual growth and maturity;
thank You that it ends in the tranquillity and fulfilment of fall.
During this season of change,
help us to reflect on how the world changes
and how You remain the constant source of love and life.
Just as it was yesterday and just as it will be tomorrow,
Your grace is sufficient.
In profound gratitude I dedicate myself anew to You:
body, soul, and spirit.
Guide me through this month; make me Your faithful disciple
and a fearless witness of Your love.
Through the cross, let me realize the wretchedness of sin,
so that I will flee from it to Your grace.
This month, let me see Your love
so that I may take refuge in You.
For Your love's sake.

Amen.

Read Colossians 1:15-20

THE PURPOSE OF CHRIST'S MISSION

God gave us the ministry of reconciliation: that God
was reconciling the world to himself in Christ,
not counting men's sins against them (2 Cor. 5:18-19).

The great separation between God and man took place when man in disobedience declared himself to be independent of God. He thought that through this he would be liberated, but in reality he became the slave of influences stronger than himself. The self replaced God; love turned into sensuality and self-satisfaction. Man's one-sided declaration of independence from God was disastrous, because subsequent events proved that man cannot control the world in his own wisdom and strength.

Even though man turned away from God, God did not turn away from man. He descended to the level of mankind and came as the man Jesus Christ. The purpose of Christ's coming was to bridge the gap that separated man from God.

Through Christ's worldly ministry God revealed to us what we may become through His strength. We can be liberated from sin, share in the enriching experience of His Spirit living in us, and experience an ever-increasing communion with Him. According to the New Testament it is God's earnest desire to rehabilitate those separated from Him.

God has not changed. His love is eternal and those who accept Christ and His standards find that their relationship with God is fully repaired.

I kneel in gratitude and wonder before Your love,
O God, because You reconciled us with You through Jesus Christ.

LIVE YOUR FAITH

If I say, "I will not mention him or speak any more in his name,"
his word is in my heart like a fire, a fire shut up in my bones.
I am weary of holding it in; indeed, I cannot (Jer. 20:9).

Any true disciple of Christ will know the ecstasy of having a personal relationship with his Savior. It creates such an intense feeling of joie de vivre that your heart brims over with joy in the knowledge that the living Christ lives in you.

In many cases people also experience an irrepressible urge to tell others of the wonder of Christ. They bubble over with enthusiasm and give testimony in front of friends and acquaintances, business partners and even strangers. They want to tell everyone of their wonderful Lord and His marvelous deeds of love and grace. Their sincerity is beyond question. In today's world there is a definite need for this kind of testimony to be given and heard.

But perhaps you feel that you are unable to speak about Jesus. Don't be discouraged by this, because there is another, just as important way to share the gospel, and this is through the way in which you live and behave in your interactions with other people. Jesus is the incarnate Word and if He takes possession of your life, it will be reflected in your deeds. His acts of love and compassion will be evident in your behavior. Share your feelings of joy with the people you encounter in your daily relationships. In doing so you will lead them to Jesus by your example.

Heavenly Example, come and fill my life, so it will reflect Your love.

Read Luke 24:13-35

WALK WITH JESUS

As they talked and discussed these things with each other,
Jesus himself came up and walked along with them (Lk. 24:15).

Tragic events paralyzed Jesus' first disciples. Their spiritual perception was unable to see beyond the darkness of the crucifixion, and therefore they could not remember Jesus' promises. Consequently, the road to Emmaus was shrouded in despondent darkness for the disciples.

Jesus joined them on this journey, but they did not even recognize Him. Initially He was only a stranger who astonished them with His ignorance of recent events. But when He started to explain the Scriptures, He became a prophet to them, and they listened to Him with interest. Only after they had invited Him to spend the night with them did they recognize Him as the Master they loved.

The events on the road to Emmaus were not unique in Christian experience. Many have walked this path in His company without recognizing Him. He showered His blessings on them and they did not respond to His love. They may have listened to the gospel for years without grasping its full meaning. They may even claim to have been converted, and yet the joy and reality of true faith has passed them by.

The wonderful truth is that the Master is with you every step of the way. Even when He is regarded as a stranger, He remains your Friend; even when His blessings aren't recognized, He keeps giving, and if you listen to His Word He reveals Himself to you. The living Christ wants to walk the road with you; do you want to walk the road with Him?

Powerful Redeemer, I no longer want to treat You as a stranger,
but I accept You completely as my Savior and Redeemer.

LET YOUR LIGHT SHINE

[Joseph] reassured them and spoke kindly to them (Gen. 50:21).

Different people respond to other people's approaches in different ways. Some people respond favorably to a friendly approach, while others respond better to a command rather than a request. In some cases discipline causes fear, while in others it brings about respect and efficiency.

No one, not even the most hardened person, can resist friendly reassurance indeterminately. An overview of Jesus' life reveals that He was held in high esteem and treated respectfully by people, even by His worst enemies. Everything that He said and did was characterized by love.

The gospel shows us that even when He firmly admonished people, He always spoke in a friendly and charming manner. Whatever He said was always to the advantage of the person He spoke to, and His words sprung from His deepest concern for their welfare. Even at the moment of His gruesome death on the cross, His loving reassurance conquered the hardened hearts of the murderer and the Roman soldier.

In your relationships with others it is crucial to follow the example of the Master. Display His love and understanding in the way that you treat them and their problems. Assure them of your interest in them and your concern for their welfare. Let the love of Christ shine through you so that they may find His peace in you. In this way you are following His command to be the light of the world (see Mt. 5:14).

*Lord Jesus, may I reflect Your perfect
love in everything that I say and do.*

WHY SHOULD WE PRAISE AND GLORIFY GOD?

Praise, O servants of the Lord, praise the name of the LORD. Let the name of the Lord be praised, both now and forevermore (Ps. 113:1-2).

Why should God be praised and glorified? Why should we tell Him how almighty, all-knowing, and omnipresent He is? Why should we waste time telling Him things that He already knows? And yet He commands us to praise Him. God never channels our energy into dead-end streets. There is more to praising and glorifying God than simply repeating His divine attributes.

The complexity of the human temperament compels it to reach out to something higher and greater than itself. This yearning can be fulfilled by praising and glorifying God, through which we connect ourselves to Him who knows and understands the desires of our hearts. God can manage fine without our praise, but we cannot manage without the uplifting strength and inspiration that emanates from our praise for Him.

True praise is one of the greatest inspirational forces in life. It raises you up from your spiritual despondency and enables you to live in communion with your heavenly Father. Praise can occur in many different ways: during the excitement of a revival service; during the sanctification of the communion; or in those quiet moments when you are alone with your heavenly Father. The method is of little importance, as long as it allows you to enter into the holy presence of God.

Holy Father, I enter Your gates with adulation, with praise I go into Your temple court. In so doing I enter into Your presence with joy and thanksgiving.

DON'T TURN BACK

From this time many of his disciples turned
back and no longer followed him (Jn. 6:66).

For Jesus' disciples life with Him was filled with excitement, and they were witnesses to many of His mighty deeds and miracles. They were with the Master when crowds flocked around Him to listen to His words and teachings. As part of His following they must have been swept up in the radiance of the mystery and wonder that surrounded this exceptional Man.

However, at some point their enthusiasm suddenly started waning. For a moment they came to a standstill to think, and inner doubt started gnawing away at them. The excitement made way for worry, which became so overwhelming that many of them decided no longer to walk with Him, as John recounts. How is it possible that such enthusiastic followers lost interest and returned to their old ways of life?

The Master was busy explaining to them exactly what the price of complete surrender and commitment to Him entailed. He emphasized the things which God expects of His people, so that they may obtain the abundant life that Christ offers. These expectations were too high for some, and they felt that more was expected of them than what they were willing to give.

The same challenges confront us today, and the temptation to turn back is a reality to each Christian. Meanwhile, the Devil continues to try and sow the seeds of doubt and discouragement. Don't turn back, but rather open your life to the influence of the Holy Spirit. He will give you the ability to follow Christ to the end.

Leader and Master, I accept the challenge of following
You to the end. Guide me, so that I will not lose my way.

YOUR ATTITUDE IS EXTREMELY IMPORTANT

I do not hide your righteousness in my heart; I speak of your faithfulness and salvation. I do not conceal your love and your truth from the great assembly (Ps. 40:10).

Despite appearances to the contrary, we are all endowed with a sensitivity that makes us deeply aware of other people's attitudes towards us. For example, you may be introduced to a person who smiles amiably and has a friendly handshake, and yet you instinctively distrust him. You can't explain your distrust, but it is there as a reality and therefore you approach that person carefully.

The fact is that when you meet someone for the first time, your smile and your handshake are not adequate proof of your sincerity. People pick up your invisible, though essential, nature as a radio picks up sound waves from the air, and they instinctively know you.

When you meet someone for the first time, your attitude should be one of goodwill and sincerity. When you are involved in an interview with someone, let your love towards the interviewer replace your fear. Remember the words of the Scriptures: "There is no fear in love. But perfect love drives out fear" (1 Jn. 4:18). When you find yourself in a situation where you are expected to venture an opinion, let there be no bitterness in your heart so that love may be the dominant emotion.

What you feel in your deepest being is reflected far beyond your appearance or the personality that you present to the world. Approach all people with an attitude of love, and you will be astonished at the joyful and trusting response that you elicit.

Only through Your grace, Lord my God, is my heart filled with Your love that is revealed in my attitude towards my fellow human beings.

TRANSFORM YOUR FAITH INTO DEEDS

In the same way, faith by itself, if it is not accompanied by action, is dead (Jas. 2:17).

You may be finding it difficult to transform your religious theories into deeds. Perhaps you spend some time with God early in the morning and find His presence to be a glorious reality, so that you are able to face the day in the firm conviction that He will be with you at all times.

Then you begin your day with its changing circumstances and continual demands, and hours pass without your giving the Lord a single thought. When you suddenly remember that it has been some time since you have had contact with Him, a feeling of guilt saturates your being. Don't be discouraged. Your mind can handle only one thought at a time, and when you focus on the task at hand, you can't think of anything else. Remember that He is with you even when you are immersed in a task that leaves no opportunity for other thoughts. If you complete a task to the best of your ability, you are doing it in His honor, and when your mind is focused on Him once more, you will hear Him saying, "Well done, good and faithful servant!" (Mt. 25:23).

The Holy Spirit who lives inside you creates an attitude that makes every ordinary task an act of worship. If your spirit is in harmony with Christ, whatever you do in your practical life will be transformed into an act of practical faith.

Master and Savior, Your immanent presence enables me to express my faith in practical terms.

REMEMBER WHO
YOU ARE!

*So God created man in his own image, in
the image of God he created him (Gen. 1:27).*

When it seems as if nothing in your life is working out, when loneliness
takes hold of you and despondency descends upon you, it is time to call
into remembrance a few spiritual facts.

You were created in the image of God. Yes, this image has been
damaged and perhaps you have forgotten your rich spiritual heritage.
But the fact remains that you are irrevocably a spiritual being. Knowing
this should let new hope and inspiration flow through your mind and
spirit. You were not created to be the plaything of moods that are beyond
your control. Because you have been created in the image of God you
have also been created for spiritual greatness, and you will know no
rest or fulfillment before you live in the awareness of His presence, thus
growing and developing spiritually.

This may sound very theoretical, but actually experiencing it brings
forth practical results. If you are afflicted by feelings of inferiority, you
will find great comfort in remembering that you are a spiritual being
meant to live in the presence of His holy countenance. If your life is
impaired by the stress and tension created by feelings of inadequacy, you
will find liberation in drawing on the abundance of God's strength. This
will enable you to face life confidently, because you will be assured that
His Spirit is working in you.

*My Savior, Jesus Christ, because of my spiritual
heritage and the awareness of Your living presence,
I go forward to meet life with confidence.*

REJOICE IN THE LORD!

*Then the people of Israel—the priests, the Levites
and the rest of the exiles—celebrated the dedication
of the house of God with joy (Ezra 6:16).*

Unfortunately, there are many people in the world who associate worship with despondency, cheerlessness, and even fear. Their attendance of church services is little more than a duty done merely for habit's sake. It is expected of them and they believe that they will be punished if they neglect doing it. The tragedy of an attitude like this is that it deprives people of the greatest of all joys: joy in the Lord.

Through Christ God invites you to find repose in Him and to receive the fullness of life that He offers you. If you turn to Him you become increasingly aware of His life-giving Spirit that works in you. Seemingly unattainable goals are suddenly within your reach; adversity does not overwhelm you because in Him you find the strength to overcome it; a newly found confidence replaces your nervous pessimism and feelings of failure. Day by day your faith grows stronger.

As you open yourself to the Holy Spirit, you will find that your worship, Bible study, and prayer life gain new meaning. If you place your trust in the living Christ, you will discover that God is no longer a faraway figure but an integral part of your life. He will lead you on the path that He has mapped out for you.

Worship ought to be a joyful experience. Open yourself to the Holy Spirit, and He will raise you from despondency to ecstasy in Christ.

O Holy Spirit, come into my life and fill me with the joy of the Lord.

LISTEN TO YOUR CONSCIENCE

*"I heard you in the garden, and I was afraid
because I was naked; so I hid" (Gen. 3:10).*

There are times in our lives when we are burdened by feelings of guilt. In these times we find it very difficult to live with our conscience. The most common causes of these kinds of experiences include acts based on half-truths, deception, jealousy, and envy, but there are many other causes, too numerous to list. Some of these acts may seem trivial, but whatever form they take, the human conscience will reprimand the wrongdoer in no uncertain terms.

Because of these feelings of shame and self-reproach, most of us instinctively try to hide from our wrongdoing by turning our backs on it or excluding it from our thoughts. Some people try to justify their behavior, while others think that an external façade of bravado will calm their inner storms.

One thing is absolutely sure: whatever you do and however hard you try, you cannot hide from God. Whatever you do to erase your footsteps, you can be sure that the blinding light of Jesus Christ will reveal it before your heavenly Father.

Never try to hide from God. Be assured of His undying love; confess to Him in repentant prayer those things that cause you shame and fear; then receive from Him the peace of mind that springs from the true confession of your sins. Listen to your conscience!

*Lord Jesus, because I am assured of Your loving
forgiveness, I reveal my soul to You in confession.
Thank You for Your boundless forgiveness.*

WE CANNOT PLACE DEMANDS ON GOD

Teach me your way, O LORD; lead me in a straight path (Ps. 27:11).

There is an essential difference between laying your requests before God and making aggressive demands of Him. To ensure that God will be present in the inner sanctuary of your heart, you need to be obedient to His demands and rejoice in His answers to your requests. You must believe that He knows what is best for you and willingly submit yourself to His judgment. This acceptance creates a firm bond between you and your heavenly Father. As your faith grows, you will be increasingly willing to meet the demands that He puts to you.

When you are tempted to approach His throne of mercy with demands, you should remember that sincere humility is a virtue. However strongly you may feel about the matter, you really have no right to demand anything from Him. Irreparable damage has been caused by people making aggressive demands of God that He has chosen to leave unanswered. In such cases it is easily said that people's prayers are not answered because they lack faith.

It is not the person who storms the gates of heaven, but the disciple who in humility lays his requests before God who experiences the joy of God's guidance in his everyday life—those who say, "Lord, this is my humble prayer, but let Your will be done."

This is not an approach of blind fatalism, but one of deep trust born from the profound conviction that God knows best and that He wants to do what is best for you.

O Hearer of prayers, help me not to walk my own path, but Yours, so that I can come to a deeper understanding of Your love and Your purpose for my life.

FOR DAYS WHEN
YOUR FAITH FALTERS

My soul yearns, even faints, for the courts of the Lord;
my heart and my flesh cry out for the living God (Ps. 84:2).

If you have experienced the love of God in your life, encountered His power, and walked in His presence every day, but have allowed all these wonders to become nothing more than beautiful memories, then you are truly experiencing a tremendous tragedy.

There are many Christians who look back on the road they have traveled and wonder where they lost the glory and the reality of their faith. They still possess some form of Christian faith, but only they and God know that it is merely a shell of their faith.

Very few people are really content with this unfortunate situation, because they know what they once possessed, and they are challenged to once again become what they used to be. To know what they are now and what they ought to be causes an intense disappointment within themselves and a deep yearning for a more profound experience of God. People who once experienced the deep waters of God's grace can never be content with sloshing around in the muddy waters of mundanity.

It is not God's will that anyone should be separated from Him. However, to return to God is something that many people find extremely difficult. Nevertheless, be assured that if you return to God He will still be waiting with the outstretched arms of His Son on the cross. If you become estranged from God, it is through your own fault and not His.

Holy Lord Jesus, in simple faith I return to You and ask that
the awareness of Your love and strength will once again fill my life.

LIVE VICTORIOUSLY
FOR CHRIST!

*This is what the LORD says: "Maintain justice and
do what is right, for my salvation is close at hand
and my righteousness will soon be revealed" (Is. 56:1).*

When casting an eye on the things happening in contemporary society, there are many people who feel that it is simply no longer worth the trouble trying to maintain standards. They see good people suffering while criminals prosper; honesty is not rewarded, while dishonest people get off scot-free. All things considered, is it still worthwhile to maintain Christian standards? So often we are tempted to compromise or abandon our principles in order to follow the popular opinion rather than Christ's standards.

Despite the fact that it sometimes appears as if everything is turned against the righteous, we should never lose sight of the fact that God ultimately judges everything. We might manage to get away with compromising our principles in this life, but the fact remains that we are also busy preparing ourselves for eternity, when all people will be held accountable for their deeds.

Never tire of doing what is right, and open yourself to the influence and power of the Holy Spirit. He will enable you to weather life's storms and live in victory.

> *O Holy Spirit, in You I find the strength to live
> victoriously for Christ. For this I praise and thank You.*

COPE WITH YOUR WOUNDED FEELINGS

You will increase my honor and comfort me once again (Ps. 71:21).

Many people claim to believe in an almighty God, but their lives do not reflect this faith. They see the wonders of creation or try to fathom the mysteries of their own personalities and feel that this knowledge is out of their reach. The greatness of God in nature and in wisdom overwhelms them, and they recoil into the pettiness of their own personalities. Consequently their perspective becomes confused and narrow-minded.

If your concept of God is large enough, there can be no space for pettiness or narrow-mindedness. If someone hurts you with a snide remark or an unfriendly gesture, you can either take revenge or accept it in the spirit of God's forgiveness. If you take it personally and nurse a grudge, your life will become miserable. However, if you simply accept these incidents against the background of God's omnipotence, they will become inconsequential and you will grow spiritually.

You can only experience mental and spiritual greatness if God is the center of your life. It is only when you accept everything that comes your way in the Spirit of Him who lives inside you that nothing can undermine your spiritual stature. In this case God becomes of greater importance than your feelings or desires. If God comes first in your life and you aim to please Him alone, what other people say and think will be of little importance to you.

I praise and thank You, holy Master, that I am able to handle even my injured feelings constructively and positively through the grace that You grant me.

WHAT DO I OWE GOD?

*"Here I am, living in a palace of cedar, while
the ark of God remains in a tent" (2 Sam. 7:2).*

The issue of stewardship has, throughout the years, been a thorny one among Christians. People have argued and debated about tithes and offerings, and a variety of different standpoints have been held. Many of the arguments are completely transparent and do little to hide people's unwillingness to give an offering to Christ. On the other hand, there are also people who truly find this matter extremely problematic.

While people continue to argue about whether you should give ten percent of your net or gross income to the Lord and about what is lawfully deductible, the fact remains that the Scriptures are very clear about what the Lord expects of His disciples.

As a Christian you and everything that you own belong completely to Christ. In His grace He has trusted you to be the steward of your life and your possessions. It then follows as a matter of course that you, as a good steward, should be extremely careful to perform your task well. Consequently, God should have the first priority over anything else in your life. Once you have accepted this, you will find that all arguments are pointless, because God's cause must come first. If you honor Him in this way, He will bless you and guide you in how to use your life as well as your possessions.

*My Lord and my God, I want to profess my faith anew.
May I have a love as perfect as Yours, in body, mind, and spirit.*

ALL IS WELL WITH MY SOUL

*Why have you rejected us forever, O God? Why does your
anger smolder against the sheep of your pasture? (Ps. 74:1).*

There are many people who feel that they are abandoned and completely
alone in the world. Circumstances cause things in their lives to go
wrong; illness and death dominate their thoughts and the only thought
in their minds is: "Why?" As far as one can see they seem to live worthy
lives, keeping God's commandments, and yet now in their times of trial
and tribulation, they feel that God has forsaken them.

It is an absolutely false concept to think that you are abandoned or
forsaken by God. He has promised to be with you always and to not
forsake you (see Heb. 13:5). He has proved the unfathomable depth of
His love in your life by offering His Son on the cross.

God has a divine purpose with all the things that happen in your
life. Even when you are the victim of adversity or disappointment, don't
despair. He wants to, and can, use these circumstances to bring about
His perfect will in your life.

There was a brief moment on the cross when Jesus felt abandoned
by God, but the humiliation of Good Friday was transformed into the
triumphant victory of Easter Sunday. Know under all circumstances
that the living Christ is with you, place your trust in Him, and in His
good time you will experience victory.

*Be still, my soul, the Lord is on your side. Patiently carry
all your sorrow and grief, and leave all decisions in His
loving hands. When everything else fails us, He remains faithful.*

DON'T BE IMPATIENT

*Grow in the grace and knowledge of
our Lord and Savior Jesus Christ (2 Pet. 3:18).*

When some people commit themselves to Christ, an immediate transformation of their personality takes place. The weakness of their character is replaced by strength, and an indescribable confidence fills their entire life. Becoming a born-again Christians can indeed be a joyous experience. But with the passage of time the wonder and enthusiasm of this initial phase sometimes abates, and the spirit that was once aflame for Christ starts to wane. Unfortunately this is not an uncommon occurrence among relatively new Christians.

When one surrenders oneself completely to Christ, one becomes a new creation, but old habits die hard. Even though the freshness of Christianity is a glorious reality to new Christians, they are still infants in Christ, and in the process of growing, old habits may easily make their influence felt once again. Therefore it is imperative that the young Christian begins the process of growth immediately after his conversion to Christ. The excitement of conversion, which is undoubtedly a legitimate spiritual experience, should be strengthened by the foundation of Bible study, prayer, and communion.

Without worship, prayer, and Bible study there can be no growth. If a piece of coal is removed from the fire it cannot retain its heat. It is God's desire that you will grow spiritually, but the responsibility to actually do so belongs to you.

*Thank You, Lord Jesus, for starting me on my
Christian pilgrimage. With Your help I am determined
to work hard at my growth and development.*

FIND JOY IN THE SMALL THINGS

*Everything God created is good, and nothing is to
be rejected if it is received with thanksgiving, because it
is consecrated by the word of God and prayer (1 Tim. 4:4-5).*

Many people tend to take things for granted. This is an unfortunate attitude, because it causes people's sense of value to be skewed so that they can no longer appreciate the intrinsic value of things. The colors of the flowers, the song of the birds, the beauty of a sunrise or sunset are all things that many people barely notice. They regard these things as mundane occurrences that do not deserve special attention.

It is only when you start pondering a life without these blessings that you begin to realize how drab and mediocre your existence would become. Life without these gifts of God would be colorless and uninteresting. It is difficult even to imagine a situation like this. We ought to cherish and appreciate every blessing in our lives, be it large or small. We should learn to appreciate the wonders of God's creation, especially in nature, because it adds meaning, beauty, and purpose to our lives.

We should therefore appreciate everything that God has granted us in His grace, but we should also realize that we must carefully protect and conserve the wonders of creation, because we are its keepers. This is the most practical way of thanking God for His greatness and benevolence.

*Heavenly Father, I thank You for the everyday things
in my life and for everything that they mean to me.*

THE SIMPLICITY OF JESUS' TEACHINGS

Then he told them many things in parables (Mt. 13:2).

One of the most marvelous things about Christ is the simplicity of His teachings. He expressed the great truths of His heavenly Father in such a way that illiterate people could understand it. He also confronted the scholars of His time and stunned them into silence with the quality of His wisdom. The difference between Jesus and the scholars who questioned Him from time to time was that He was from above and so understood heavenly things, whereas they were of the earth.

He challenged people to forgive their enemies and spoke of turning your enemies into friends. In His teachings, as well as through His example, He conveyed the importance of love, and He clearly showed that a dynamic religion encompasses more than a rigid moral code that leaves no room for love. The simplicity of faith, as He taught it, leads to a practical, devout lifestyle that embodies its beliefs. Everyone who was willing to listen to Him and learn from Him understood what He wanted to tell them.

In the midst of clashes between different theological ideologies, it is advisable to remember that the simple elements of Christ's teachings are such that everyone can understand and take joy in them. To love Him and to love your neighbor through Him; to experience His strength in your spirit; to know that eternal life is through faith in Christ alone—these are simple yet profound truths that ultimately become a glorious reality in your life.

Loving Master, grant me the wisdom to develop a faith that is simple yet powerful.

USE GOD'S GIFTS

Timothy, guard what has been entrusted to your care.
Turn away from godless chatter and the opposing
ideas of what is falsely called knowledge (1 Tim. 6:20).

As a child of God you are blessed with a precious gift: the ability to reflect the nature of Christ in your life. As is the case with all things of great value, this blessing also involves great responsibility. You have to cherish it, look after it, and use it in the way it was intended to be used. After His death and triumphant resurrection Jesus gave His disciples the great commission for missionary work (see Mt. 28:19-20). To enable them to follow His instructions He sent the Holy Spirit to assist them. This gift and the strength of the Spirit are as available today as they were to His first disciples. All that Jesus asks of you is your complete surrender to His sovereignty and your willingness to serve Him in the way that He calls you to.

This may appear to be an immense challenge, and you may doubt your ability to meet its demands. However, remember that history proves that Christ has always provided His disciples with the strength to accomplish their tasks. Allow His Spirit to possess you completely, and you will experience the fullness of Jesus Christ in wonderful ways.

Leader and Master, I dedicate myself to Your
service and am grateful that You wish to use me.

JOY IN THE SERVICE
OF THE MASTER

*The seventy-two returned with joy and said, "Lord, even
the demons submit to us in your name" (Lk. 10:17).*

Those who are familiar with the Scriptures will know how Jesus sent
out seventy-two of His disciples. Luke tells how Jesus sent them out to
preach the gospel in His name and how they returned joyfully to tell of
what they had achieved.

People often think of their work in Jesus' name as a necessary but
tedious calling. They do their work with a grumbling attitude and consequently find no joy in it. Your attitude towards your work for the Master
will play an important role in the way that you work for Him. It makes
the difference between happiness and unhappiness in His service. Your
attitude will have an amazing effect on you as well as on those you serve.

Remember that the living Christ is always willing to be your heavenly
partner in everything that you undertake in His name. If you devote
all your time and labor to Him, you will not only go about your work
with confidence, but you will also experience the joy that gives you peace
of mind, because you are performing your task in His strength and to
His glory.

*Faithful Lord Jesus, with You at my side I perform
every task You entrust to me with joyful self-confidence.*

THE UNSEEN THINGS

So we fix our eyes not on what is seen, but on what is unseen.
For what is seen is temporary, but what is unseen is eternal (2 Cor. 4:18).

Many people find that their experience of the beauty of life is spoiled by the narrowness of their spiritual perspective. They cannot appreciate beauty or any form of goodness unless it conforms to their religious convictions. However, a life and character that have been created by inner piety cannot be narrow in either perspective or in practice. The beauty of piety transcends narrow-mindedness and reflects the glory of God in the life of His disciple.

When your thoughts are focused on Christ and you try to live to His glory, your spirit is elevated beyond place and time and you develop a greater understanding of eternal truths. You appreciate love, honor, purity, unselfishness and other noble qualities, despite the fact that they reside in the realities of a rough and often crude life.

As your appreciation for the intrinsic values of life increases, you develop the ability to distinguish between that which is genuine and that which is feigned; between the wheat and the chaff. And then you realize that the things that you cannot see or touch are actually the most important things. He who claims only to believe in what he can see, touch, and understand has a very limited perspective on life, because the great wealth of God does not fall only into these categories.

Beloved Lord, may I always have a deep
appreciation for the value of the spiritual forces that
surround me, which remain unseen and untouched.

GOD'S STANDARDS

"A man can receive only what is given him from heaven" (Jn. 3:27).

In today's world material possessions play an important role in most people's lives. Things that used to be regarded as luxuries have become necessities in people's attempts to keep up with their neighbors.

Indeed, over the years things have changed radically, but it would be a foolish mistake to say that life ought to continue at the same pace as a century ago. Progress simply does not allow for this, however much we long for "the good old days."

If we accept that things have changed and will continue changing, we will also have to accept that we now have a new way of life. However, we dare not allow our value system to change. Despite modern progress and changes in lifestyle, the age-old truth remains steadfast and sure: any worthwhile undertaking must have the blessing of God, otherwise it is doomed to failure.

When you are challenged to change your lifestyle or when you are guided towards a new path of life, you should humble yourself before God before making a final decision. Pray that His way, the only true way, will be made known to you.

Eternal and immutable God, in this changing world I hold on to You in the knowledge that You are God from eternity to eternity.

THE ART OF CHRISTIAN CONVERSATION

Let your conversation be always full of grace, seasoned with salt,
so that you may know how to answer everyone (Col. 4:6).

People often underrate the powerful effect of the spoken word. So much depends on the way in which things are said. The tone of voice, the timing, and the circumstances in which words are spoken are all of cardinal importance. The same words can be interpreted in different ways and can create wrong impressions, which can, cause much damage.

There are few things worse to behold than to see someone snubbed by a sharp reprimand or a condescending remark. Because of experiences like these, shy or modest people rather keep quiet for fear of being ridiculed or humiliated by words. Insensitive and intolerant people often speak cruel words, not taking other people's feelings into consideration.

Take a minute to ponder how Jesus spoke to the people with whom He interacted. Whether He agreed or disagreed; whether He attacked or defended; whether He addressed friends or enemies; beggars or rulers, there was often a tenderness in His voice—a tenderness not to be confused with weakness. He spoke with authority but without being harsh. He was always understanding, sympathetic, and loving. When you speak to other people, follow Jesus' example and you will find that your conversations will elicit responses of love and understanding.

Beloved Savior, may what I say always be acceptable
to You. Please use my words for Your honor and glory.

ARE YOU TRYING TO CARRY YOUR BURDEN ALONE?

*"I will come down and speak with you there, and I will
take of the Spirit that is on you and put the Spirit on them.
They will help you carry the burden of the people so
that you will not have to carry it alone" (Num. 11:17).*

There are many devout and zealous servants of the Lord who serve Him with enthusiasm—to the detriment of their personal health. They never refuse a request to serve on a committee and willingly take on any task; even if they are not equipped for it. Ultimately their responsibilities become so numerous that they can do nothing properly. Their mental and spiritual tension becomes so intense that it affects their health. And yet still, they are reluctant to share their responsibilities with others.

Many ministers, pastors, priests, and lay preachers are so conscientious and concerned about their God-given tasks that they are unwilling to share them with anyone else, because they are afraid that they will not be done properly. With so many things to do in the limited time at their disposal, however, nothing can be done effectively and they become frustrated and discouraged.

If God has called you to do a specific task, it is your duty and privilege to do it to the best of your ability. This does not mean that you are not allowed to call upon others to help you accomplish the task. Accept your God-given responsibility, but never think that by sharing it with others you are evading your duty towards God. With others' help you may, in fact, serve God more effectively.

*Loving Master, when You entrust me with a task, please
give me the wisdom to use others' help to accomplish it.*

RELIVE YOUR MEMORIES

*Early the next morning Abraham got up and returned
to the place where he had stood before the* LORD *(Gen. 19:27).*

All Christians face the danger of becoming smug and self-satisfied about their religion. We so easily lapse into a comfortable pattern of worship and personal quiet time with God. It may be a very gradual process, but you will soon see its effects when something of the dynamism starts disappearing from your faith. Your sense of purpose and joy is replaced by apathy and disinterest.

It is therefore beneficial to look back on your pilgrimage from time to time. Remind yourself of the mountaintop experiences as well as the times spent in the valleys. Relive the time when you were filled with ecstasy in the presence of God; remember those times when it seemed as if you were walking alone through the valleys of despair and suddenly found yourself surrounded by the love and peace of God.

When you feel that the flame of faith is burning low in your life, turn to God and remember how He helped and encouraged you in the past. Ask that He will once again fill you with His Holy Spirit so that the spiritual strength and purposefulness of your Christian calling will be revived.

*Merciful Lord, please keep my faith from weakening
and help me to follow You with enthusiasm. Grant me
the full measure of Your Holy Spirit to inspire me.*

BE SINCERE BEFORE GOD

Search me, O God, and know my heart; test me and know my anxious thoughts. See if there is any offensive way in me, and lead me in the way everlasting (Ps. 139:23-24).

There are some people who appear to be very religious but whose lives do not correspond with the example that Jesus set. They speak in an intimate way about God, and yet they maintain an unforgiving spirit; they ignore the truth that God's forgiveness of their sins should lead them to forgive others; they boast of speaking to God, but cannot speak to their fellow human beings in a loving and civil way.

The fact is that such people may manage to deceive others for a while, but they can never deceive God. He knows their thoughts and emotions and knows just as well as they do that they are living an unsatisfying life. And yet God continues to love them. God's love does not fluctuate, and even those who are spiritually immature do not fall outside the sphere of His love.

The tragedy of such "imitation" Christians is that they miss out on the joy and peace of a life in the abundance of Jesus Christ. If people are not sincerely and completely devoted to God, their faith will always be of an inferior quality. God expects you to be honest with Him. Confess everything in your life to Him, and all the hidden inhibitions that hinder your spiritual growth will disappear.

Teach me, O perfect Example, to live for You alone, because only in doing so will I find complete satisfaction in my life.

BE POSITIVE IN TEMPTATION

When tempted, no one should say, "God is tempting me."
For God cannot be tempted by evil, nor does he tempt
anyone; but each one is tempted when, by his own
evil desire, he is dragged away and enticed (Jas. 1:13-14).

Temptation assumes many guises, but it will always come to you in moments of weakness or when you least expect it. There are many ways to resist temptation. Some disciples try simply ignoring it, but this is seldom an effective solution.

Moments of futility are an open invitation for temptation, and the consequences can be disastrous. Never allow destructive thoughts to take possession of your mind, because they will fester and affect your attitude towards life. Initially all temptations seem reasonable and even acceptable, but do not be deceived: the ultimate goal of all temptation is your spiritual degeneration and destruction.

Prayer, Bible study, and contemplation all play an important role in your fight against temptation. In prayer you enter into the presence of God and you can draw on His strength; the Bible teaches you what God has done to rescue you from sin through His Son; in contemplation you allow sanctified and constructive thoughts to fill your mind.

When you have completed these spiritual disciplines, it is of the utmost importance that you will live them in practice. Keep yourself constructively occupied under the guidance and strength of the Spirit, and you will be able to triumph over temptations.

Lord, my Redeemer also in temptation, make me sensitive to
the danger of temptation through the ministry of the Holy Spirit.

GOD'S GRACE IS SUFFICIENT

The days of the blameless are known to the Lord,
and their inheritance will endure forever (Ps. 37:18).

One often hears of people who apparently live a virtuous life and yet are pursued by disaster. They live frugally, are careful with their expenses, and make provision for a safe future, and then, through no fault of their own, they are struck with disaster and face financial ruin. There are those who generously give of themselves in the loving and compassionate care of others, and then find themselves or a loved one struck by illness or death. These are but a few examples of virtuous lives that appear constantly to be followed around by disaster.

When you become entangled in such a situation, it is difficult to agree with Paul when he says, "We know that in all things God works for the good of those who love Him, who have been called according to His purpose" (Rom. 8:28). The human reaction is immediately to question God's actions and to wonder whether it is, in fact, worthwhile to live a virtuous and honorable life.

In such circumstances it is important to remember that God's perspective on life is eternal, and that it is true that He wishes all things to work for your own good. Paul also says that our present suffering does not outweigh the glory that will be revealed to us (see Rom. 8:18). Take courage and let your heart be peaceful: God's grace is sufficient!

I thank You, all-knowing God, that I am always
assured of Your grace, despite my problems.

October

God of love and grace,
today we kneel before You for the sake of the elderly;
those whose tent-dwellings look more dilapidated day after day,
but who possess an inner strength and power.
Thank You that when all we seem to see around and in us
is change and decay,
You remain the immutable One!
We worship You as the God who controls our lives:
our youth with its strength and invincibility,
its passion for life and its fearlessness.
And yet, when we grow older, You bless us with
calmness, peace, wisdom, and maturity.
We praise You for this most beautiful of months that You have created:
the daybreak and the sunrise;
the full ripeness of the noontide;
the glory of the sunset;
the twilight and the quiet of night-time.
Thank You, good Shepherd, that You remain with us
even to the very last stretch of our journey;
that You do not forsake or abandon us, even in our old age;
that You are with us as You were in our youth;
that we only become more aware of Your eternal arms beneath us.
We pray this in the name of Jesus, our Savior and Redeemer.

Amen.

YOUR DIVINE SUPPORT

Immediately Jesus reached out his hand and caught him.
"You of little faith," he said, "why did you doubt?" (Mt. 14:31).

There are times in all of our lives when our problems threaten to become too much for us, and we feel that we are in danger of drowning in the waves of doubt and despair.

One moment we are completely sure of our faith, and the next we are overwhelmed by a tidal wave of fear and unbelief. This is especially true when we have experienced Jesus' peace in our personal time with Him and then lost our faith when we had to cope with difficult life situations.

Peter had exactly this kind of experience. He was overcome with joy when he saw Jesus walking on the water towards him. In his excitement he left the safety of the boat and walked across the water towards Jesus. Then he was suddenly overwhelmed by fear when he saw the wind and the waves. His faith failed him, and Peter started sinking into the water.

When the storms of life threaten, there is only one thing to do, and that is to follow Peter's example and to call on Jesus for rescue. He will take your hand and lead you safely through. Place your trust in Him, because He will never disappoint you. Even though you may not be aware of it, Jesus is at your side at this exact moment, ready to help you, should you call upon Him.

My Savior Jesus, grant that I will retain my faith in You through the work of the Holy Spirit, even in the most trying circumstances.

CHRIST'S GIFT TO YOU

But now a righteousness from God, apart from law, has
been made known…This righteousness from God comes
through faith in Jesus Christ to all who believe (Rom. 3:21-22).

There are, unfortunately, many people who deny themselves the privilege of a Christ-fulfilled life, because, at times, they are convinced that they are not worthy of it. Because of something they have said or done in the past or because they have drifted from their faith, they claim that they cannot simply turn to Christ for help. Consequently they deprive themselves of Christ's greatest gift to humanity: God's love.

The greatest wonder of the Christian faith is that, regardless of what you have said or done in the past, God has still chosen you to be His property. Nothing qualified you for this privilege, except for the fact that you believe in Jesus Christ. His love cannot be earned and nothing that you do can make you worthy of it. It is God's gift to you, given in unrestricted grace.

If you find it difficult to understand or accept this fact of salvation, just think back to the crucifixion of our Savior. A thief, who lived a life of lawlessness and sin, was crucified with Jesus, and at the very last moment he turned to Jesus for mercy. He was accepted and assured that he would be in paradise with the Redeemer.

Regardless of who you are or what your past involves, the love of the living Christ is God's gift to you, if you accept Christ as your Savior.

Just as I am, dirty and black of heart, I come to You,
Lord, in my distress. You are the One who never rejects
any sinner, and therefore, O Lamb of God, I turn to You.

LIVING IN ACCORDANCE WITH GOD'S WILL

The LORD said, "Look, I am setting a plumb line among my people Israel; I will spare them no longer" (Amos 7:8).

Most of us have become so adept at making excuses. When we are challenged, we will usually find some excuse for what we have said or done. How often do we hear: "I didn't mean it like that" or "I was told to do it"; "You probably misunderstood me" or "I thought you wanted me to do it like that." These are but a few of the well-known expressions that we often hear as excuses.

In your Christian faith there is no room for excuses not to do what God has called you to do. He always specifies exactly what He wants you to do. Just as He, through his prophet, set a plumb line among His people, from which there could be no deviation, so God gave humanity the living example of Jesus Christ to show us the kind of life that every Christian should live. His doctrine is clear and unavoidable and leaves us with no doubt about the standards that He has set for us.

In His great grace and understanding God goes even further. Because He is aware of human fallibility, He gives us the Holy Spirit to equip us for leading this life. Without this assistance we would never be able to succeed, but in the strength of the Holy Spirit we can grow. Therefore, follow God's path and enjoy a life of abundance in Christ.

Grant me the ability and the will, beloved Father, to live as You want me to live.

DON'T BE MISLED

See to it that no one takes you captive through hollow and deceptive philosophy, which depends on human traditions and the basic principles of this world rather than on Christ (Col. 2:8).

Some people can be tremendously convincing in stating their particular theories. This is especially true in the case of religious matters, and exceptionally so in the case of the Christian faith. Much unhappiness has been caused by such people, whose attitude is both destructive and divisive. It is all too easy to take a passage from the Scriptures and to use it out of context to support a particular theory. However, the consequences can be extremely far-reaching and disastrous.

In your prayer life, never neglect to ask God for the wisdom to understand certain passages from the Scriptures, and also ask the guidance of the Holy Spirit in assessing the theories and arguments that other people force upon you in their quest to get you to share their views.

Continually develop the skills and habits of a good reader of the Word, understanding each passage according to its context and genre. And always ask for the help of the Holy Spirit, without whom you cannot truly understand Scripture. However convincing others may appear, unreservedly place yourself in the care of Jesus Christ, and He will always make His will known to you.

Thank You, O Holy Spirit, for Your light and guidance in my understanding of the eternal truths that You impart to me through the Word.

NEVER UNDERESTIMATE YOUR THOUGHTS

I have considered my ways and have
turned my steps to your statutes (Ps. 119:59).

If you are sensible, you will take some time to study the path that you have traveled and consider the direction in which you are going. If you neglect to do this, you may find, to your regret, that you achieve little in life. Eventually your daily routine may become the grave of your ideals and ambitions. There are too many people who blame their circumstances for their lack of accomplishment and refuse to admit that their circumstances are the direct consequence of their lack of mental power and planning.

The fact is that your thoughts possess an immense power. Negative thoughts not only create an ineffectual life, but can sometimes be extremely dangerous, because they easily cause one to act irresponsibly without taking into consideration the rights and feelings of other people. Negative and immature thoughts are the basic cause of disrespectful behavior towards other people.

To think positively is to act creatively in every situation. However dark the future may seem, the positive thinker always plans constructively. Constructive thinkers have developed the ability to look beyond the darkness and to continue cherishing high ideals. They are not distracted by their immediate circumstances, because they are able to focus on the final goal. This may seem to be an unattainable ideal, but many people have proved that it is possible if we only place our faith in God. A living faith produces positive and creative thoughts.

Leader and Finisher of my faith, in living close to
You I always have a positive attitude towards life.

Read Colossians 3:5-17

STRENGTH IN DIFFICULT TIMES

Let the word of Christ dwell in you richly (Col. 3:16).

How do you survive when things go horribly wrong? How do you cope with financial setbacks, family crises, illness, or death? Can you maintain a calm and poised attitude, or do you go to pieces in a turbulent sea of doubt, confusion, and despair?

Any of the mentioned circumstances can cause you serious anxiety and concern. Your perspective can easily become obscured, and your disorganized thoughts may be unable to handle the situation logically or sensibly. There is a fundamental danger that you will make the wrong decision or follow an inappropriate course of action, which will ultimately turn out to be nothing but damaging and will leave you with great self-reproach.

In order to live in peace and to be prepared for any eventuality, it is essential for you to maintain an intimate relationship with your Savior. To know of Him is one thing, but for the sake of your peace of mind you should know Him personally. Develop an ongoing trust in Him at all times and in all places. In this way you will ensure that His Spirit will continually work in you and sustain you in your difficult times.

Lord Jesus, You call everyone who is tired and overburdened to You. I accept Your invitation with gratitude and praise.

DISCOVER GOD'S WILL FOR YOUR LIFE

Now to each one the manifestation of the Spirit
is given for the common good (1 Cor. 12:7).

Sometimes it feels as if you are drifting aimlessly through life, and that it doesn't really matter whether you are here or not. Day after dismal day passes without accomplishing anything worthwhile. The sparkle seems to have disappeared from your life long ago. This unfortunate state of affairs by no means comes about through any fault of God.

To prevent it, you should, in the first instance, relive the glory of your faith in Christ. Then seek God's plan for your life so that you may strive towards a positive goal in your life. When the living Christ takes control of your life and reveals Himself through you, you will cease drifting aimlessly and become a positive and inspired Christian disciple.

A renewal of your spiritual experience with Christ occurs when you invite the Holy Spirit in and allow Him to take complete control of your life. You will discover that while you are living in harmony with the Spirit, new avenues of service open up to you, and you are guided towards new dimensions of holiness.

When you sense that God is busy guiding you, you should confirm it through continual prayer. Dare to trust God unconditionally. To discover God's will for your life not only requires faith, but also positive actions.

With renewed faith and fervor, O Master, I step into
the future with the confidence that only You can give me.

ALL THINGS WORK
FOR THE COMMON GOOD

*"For there is nothing hidden that will not
be disclosed, and nothing concealed that will not
be known or brought out into the open" (Lk. 8:17).*

One often hears the complaint that it is always the wrong people who achieve success in life. People who are involved in dishonest practices become very wealthy, while honest people struggle financially. People who deliberately harm their bodies never become ill, while health-conscious people contract all kinds of illnesses. Examples of these kinds of situations abound, and the complaint continues to resound: good people suffer while corrupt people prosper.

Before you join this choir of voices, it is necessary to remember that life as we know it is not the end. What we experience now is transient, but the true life to which Christians aspire is eternal and lasting. In the spiritual life, people who cling to their faith and keep to their course will receive their just rewards, not from people, but from God.

Nothing that happens in this world is hidden from God. The most insignificant event is known to Him. We will all be called to account for our lives, in God's own perfect time. So if it seems as if you are ill-used by life, don't be discouraged or succumb to the temptation of throwing in the towel. Renew your trust in Jesus Christ and remember, "Be faithful, even to the point of death, and I will give you the crown of life" (Rev. 2:10).

*I praise and thank You, Lord my God, that because of our faith
in Jesus Christ everything in life and death will turn out well for us.*

UPHOLD THE DAY OF REST

*"Keep the Sabbath day holy, as I commanded
your forefathers" (Jer. 17:22).*

The day of the Lord is slowly but surely beginning to lose its importance—even in Christian countries. There was a time when keeping the Sabbath holy was a way of life among Christians. This holiness has gradually been worn away and today there is little difference between the day of the Lord and an ordinary weekday. Shops are open for business, entertainment centers operate, and big sport events are the order of the day.

Many people argue that keeping the Sabbath holy is nothing but the Puritan attitude of some people who are out to spoil other people's fun. They say that because you have worked the entire week, you have earned the right to enjoy life on a Sunday in any way you choose.

We do not want to deny anyone's right to some time of leisure for even a moment. However, remember that the Sabbath calls the completion of God's miracle of creation into remembrance, and as such it should be regarded as a day of rest, used to devote ourselves to praise and contemplation.

It is impossible to remain active for seven days of the week without paying the spiritual, mental, and physical price. God set aside a day of rest for you—for your own sake. Uphold it as such!

> *This is the day the Lord has made;*
> *let us rejoice and be glad in it (Ps. 118:24).*

DYNAMIC CHRISTIANITY IS MORE THAN A FEELING

Just as you received Christ Jesus as Lord, continue to live in him, rooted and built up in him, strengthened in the faith as you were taught, and overflowing with thankfulness (Col. 2:6-7).

The experience of the living Christ residing inside your spirit provides you with inspiration and strength for your everyday life. This experience initially changes your entire way of life and fills you with an indescribable joy. There is something very attractive about a Christian with a joyful spirit. Many of Christ's more reserved disciples feel that something essential is lacking from their spiritual lives because they are not as demonstrative as some of their fellow believers.

The danger of such an extroverted faith is that it feeds on emotion. In times of despondency or failure it is shown to be insufficient, because it lacks those qualities that fortify the basic needs of the spirit and the heart. There are many who started out on their Christian pilgrimage with great joy and enthusiasm, but once the initial excitement faded, they started to drift and eventually became spiritual wrecks.

Emotion is based on your physical state and your temperament and fluctuates according to your feelings and your responses to your environment. We dare not put our trust in them. Dynamic Christianity transcends feeling and emotion. It is obedient to God's call for a life of complete devotion and surrender to His will. It means that you will never lack the Christian qualities of goodness, forgiveness, tolerance, understanding, and humility. Ultimately everything you do is dedicated to the glory of God.

O Lord, grant me a faith that is sensitive to the voice of the Holy Spirit and practical in the application of His message.

TRUE LOVE

Love must be sincere (Rom. 12:9).

The word "love" is probably the most used and least understood word in any language. Through the years it has been used to express people's feelings towards art, food, leisure, and relaxation. On a personal level it is used to express one's feelings of affection. It is even used in connection with clothes and other material possessions.

When you are professing your love towards someone, it would be beneficial to take a moment to consider the actual depth of your love. To what lengths would you go and what sacrifices would you be willing to make for the sake of love?

Jesus Christ came to demonstrate to us the meaning of true love when He willingly gave His life for you and for all of humanity. To redeem mankind of its sin, He was willing to die for all of us and to take our punishment upon Him. As Jesus said, "Greater love has no one than this, that he lay down his life for his friends" (Jn. 15:13).

True love involves making sacrifices for the sake of another. It is tolerant, patient, and understanding, even in the most trying circumstances. It comprises forgiveness and giving of yourself for the benefit of others. It means to love others as Jesus loves you.

Loving Lord Jesus, help me to distribute
Your love in the world around me.

THE POWER OF WORDS

How good is a timely word! (Prov. 15:23).

Words possess a dynamic power. If used correctly they can inspire and provide courage; they can supply hope and encouragement; they can express understanding. But words are also neutral. It is the way in which they are used and the emphasis which they are given that convey their meaning and influence communication. "I love you!" can wound and hurt if it is said in sarcasm or insincerity. Words are extremely personal and to a large extent emanate from the personality who uses them.

The receiver of the spoken word is either blessed or tormented by it, but the speaker is similarly influenced by words. If you regularly disparage yourself in front of others or belittle everything you do, you will eventually believe your own words, and your low opinion of yourself will become a conviction. Words give power and purpose to life. You become what you say.

If you are experiencing a time of discouragement and are feeling despondent, admonish yourself with these words from Scripture, "Be strong and courageous; do not be terrified; do not be discouraged, for the Lord your God will be with you wherever you go" (Josh. 1:9). Repeat this to yourself out loud, so that it becomes indelibly imprinted on your mind. Always consider the power and the influence of the spoken word. Think before you speak and ask yourself whether that which you are about to say is true, friendly, and sensible.

Holy Master, let the words I speak be pleasing in Your sight.

GUARD AGAINST PRIDE

Humble yourselves, therefore, under God's mighty hand,
that he may lift you up in due time (1 Pet. 5:6).

In Proverbs 16:18 Solomon says: "Pride goes before destruction, a haughty spirit before a fall." This is an irrefutable truth about life. Throughout the ages there have been many people—in widely diverse circumstances and from all walks of life—whose lives attest to this truth. Their own bitter experience confirms the truth and caution of these wise words.

There are many occasions in life when you feel compelled to stand upon your dignity or to maintain an attitude of cool aloofness. The circumstances in which you choose to act in this manner may serve as justification for your behavior. Whatever the situation, it would be sensible to say to yourself, "There but for the grace of God go I."

Jesus' humility was a salient feature of His earthly existence. Even in His death and resurrection, He moved among all classes without pride or superiority. Follow the Master's example. Even in those moments when you stumble, He will be there to support you and guide you towards the right path.

> *Beloved Lord and Savior, help me never to think*
> *too much of myself, so that I will not come to a fall.*

GOD'S SILENCES

Yet when he [Jesus] heard that Lazarus was sick,
he stayed where he was two more days (Jn. 11:6).

There are many devout Christians who, like Peter, constantly want to remain on the mountaintop with Jesus. When they occasionally become despondent, they feel that they have somehow disappointed God. The Christian life is lived by ordinary people who are subject to the fluctuations of the human spirit. There may be times of mountaintop experiences, shortly followed by a plunge into the valley of despair. As a matter of course we tend to link our spiritual peaks to the presence of God and our depths to His absence. This need not necessarily be the case.

Whatever your changing moods, God remains unchanging. The question you should ask yourself when you are in the depths of despair is: "What is God trying to tell me or teach me in this situation?"

Many of God's most devout followers on earth have found that His will became known to them when they were struggling through the dark valleys. Never regard yourself as a spiritual failure just because you are passing through a time of despondency. Become still in the midst of your sorrow and self-pity and try to understand God's will for your life. Don't become afraid in those times when God is silent and appears to be distant. In these moments He is just as close to you as when you were with Him on the mountaintop.

Ever-present God, help me always to experience the
reality of Your presence, even when I feel far away from You.

TRUST IN GOD

*"My grace is sufficient for you, for my power
is made perfect in weakness" (2 Cor. 12:9).*

There are very few people who have not upon occasion experienced the inadequacy of their own resourcefulness and who feel that they simply cannot continue. These feelings may be the result of illness, death, loneliness, financial insecurity, or any of the numerous setbacks that can have a destructive influence on the human spirit and emotions.

In so many cases people regard their situation as hopeless, and then they run the risk of becoming completely discouraged. Whatever the predicament in which you find yourself and however dark the outlook, never underestimate the scope of God's love for you and the expanse of His grace.

Take a moment to consider the innumerable instances in the Bible and in world history when God transformed despair into hope and defeat into victory through His grace. However desperate your circumstances may seem to you, always remember that God loves you with an eternal love and that He is waiting for you to turn to Him and trust in Him. Your faith will be rewarded, and in His own wonderful way He will deliver you.

*Faithful God and Father, through the years You have proved Yourself
to be faithful, even when I found myself in extreme difficulties.
Therefore I will hold on to You in the future, because Your grace
is sufficient for me at all times and under all circumstances.*

EFFECTIVE CHRISTIANITY

We have been released from the law so that we serve in the new way
of the Spirit, and not in the old way of the written code (Rom. 7:6).

We might as well say it once again: there are many people who are dis-illusioned by Christianity. Or maybe it would be more accurate to say that they have become prejudiced against the Christian faith because of the way in which it was presented to them, because no level-headed person could reject the basic tenets of the living Christ. When zealotry and hypocrisy taint the principles of the Master and transform them into a fixed set of man-made rules from which His love and compassion are absent, the love and power of Christianity become a mere stereotype.

Effective Christianity only emerges when the words of Romans 5:5 ring true: "God has poured out his love into our hearts by the Holy Spirit, whom he has given us." It cannot be limited to religious formulas but must be free and validated by the Holy Spirit.

It is the Holy Spirit that breathes life into Christianity, because with-out the Holy Spirit our religion becomes a set of dogmatic percepts that lack inspiration and are virtually impossible to follow. Therefore true Spirit-filled Christianity is intensely personal. It is a matter of the heart and personal trust in God. While your mind is certainly important in the formation of your vision of God, the full power of your faith is not revealed unless your emotions are touched also, unless you have tasted the reality of your faith and lost yourself in the wonder, love, and praise of God, brought about by the Holy Spirit.

Holy Spirit, open my life to Your influence
so that my faith may be meaningful and vital.

INNER DISCORD

*What I do is not the good I want to do; no, the evil
I do not want to do—this I keep on doing (Rom. 7:19).*

To a greater or lesser extent, everyone is familiar with the inner conflict of a divided personality. There are times when you are possessed by an overwhelming desire to live an honorable and uncompromising life. In these times spiritual matters have a strong appeal for you. You are confident that you will harbor no mean or unworthy thoughts, and you experience God as a reality.

It may be precisely while you are experiencing these feelings of ecstasy that your spiritual defenses start to relax, and religious pride and conceit start to undermine your faith in your heavenly Father. You start to weaken spiritually and no longer enjoy the strength you once knew.

Under such circumstances it is difficult to maintain your spiritual enthusiasm. You know what you have to do, but you find it impossible to do it. Your sinful nature is engaged in a struggle with your mind, wins the battle, and turns you into a slave of sin.

An endless battle between right and wrong may ensue in your spirit, and it will only be settled if Christ is in complete control of your life. Once you have completely surrendered to Him and live in the assurance that His living Spirit is with you, His unifying and triumphant power will be at your disposal.

*Lord Jesus, through the guidance and inspiration of Your
Holy Spirit, I become a completely integrated personality.*

HOLD ON TO YOUR PRINCIPLES

"The day of the Lord is near for all nations. As you have done, it will be done to you; your deeds will return upon your own head" (Obad. 1:15).

Because of the events taking place around us, there are many people who question whether it is worthwhile to live a virtuous and honorable life. They give examples of people who achieve success through dishonest practices. They refer to criminals who manage to evade justice and to their victims who have to endure the suffering inflicted upon them. They draw attention to the violence, oppression, and injustice of the world. And then they want to know why it appears as if injustice reigns supreme.

It is extremely important not to give in to temptation and not to allow yourself to be influenced by these circumstances. You must never compromise with the Evil One or give up on your Christian principles. What happens around you is of a transient nature, but God's will remains eternal. Therefore justice will ultimately prevail and evil will be conquered by good.

Seek your strength in Jesus and take a stand against an evil world. Open your life to the influence of the Holy Spirit so that He may empower you to stand firmly and to be strong in your faith. In the strength of the living Christ, you can and will triumph. If you remain faithful to Christ, the day will come when you will experience victory together with Him.

Holy Jesus, I so much want to receive the victor's crown from Your hands. Help me through Your Holy Spirit to hold on to my Christian principles.

THE NEVER-ENDING QUEST

"If only I knew where to find him;
if only I could go to his dwelling!" (Job 23:3).

Man's inborn yearning for God may be revealed in a multitude of different ways. The first indication of spiritual hunger is a restlessness that refuses to be appeased. It often manifests itself in dissatisfaction with a church that has served you faithfully for many years. When this happens you run the risk of becoming a spiritual drifter who fruitlessly seeks "the peace of God, which transcends all understanding" (Phil. 4:7).

One of the encouraging facts about our spiritual hunger, which is often overlooked or ignored, is that God is always waiting to fulfill every person's spiritual hunger and yearning. It is not the Father's will that any of His children should drift from the sphere of His love and become unhappy with the lives that He granted them.

The message of the gospel is precisely that our heavenly Father is waiting to receive every one of His children into a full and enriching union with Himself. This is His fervent desire for all people, and it is for this purpose that He sent Jesus Christ to earth.

In order to experience this profound unity, it is essential to turn away from your stubborn disobedience to God and to accept the gift of Jesus the Savior in faith. Allow God's Spirit to guide your life so that Jesus can be your Lord. It is the only way for your hunger for God to be appeased.

By unconditionally accepting You in my life,
Lord Jesus, I enter into a spiritual union with
my heavenly Father. For this I praise and thank You.

TRUE CHRISTIANITY

Examine yourselves to see whether you are in the faith; test yourselves.
Do you not realize that Christ Jesus is in you? (2 Cor. 13:5).

Many people perceive Christians to be generally weak and ineffective. Christians are often regarded as living in an isolated world of their own, removed from the realities of life. They are seen to be banding together in excluding the world while spending their time in prayer and Bible study. Of course, this is a misconception of the Christian faith.

There was nothing weak or ineffective about Jesus Christ. The Scriptures, and especially the Gospels, are witness to His humanity and His divinity; to His firmness and His tenderness; to His courage as well as His humility; and above all, to His love, even when He was subjected to bitter hatred and barbaric torture and death.

This is the example that our Leader set for all Christians to follow if we wish to be faithful to our highest calling as Christians. It is an accepted fact that you cannot accomplish it in your own strength. Therefore God granted us the Holy Spirit, and if you give Him complete control of your life, the transformation that He brings about will undoubtedly reveal you as a true Christian to the world.

Thank You, heavenly Father, that we are more than
conquerors in Your Son and through Your Holy Spirit.

CONFLICTING PERSONALITIES

A hot-tempered man stirs up dissension,
but a patient man calms a quarrel (Prov. 15:18).

No two human personalities are exactly alike, and therefore it is inevitable that we will experience a conflict of personalities somewhere along the road of our pilgrimage through life. The vast majority of God's heroes of faith had to contend with someone who was difficult to love—and most of us are not heroes of faith!

How does one handle such people and at the same time maintain one's Christian testimony? The first important step is to pray for people who you find difficult to live with in love. Praying destroys the destructive power of hate that has such a negative effect on your spiritual life.

After you have prayed for the person, only speak well of him to others, and never be destructively critical. This may sound idealistic and even hypocritical to you, but it is really just common sense. Acting in this way destroys bitterness and hate and addresses the problem of human relationships in a constructive way.

When you, as a disciple of Christ, find that you dislike someone, do not disparage him. Do as much good to that person as you possibly can. In so doing you will discover that you can transform enemies into friends. It is the practical application of the Christian faith. While people are easily critical of the Christian faith, they can also not deny its strength, because they see it in the practical lives of devout disciples.

Loving Teacher, teach me to apply Your wisdom
in every human relationship in which You place me.

THE LORD WILL PROVIDE

The desert and the parched land will be glad; the wilderness will rejoice and blossom. Like the crocus, it will burst into bloom (Is. 35:1-2).

Throughout the ages people and nations have experienced difficult times. The future often seems dismal and hopeless and the outlook appears grim. The reasons for these difficulties are too numerous to mention, but the consequences can be extremely destructive, because many give up hope and see no possibility for the future to improve. In these circumstances many lives may be adversely affected.

We must always remember that God loves His creation. He loves the world and He loves humanity; man is, after all, created in His image. The love of God is so vast that He sacrificed His only Son so that those who believe in Him may be saved from despair and death and be assured of eternal life. It is because of this great love that God has always restored the ruined hopes and expectations of people. He takes pity upon His people, answers their prayers, and provides in their need.

The living Christ is your faithful Friend to whom you can turn in your moments of distress. If you are worried or have struggled through some unpleasant times, place your trust in Him and lay your needs before His throne of grace. Do not despair, but trust Jesus to lead you from your present darkness towards light and hope for the future. Remember, He promised never to forsake or abandon you (see Heb. 13:5). Hold on to this promise and believe that the Lord will provide.

Benevolent Father, I place my trust steadfastly in You and step into the future in the knowledge that You will provide.

THE ONLY TRUE GOD

"Who among the gods is like you, O Lord? Who is like you—majestic in holiness, awesome in glory, working wonders?" (Ex. 15:11).

From the earliest times people with different religious convictions have worshiped a variety of different gods. Some of these gods are feared, while others have to be placated with gifts and sacrifices. We encounter these idols in all shapes and sizes, and every one of them is supposed to possess its own unique power. However, one thing that is true of all of them is that they are dead, lifeless objects. They possess no feeling or love and are feared by those who worship them.

There is another kind of idol, which is created by man. Anything to which man becomes addicted assumes the stature of an idol. Many people's souls are enthralled by the accumulation of wealth and possessions, power and status; others become drug addicts. If you find that you cannot manage without any of these or other things, you can be sure that you have created an idol that demands your faithfulness above all other things, and this may eventually lead to your destruction.

On the other hand, Jesus offers you life in all its abundance as reward for your surrender and commitment to Him (see Jn. 10:10). He offers you freedom, sanctifying grace, joy, and flourishing that wells up to eternal life. The Lord gave you the free will to make your own choice.

Once you have accepted the living Christ as your Savior, you will experience a rich fulfillment and joy. Ultimately no other form of worship or devotion will be acceptable to you, because you have met the only true God.

Holy God, I worship You and only You.

WHEN THINGS
NEED TO BE SAID

In him you have been enriched in every way—in all
your speaking and in all your knowledge (1 Cor. 1:5).

We often find ourselves in a situation where something needs to be said. Our words may express encouragement or sympathy; they may be words of admonition or of praise; we may be expected to deliver criticism.

Whatever we say, it may have far-reaching consequences for our relationships and our feelings, and therefore we have a profound responsibility to choose the right words and the right time when we speak.

Our words should also carry the hallmark of honesty and should be spoken in the spirit of sincere Christian love. Love without honesty is mere sentimentality, and honesty without love can border on brutality. Unless the occasion requires us to comment in public, our conversations should always take place in private and should always occur at the most appropriate time.

There is only one way to ensure our adherence to these basic rules, and that is through a steadfast relationship with Jesus Christ. If we have such a relationship with Him, we become sensitive to the promptings of the Holy Spirit who will guide us in all our relationships. In so doing we can be sure that all our words will be inspired by Christ and spoken in love.

Holy Spirit, Teacher and Leader, guide my thoughts and
restrain my tongue so that I will never intentionally hurt someone.

LET YOUR LOVE
BE PRACTICAL

Dear children, let us not love with words or
tongue but with actions and in truth (1 Jn. 3:18).

True love is not something that can be fathomed by the human mind
or experience. It cannot be sufficiently explained, and yet it is the most
important and dynamic human emotion.

Because of the unique quality of love and the ineffectuality of human attempts to express it in distinct terms, words remain incapable
of explaining it. Compassion, goodness, tenderness, and many other
beautiful and highly emotive words cannot succeed in describing the
strength and power of love. However, there is an unfortunate tendency
to equate love with sentimentality, and then this dynamic force becomes
weak and ineffectual.

The foundation of true love is compassionate identification with the
beloved. The same joys, sorrows, temptations, and failures are experienced. True love entails sacrifice and often includes sadness. The quality of love transcends sympathy and comes to expression in loyalty and
faithfulness, even if the whole world should turn against the beloved.

Love in action is more than just the performance of good deeds, even
though such deeds may be an expression of love. True love is deep and
unselfish and encompasses qualities such as faithfulness, trust, noble
principles, and many other similar values that enrich the mind and
spirit. It cannot be bought, and it is precisely for this reason that love is
so precious.

Eternal God of love, help me to love without calculating the cost.

YOUR HEAVENLY LEADER

You must serve faithfully and wholeheartedly
in the fear of the LORD (2 Chr. 19:9).

It is a great source of frustration when your careful planning goes awry. You are deeply disappointed when your best attempts come to nothing and all your hopes are dashed. Often you become disillusioned as a result of this kind of experience, and sometimes you become so discouraged that you threaten to throw in the towel. You are convinced that everything you undertake is doomed to failure.

It is scant consolation to say that you are not alone in going through this kind of experience. However, the solution to your problem does not lie in accepting your failure, but rather in finding the reasons for it. And then it is a good time to ask yourself: "Where does God fit into my planning?"

When you embark on a venture, however minor or insignificant it may appear, you dare not underestimate the importance of seeking the will of the Lord before proceeding with your project. He knows what is best for you, and though it may initially seem as if His will does not fit in with your plans, you have to realize that His perspective on your life is eternal. Therefore He is able to lead you into a future that may be unknown to you but is perfectly clear to Him.

You would not risk venturing blindfolded into the street unless you had a trustworthy guide. Make Jesus your partner and your leader in everything that you undertake. If you do, you can be assured that you will ultimately achieve success.

> *Heavenly Leader, in the past I have tried to choose*
> *my own path, but now I am guided by You.*

YOUR CALLING
TO BE CHRISTLIKE

*"On that day you will realize that I am in my Father,
and you are in me, and I am in you" (Jn. 14:20).*

The life and teachings of Jesus Christ pose the greatest challenge that anyone can accept. Many people who accept Him as their perfect example try to follow Him by committing themselves to good works. They make great sacrifices in the hope that this will help them to become like Him.

While all disciples should have a sincere desire to be like Jesus, all the effort and toil in the world will not help them to achieve this goal. Being Christlike must have its origins in the heart and mind.

It is only here where the awareness of the presence of the living Christ is to be found; where He becomes the source of the strength that enables them to grow spiritually in strength, beauty, and truth. Unless the presence of Christ is a living reality in their hearts, it is impossible to reflect His personality in their lives.

The challenge and call to be more Christlike is intensely personal. It is a challenge to a deeper and more intimate relationship with the Master, in which you allow Him to reveal Himself through your life.

*Holy Master, through Your great grace and immanent
presence I grow every day to become more like You.*

SCRUTINIZE YOURSELF
THOROUGHLY

"When he came to his senses" (Lk. 15:17).

Few people have the courage to engage in some painfully honest self-examination. They defend their own weaknesses and are always quick to justify their own shortcomings. They even ignore their sins in an attempt to evade the consequences thereof.

An honest evaluation of yourself is the first step towards spiritual and moral renewal. The picture that you see when you look at yourself honestly may be very discouraging. Hidden sin, pettiness, jealousy, greed, lust, and a multitude of destructive forces that only you are aware of are revealed in the hidden depths of your soul. And you are standing in the bright, white light of God's perfect holiness. It is an experience known only to those who have enough courage to be completely honest with God and with themselves.

Fortunately God not only sees you for what you are but also for what you can become through His grace and the work of the Holy Spirit. When you have reached this low-water mark, you should look up and see yourself as God sees you. It is an astonishing sight! You realize that you are His child, who was made for the mountaintops of faith and not for the valleys of sin.

Through Jesus you are redeemed from the power of sin, your love for Him intensifies, and you view life from a completely new perspective. You suddenly discover that you are a new creation through the strength of the immanent Christ.

I rejoice, merciful Father, because I am Your child and nothing and no one can tear me from Your hands.

MAKE A RIGHT JUDGMENT

"Stop judging by mere appearances,
and make a right judgment" (Jn. 7:24).

There are so many people who think that they can determine the quality of a person's character from a brief encounter: "I liked him from the beginning" or "I mistrusted him from the moment I met him." These are common expressions, but it is often foolish to judge in this hasty fashion.

As a Christian disciple you should not judge people according to outer appearances. If you do, you are bound to be prejudiced when you meet an apparently unpleasant person. If you have a sensitive spirit and remember that precious diamonds are often found in mud, you will first spend time in prayer and contemplation before criticizing someone. Always try to discover the hidden personality.

Our Master had the marvelous gift of penetrating beyond the external façade to meet the true person inside. When He touched someone's inner being He showed love and compassion. In doing so He restored people's self-respect.

During your journey through life you are constantly forming opinions about people and classifying them in your subconscious. Ask the Master to impart to you His gift of perception so that you will be able to see people, not according to your own judgment, but rather in the same way as the heavenly Father sees their potential. After all, He is able to see the human heart.

> *Merciful Father, help me to assess and judge*
> *others in the light of Your love and compassion.*

THE BEAUTY OF
A LIVING FAITH

*Let us not become weary in doing good, for at the proper
time we will reap a harvest if we do not give up (Gal. 6:9).*

It is sad to see what some people do to their faith. God has intended it to be a life-giving relationship, but they allow it to degenerate into a limiting, depressing, and dismal burden that warps their lives into an atrocious lifestyle, and then they believe that this is God's will for them. God intended faith to be an experience of His love, strength, and presence.

If the Christian faith has lost its allure for you, it is time to contemplate the matter honestly. Jesus created something that should radiate beautifully in you. It touches your deepest being and impels you towards spiritual growth. It enriches your personality. It is not the product of emotion or superficial thought, but the result of steadfast devotion and continual prayer.

The experience of the living Christ in your deepest spirit brings forth a quality of life which is so genuine that it has the potential to convince skeptics of the authenticity of Christ. A colorless and lifeless faith is a catastrophe that is of little value to both you and God. A dynamic, living faith glorifies God and blesses the person who possesses it.

*Lord my God, preserve me from the laziness and the happy-go-lucky
attitude that are the causes of a drab and ineffectual faith.*

COME, LET US PRAY

There on the beach we knelt to pray (Acts 21:5).

One is often reminded of the saying that there is a time and a place for everything. It is also often applied to religion. In many segments of society the matter of a person's faith is regarded as a taboo topic of conversation. Furthermore, there are also people who believe that prayer should be limited to the church or to the privacy of your inner room. They regard any form of public prayer in the run of daily life with uneasiness or even disapproval.

Prayer is as much a form of communication as conversation. The difference is merely that conversation is a form of communication between people, while prayer is a conversation between us and our heavenly Father. There is nothing more natural than this.

There are moments in our lives when it is both essential and desirable to draw near to God. In these circumstances, prayer is normal and appropriate as a form of communication.

While you should never be too shy to pray, it is also necessary to be careful and discreet in terms of the time and the place in which you choose to pray. Trust in the guidance of the Holy Spirit and your prayers will at all times be a blessing to you as well as to others.

O Hearer of prayers, thank You that I may draw near to Your sacred throne at all times and under all circumstances and know that You will always listen.

November

All-knowing Teacher,
during this month we worship You as the source
of all true wisdom and knowledge.
Thousands of students will write examinations in this month—
while thousands of others will struggle with
the examination of life.
Please give all of them Your peace in these days;
the peace that is beyond human comprehension.
Strengthen them physically and make them calm
when they are under pressure.
Be in their hearts so that they will be calm and peaceful
when they are required to give account.
Be in their eyes so that they will be able to
read and understand with discretion.
Be in their thoughts so that they will be able to
think logically and orderly.
Be in their hands and make them strong and steady
so that they will be able to do what is expected of them.
Be, now and forever,
the road they have to travel;
the truth they have to know;
and life in all its fullness.
In the name of Him who makes everything possible, Jesus Christ.

Amen.

PEACE IN THE STORM

You will keep in perfect peace him whose mind
is steadfast, because he trusts in you (Is. 26:3).

If you allow your thoughts to dwell on the things that happen in the world today, you run the risk of being caught up in feelings of hatred, bitterness, fear, and negativity. God definitely does not want this for you.

To enable you to remain steadfast in these changing times and to overcome personal fear amidst wars and tidings of war, God has given Himself to you as a wonderful gift. He grants you His eternal life; because He is love, He plants His love into your heart and gives you the peaceful assurance that this love can never be destroyed—not even by the combined forces of hatred.

When disturbing influences threaten your faith, He gives you the power to believe that all things are working for the good of those who love Him. If you focus your energy on God and surrender your life to Him, His peace will be your glorious possession at all times and under all circumstances (see Jn. 14:27). This peace is the direct result of trust.

When your faith in God exceeds your faith in everything else, you possess an inner calm and balance that imparts equilibrium to your life. Put God first in all things, and you will know His peace and joy even in the most trying circumstances.

Almighty God, with You at the center of my life
I fear no storms, not even those that grow into hurricanes.

IDENTIFY YOUR FEAR

*The LORD is my light and my salvation—whom shall I fear? The LORD
is the stronghold of my life—of whom shall I be afraid? (Ps. 27:1).*

Fear in any of its dreadful forms is a powerful and negative force in
the lives of many people. It may be caused by economic and social circumstances, racial tension, or a multitude of other factors that are too
numerous to list. However, it is an undeniable fact that fear causes
irreparable harm to many people's lives.

Somebody once remarked justly that there is nothing to fear but fear
itself. If fear is casting its shadow over your life at the moment, ask yourself honestly what the source of your fear is. If it is a passing fear, it will
disappear before long without causing too much damage. However, if it
is a fear that gnaws at your spirit and confuses your mind, it is essential
to deal with it immediately.

In order to manage fear effectively, you have to identify it properly. It
could be caused by a vague influence that is casting a dark shadow over
your spirit, thus rendering you as someone suffering from habitual fear.
If this is the case, now is the time to ask God to help you to rid yourself
of this destructive ailment through His Holy Spirit.

By becoming aware of the mighty presence of God, your fear will
gradually diminish. Allow Him to erase the dominance of fear from your
thoughts. He will control your fear and guide you towards a peaceful life
without fear.

*Almighty God, with Your guidance and through
the influence of the Holy Spirit, I will conquer all the
destructive fears in my life. For this I praise and thank You.*

THE LITMUS TEST
OF YOUR FAITH

"My command is this: Love each other as I have loved you" (Jn. 15:12).

Fanaticism is a common sin among spiritually attuned people. They have fought their way through many problems to reach a state of faith, and then they suddenly believe that they are the only ones to have found the full truth. Their faith is the product of their personal thinking and possibly also of their individual experiences.

However, when they claim to be the only ones to possess true faith and knowledge while denying other people the same privilege, their lives are no longer reflective of God's love. Their fanaticism and narrow-mindedness prevent the love of God from spreading to their neighbors.

It is vital to know exactly what you believe in. If not, you could easily fall prey to deception. But it is even more important that your love for your neighbor will transcend any dogmatic differences. For the Spirit of the living Christ to live in you and for you to realize that He can also live in those who differ from you, love has to be the dominant emotion in your spiritual experience, "By this all men will know that you are My disciples, if you love one another" (Jn. 13:35).

Unless we have become a channel for Christ's love and unless we possess the ability to embrace people who differ from us, love has not yet been perfected in us. Until it is, we will not be able to serve God and our fellow human beings as Jesus did. Love that is manifested through caring and service is the divine test for those who want to be His disciples.

God of love, Your Holy Spirit teaches us that love is the key
to each problem and each human heart. Let Your love
fill my life and allow me to reveal it to my fellow man.

MISSED OPPORTUNITIES

*"If you, even you, had only known on this day what would bring
you peace—but now it is hidden from your eyes" (Lk. 19:42).*

Few people can claim to have no regrets over some kind of missed opportunity, even just the opportunity to do a good deed or to offer a word of encouragement. Hardly a day passes without the opportunity to encourage someone who is depressed, to console someone who is experiencing profound sorrow, or simply to offer a heartening word to someone who is on the verge of succumbing to the struggles of life.

To be aware of the distress of others and to do your utmost to relieve that distress is one way of avoiding feelings of regret and self-reproach when it is too late to do something about it. Turning away from someone who needs your help and empathy is more impoverishing to you than it is to that person.

It is a law of life that you cannot bring rays of light into the lives of others without also basking in those rays yourself. To give yourself to others in love and service is a privilege that belongs to those who are disciples of the Master. It is also a certain way of building a more profound relationship with God.

Don't keep glancing over your shoulder and harp on missed opportunities. It is nothing but a waste of time. Ensure yourself of a better present and bright prospects for the future. Commit yourself to serving others with an enthusiasm born of your sincere gratitude for God's great love for you.

*God and Master, teach me never to miss
an opportunity to encourage or bless others.*

AWE-INSPIRING MIRACLE

God was reconciling the world to himself in Christ,
not counting men's sins against them. And he has
committed to us the message of reconciliation (2 Cor. 5:19).

One could ponder the question of which miracle you find most awe-inspiring. In the New Testament there is a large variety of miracles from which to choose: the feeding of the five thousand; wine from water; cripples who walk and blind people who see; Lazarus who is "woken" from the dead. All of these could be regarded as great miracles.

Your answer to this question may be more personal. The Master may have healed you; your prayers may have been answered in a wonderful manner; your life may have been changed irrevocably by the love of the Redeemer and the working of the Holy Spirit. You might view this as the biggest miracle of them all.

Could there ever be a bigger miracle than the breathtaking fact that you have received a new life from Jesus Christ? Jesus is the biggest miracle of all. All the other miracles derive their power and inspiration from Him. He came from God and revealed the heavenly Father to common people. In Him people saw what God is like.

After His time on earth He physically ascended to heaven and bestowed the Holy Spirit upon His faithful followers. Even though two thousand years have passed since, He is still alive and active in the lives of His disciples.

Jesus Christ belongs to eternity and can therefore not be limited by time and space. He is the most awe-inspiring miracle of all ages and is as real today as when He lived on earth.

I praise You, Lord Jesus, for everything
You mean to us, Your disciples.

GIVE ME PATIENCE,
O LORD

*Be still before the LORD and wait patiently for him;
do not fret when men succeed in their ways, when
they carry out their wicked schemes (Ps. 37:7).*

Sometimes you rush hurriedly and unthinkingly into an endeavor only to be deeply disappointed because your plans have been foiled. It is scant consolation to know at such times that your experience is not unique. Many people pay dearly for their impulsiveness. Consequently they become despondent, lose self-confidence, and their enthusiasm dwindles.

The cause of this situation is your inability to lay your problems before God and wait patiently for His guidance. It has been proved repeatedly in the Scriptures as well as in secular history that God's timing and methods are perfect. We only witness the temporary scene while God views matters from the perspective of eternity. We are bound to the here and now, whereas God opens eternity to us.

Before making any decision or executing any plan, first submit the matter to Christ in prayer and ask for the guidance of the Holy Spirit. Wait for Him patiently and humbly and be sensitive to the voice of the Holy Spirit. Eventually you will become aware that He is guiding you on a particular path. Walk this path in faith and with the knowledge that in all things God works for the good of those who love and serve Him (see Rom. 8:28).

*O Holy Spirit, grant us the ability to become quiet
before God and to wait patiently for His guidance.*

SERVE CHRIST JOYFULLY

"If you love me, you will obey what I command" (Jn. 14:15).

Many people regard their surrender to Christ as a strict discipline that adds an unbearable burden to their lives. They feel that the cost of being a disciple is too high a price to pay. As the demands of their faith increase, their grip on Christ weakens until they completely lose it and relapse. They consequently lead an unsatisfying spiritual life that lacks fulfillment.

You must never regard your attachment to the cause of Christ as a burden. Your life in Christ should be joyful, and as you grow in Christ, your joy should increase. If you are truly devoted to Christ, your highest desire will be to get to know Him better and serve Him more effectively. As you grow in faith you will constantly strive towards ways of serving Him better because you want to, not because you have to.

To reach this point in your pilgrimage, you have to get to know Him increasingly better through Bible study and wholesome Christian literature. However, you also have to know the living Christ personally by conversing with Him through prayer. Strive to be with Christ, and the more He becomes an inseparable part of your life, the more joy you will experience in His service.

I rejoice in Your service, O Lord,
and thank You for this wonderful privilege.

DON'T BE PREJUDICED

Where the Spirit of the Lord is, there is freedom (2 Cor. 3:17).

The vast majority of people view life through the glasses of prejudice. Their opinions are shaped by their race, color, philosophical, and religious convictions, and their views are influenced by the community in which they live. Even if they speak as individuals, their words are actually the expression of their group. This often makes it difficult for them to communicate effectively with people of another group.

Prejudice limits our spiritual and intellectual perspective. It closes our minds to the truth and smothers our spirits' yearning for God. Freedom from prejudice should be the glorious experience of every person who has felt the liberating Spirit of Christ in his life.

When you have the Holy Spirit you also receive the assurance that you belong to God's family. When this happens, all people, regardless of their race, colors, or language, become your family in Christ. You are connected with them through the unique qualities of Jesus Christ.

To be liberated from the taint of prejudice is to experience a form of intellectual broadening and enrichment in every aspect of your life. You no longer wear the blinders of hatred or pettiness, and your love is no longer limited to certain groups but is extended to those who differ from you. Through the freedom from prejudice which Christ gives you, you can attain a fuller, freer, and richer spiritual life.

> *Holy Lord Jesus, through Your Spirit who lives in me*
> *I am freed from prejudice in all the spheres of my life.*

THE PRESENCE OF CHRIST

While they were still talking about this, Jesus himself stood among
them and said to them, "Peace be with you" (Lk. 24:36).

After the terrible events of Good Friday, Jesus' followers were flabbergasted. Without their beloved Master they were scared, confused, and without a leader. Their dreams had been shattered, and life had lost all meaning for them.

All their hopes and expectations were destroyed when they had to witness how the One they regarded as the Messiah was humiliated by His shameful death. Dejected and disheartened, this sad group of people sought the consolation of each other's company—when Jesus suddenly appeared in their midst.

The transformation in the lives of those people was nothing short of a miracle. Examples of the powerful deeds that they performed in the name of the Master abound in the Scriptures. The presence of Jesus brought new energy and drive to their lives.

All of this happened two thousand years ago, but the resurrected and living Christ still has the same impact on the lives of people today. If you are depressed or disheartened; if you are in danger of giving up hope; if you are under the threat of fear; if you are experiencing problems that threaten to become too much; then it is time to invite Jesus into your life and to ask Him to support you. Trust Him unconditionally and allow Him to change your despair into hope and your sadness into joy.

I plead of You, beloved Redeemer, to send Your Holy Spirit to
change my life so that I will constantly be aware of Your holy presence.

THE WAY TO PEACE

*Jesus said to the woman, "Your faith has
saved you; go in peace" (Lk. 7:50).*

Doubt, fear, and worry are factors that are notorious for the havoc they can wreak on a person's spiritual, emotional, and intellectual well-being. Even stable and clear-headed people can be reduced to confused wrecks through acute anxiety.

How often have you, or someone you know, been confronted with an unmanageable situation? There are simply no obvious solutions, and consequently a feeling of helplessness and despair develops. In times like these you are in danger of acting abnormally, and to your detriment.

In order to handle situations like these and to prevent stumbling over the obstacles of poor advice, you have to trust Christ unconditionally. Lay yourself and your concerns before Him and allow Him to guide you in His way.

Perhaps you think that it isn't in your power to do so—and you are perfectly right. However, with God everything is possible, and as you come to live more intimately in Christ, you will find that He will guide you safely through each crisis. He will give you His peace, the peace that is beyond all human comprehension.

> *I bow in grateful worship before You and thank You
> for Your peace, which You give to Your faithful children.*

BRIDGE THE GAP

*I pray that you may be active in sharing your faith,
so that you will have a full understanding of
every good thing that we have in Christ (Philem. 6).*

Division in the church is as old as the church itself. If you read in the book of Acts about the history of the founding of the first church, you will also find an account of the first division. It remains a sad fact that the gap between the different denominations has only become bigger and bigger with the passage of time. This division has resulted in long and bitter debates, unhappiness, enmity, and even hatred.

Obviously, all of this proclaims nothing but a victory for the Devil in his merciless attack on the church of Jesus Christ. The logical conclusion is that we, as followers of Christ, are duty-bound to overcome this division, so that we can present a strong and united front in Christ against the great seducer.

It is only natural to have differences of opinion in the church. Discussions resulting from these differences can be very meaningful. If everyone always agreed, it would be a very dreary and bland way of life. Nevertheless, the important thing to remember is that the Christ we all worship sacrificed Himself for all of us. We must never forget this.

In all your interactions with other people, regardless of how much your opinions may differ, you must never allow the love of Jesus Christ to be denied—a love He has called us to share with each other. It is this love that will bridge all gaps and heal all wounds.

*Lord Jesus, You died for us because You and Your Father
loved the entire world. Please let me live in this love.*

RESTORING GOOD RELATIONS

*"If you are offering your gift at the altar and there remember
that your brother has something against you, leave your
gift there in front of the altar. First go and be reconciled to
your brother; then come and offer your gift" (Mt. 5:23-24).*

Christ's message can so easily be overshadowed by religious convictions fueled by profound emotion. When your Christianity becomes so personalized and limited that it simply ignores the evil of broken human relationships, it does nothing but ridicule the high moral standards of Christ.

Irrespective of how passionate your worship may be or of how enthusiastic you may be about matters of the kingdom of God, your praise and enthusiasm remain useless if you retain an unforgiving attitude in your heart and mind.

If there is bitterness between yourself and another person, you will be unable to appreciate the true freedom of worship inspired by the Holy Spirit and the joy and power of the living Christ in your spirit. It may be that these poor relations are not of your own making. If you have done everything in your power to mend the breach and forgiveness is still withheld, you must be careful not to harbor thoughts of revenge. You have to make sure that you not only forgive the person but also continue to pray for him or her.

When your prayers are answered and the breach has been mended, you will experience great peace and joy because you have proved once again that reconciliation is an indispensable part of being a Christian.

*God of love, through forgiveness and praise
I live in peace with You and my fellow man.*

CHOOSE YOUR WORDS CAREFULLY

There is a time for everything, and a season
for every activity under heaven (Ecc. 3:1).

Truly fortunate are those who are able to find the right word for the right occasion. There are many people who boast that they are frank, truthful, and get to the bottom of things. They say what they think without considering the consequences for themselves and for others. They tend to forget that words uttered without love lose their force, because they lack the ability to heal a broken spirit, console those who mourn, raise the spirits of the depressed, or give hope to those who are despondent.

If you have been placed in a responsible position where the happiness and welfare of others are in your hands, you must ensure that you choose your words carefully, as well as the circumstances under which they are uttered. This is particularly true if the people you talk to cannot reply without fear of reprisal. Sarcasm used towards people who are not in a position to talk back simply attests to spiritual immaturity and narrow-mindedness.

The words you use reflect the quality of your spirit. Petty and bitter words result from a small-minded spirit. Harsh and sharp expressions are the fruits of a mind twisted by disappointment and frustration. If you intend for your words to convey the conviction of truth, you have to live in harmony with the Spirit of truth. The Holy Spirit lives in the hearts and minds of those who open up their lives to Him.

Gracious God, give me the wisdom to choose my words
carefully and to always speak with love in my heart.

ACTIONS WITHOUT PLANS

The LORD said to Satan, "Where have you come from?"
Satan answered the LORD, "From roaming through
the earth and going back and forth in it" (Job 1:7).

Active lives are not necessarily the most constructive lives. You may be frantically busy from morning until night, but if this is not accompanied by definite direction and positive purpose, you are wasting a lot of energy. This could result in a feeling of futility.

Many factors contribute to this meaningless kind of activity: the suppression of a guilty conscience; the evasion of responsibility; a form of escape from a challenge—all these things could lead to futile activity.

Make sure that everything you keep yourself busy with is part of a purposeful plan that inspires and empowers you to achieve your goal. Once again this will require an intimate relationship with God through prayer and contemplation. God's joy generates positive thinking and creative action.

Activity without planning is useless. Consequently, it is wise to make time to plan your way of living in partnership with God. You will discover that your way will be the right way only if it corresponds with the way of God: in fact, God's way is the only way. Make time to discover God's way for your life. If you do, your life will become less frantic, but it will definitely also be more productive.

Lord Jesus, guide me on Your way so that
my life can be constructive and purposeful.

DON'T UNDERMINE
YOUR FAITH

Brothers, do not slander one another (Jas. 4:11).

One of the biggest disservices you could do to the cause of the Master is to put down the work of a fellow servant of the Lord. Destructive and negative criticism of another servant of the Lord is often uttered, usually based on theological or dogmatic differences. The result is inevitably a weakening of faith in one of the two persons. This in turns creates doubt in the minds of the spectators, because should the foundation of Christian faith not be love?

Everyone has the right to an opinion and this fact must always be respected. You don't necessarily have to agree with everyone, but it is essential for Christians to handle differences constructively and to avoid vicious arguments.

Too often people are carried away by their obsession of their own viewpoint, and consequently the command to love each other is discarded.

In all our dealings with others we have to remember that we serve the same God and that our ultimate goal is to glorify God, even if our methods differ. This cannot take place in an atmosphere of bitterness. If, however, you bear in mind that you are always in the presence of Jesus, and if you want to remain true to your faith, you dare not neglect to act in love.

My Example and Leader, Jesus Christ, help me always to see You before me in my dealings with other people.

SPIRITUAL PRIDE

The Pharisee stood up and prayed about himself:
"God, I thank you that I am not like other men" (Lk. 18:11).

Spiritual growth often goes unnoticed by those in whom it is taking place. When a disciple attempts to determine his spiritual quality by comparing it to the spiritual development of other people, he is in danger of becoming self-centered. The religious leaders in the time of Christ suffered from this ailment: they thought that they were spiritually superior, and consequently they opened themselves up to the judgment of Christ.

Be careful not to become self-centered and smug, irrespective of how faithful you are to God. Sincere humility and self-forgetfulness will keep you from becoming conceited over your own spiritual importance. If Christ is in you, humility is testimony of your true spirituality.

The most important testimony you as a Christian can show to the world is to be filled by Christ to such an extent that you are no longer aware of the self. This means that your thoughts must be inspired by the Holy Spirit and that all your deeds must be done to the glory of God and in the service of others.

To live a Christ-centered life is to forget yourself in the reality of Jesus Christ. The more you elevate Him in your life, the more you will discover the true meaning of life.

Keep me, merciful God, from exulting in anything
but the cross, especially not in my own humility.

YOUR GREATEST ASSET

Timothy, guard what has been entrusted to your care.
Turn away from godless chatter and the opposing ideas
of what is falsely called knowledge (1 Tim. 6:20).

As you proceed in your spiritual life, you accumulate valuable assets that can only be obtained through experience. The exuberant joy of being born again begins to wear off. Your experience with Christ, even though it is still genuine and dynamic, becomes deeper as you practice a disciplined and meaningful prayer life. You become increasingly aware of the permanent presence of Christ, and the more time you spend with Him, the more real He becomes in your life.

If you are not continually growing closer to the Master in your spiritual life, it is because of a lack of prayer and contemplation of God's miracles. Spiritual failure usually doesn't occur suddenly or dramatically, but laziness and the absence of essential spiritual discipline gradually diminish your love for the Master and your loyalty towards Him.

As soon as your love for Christ begins to wane, you may find that you begin to defend yourself with explanations and arguments in an attempt to explain the shortcomings of your love. What you need is an ever-increasing capacity for love. This is your single biggest spiritual gift: Christ's love for you and your love for Him. If you treasure this gift as a dynamic power in your life, your spiritual growth will bear witness to this fact.

Teach me, O Holy Spirit, throughout my spiritual life, to be
controlled by the essential matters and not by insignificant things.

VERBAL GYMNASTICS

Some have wandered away from these
and turned to meaningless talk (1 Tim. 1:6).

It is essential to be able to give an intelligent explanation of your faith. If not, your faith in God becomes a matter of emotion without substance, making you susceptible to any passing spiritual fad. There are so many spiritual butterflies who flit from church to church because their convictions are not founded on solid dogma.

However, there are others for whom dogma is the alpha and omega of their faith. Their biggest task is to involve others in religious arguments in an attempt to convert them to their own opinions. They make use of religious generalizations and clichés; they refer to profound theological terms; and they quote Scripture out of context.

It is easy to win an argument with uninformed people, but eloquence won't impress anyone unless the Spirit of Christ is evident. It is possible to agree with your mind while your heart remains untouched.

In your attempts to explain to others what your beliefs concerning Jesus are, begin by ensuring that you know Him as your personal Savior and Redeemer. If this is absent from your testimony, your words will be nothing but words, nothing more than verbal gymnastics. There is no use in knowing all the dogma concerning Christ if you do not know Christ personally.

My humble and sincere prayer, Lord Jesus, is that my words
will be filled with profound conviction whenever I talk about You.

FOLLOWERS OF CHRIST

Do not conform any longer to the pattern of this world,
but be transformed by the renewing of your mind (Rom. 12:2).

The difficulties and problems of this world have a marked influence on our lives. But people are also influenced by times of prosperity and peace. In times of war or economic depression, people tend to become pessimistic and depressed, while in good times they are light-hearted and cheerful.

As a responsible citizen you should feel at least partially responsible for world conditions. However, there is always the danger of being tempted to allow circumstances to affect your judgment on events in your own life as well as in the lives of those who depend on you. If you depend on world conditions for your decisions in your domestic, spiritual, and business life, you are looking for trouble.

To be able to live a well-balanced life and evaluate every situation calmly and sensibly, you require clarity of vision and mind. Surrender your life to Him unconditionally, and allow His Holy Spirit to guide you in everything in which you are involved. If you do this, you will live your life according to God's perfect will for you and not according to the dictations of a changing world.

Glorified Lord Jesus, I want to be Your follower
every day and under all circumstances. Therefore
I open my life to You and Your Holy Spirit.

REFLECT THE PRESENCE OF CHRIST

When Moses came down from Mount Sinai with the two tablets
of the Testimony in his hands, he was not aware that his face
was radiant because he had spoken with the LORD (Ex. 34:29).

People often claim that each picture tells a story, and this also applies to a person's facial expression. Often it is possible to tell at a glance what kind of person you are dealing with, what emotions he or she is experiencing, and whether this is the type of person you can trust—all by merely looking at a facial expression.

However, we often judge other people wrongly, with the result that we are disappointed. There are also those who have formed a wrong impression only to regret it later, because their perception was based on a misconception.

But you never have to doubt a person who has an intimate relationship with the living Christ. It will always be evident, because the love and compassion of Christ is visible in that person through how they treat God's people.

If you cultivate an intimate relationship with Jesus, you will become more and more like Him, because His Holy Spirit is working in you and reaches out to others through you. Allow Him into your life and allow His love to flow through you to others. Then you will live a life of plenty, which only Jesus can give you (see Jn. 10:10).

Lord Jesus Christ, grant me the privilege
of being an instrument of Your peace.

WHAT MANY FORGET

"Watch out! Be on your guard against all kinds of greed; a man's life does not consist in the abundance of his possessions" (Lk. 12:15).

People without wealth are often the ones who belittle it. Wealth itself is neutral, but it can become a blessing or a curse, depending on the priority it has in your life. It is tragic when the acquiring of great wealth becomes the driving force in a person's life.

When money is an idol it becomes so demanding that it destroys everything that is beautiful and worthwhile in terms of character and personality. Friendships are often destroyed when the suspicion exists that it is only based on personal gain. Being wealthy often causes people to become contemptuous of those who have nothing, and such people often become hard-hearted towards charity.

If money is kept in the right place on our life's agenda and if we are not servants to it, it can be a great blessing. Still, it cannot buy those qualities that are essential for true life. It might cushion some of life's blows and make your life more comfortable, but there are assets that come without a price tag that are essential for true life.

We have to remind ourselves constantly that money can buy books, but not intellect; a bed, but not peaceful sleep; food, but not appetite; entertainment, but not happiness; luxuries, but not culture; a Bible, but not heaven. People often forget that the most valuable things in life are free.

Beloved Savior, keep me from allowing money to become my master and make it a servant through Your grace.

MAKE YOUR
PRAYERS POSITIVE

So, if you think you are standing firm,
be careful that you don't fall! (1 Cor. 10:12).

There are many devout people whose thoughts contradict their prayers. They mouth prayers of thanksgiving, but fail to appreciate God's daily blessings. With beautiful phrases they tell God how wonderful and great He is, but their perspective on life remains pitifully narrow, and they are unable to understand that setbacks are merely opportunities that must be accepted eagerly. They praise God's greatness and believe that He is omnipresent, yet they mourn their loneliness. Their prayers never inspire them to confront life bravely.

Prayer should inspire us to positive action. Many Christians pray and then sit back and wait for God to perform miracles. Of course God can perform any miracle, but when you pray you open yourself to the guidance of the Holy Spirit and allow Him to work through you. In this way you become an active partner of God in the answering of your prayers.

If you are in financial trouble and ask God for help, He may stir up in you a sense of responsibility in the way you spend your money. Meaningful prayer will enable you to consider every aspect of your life positively and creatively.

Prayer is not intended as an escape mechanism from the realities of life, and it should not be reserved for those times when all other attempts have failed. Prayer makes you a partner of your heavenly Father, and surely this is the greatest miracle of them all.

Through Your perfect guidance, O Holy Spirit,
prayer becomes a practical way of life to me.

DO YOU UNDERSTAND YOURSELF?

*I do not understand what I do. For what I want
to do I do not do, but what I hate I do (Rom. 7:15).*

It is a sad fact that there are many people who do not understand themselves. They spend long and agonizing hours in self-examination, and they study psychology or regularly visit psychologists to arrive at a better and more profound understanding of their personality.

Unfortunately their studies only cause more confusion, sometimes even resulting in spiritual disaster. Psychological self-examination can lead to self-centeredness, which in turn results in frustration and dissatisfaction with the quality of your life.

In order to understand yourself, you have to accept and appreciate the fact that God created you in His image. But also you must understand that sin still haunts you, and that Christ has redeemed you from it. If Christ Jesus is Lord of your life and if you give Him priority over everything else in your life, you will discover that your personal life acquires meaning and purpose because of your intimate relationship with Him. Consequently you will also experience the fulfillment of getting to know your true self. Under the authority of Christ and the guidance of His Holy Spirit, it becomes possible to understand yourself.

It is impossible to have daily communion with Christ through prayer and contemplation and still feel confused and lonely. By getting to know Christ, you also get to know yourself.

*Holy Lord Jesus, through Your Spirit who lives in me
I have come to know my true self. I thank You for this.*

THINK BEFORE
GIVING IN TO TEMPTATION

The truly righteous man attains life, but
he who pursues evil goes to his death (Prov. 11:19).

No one has the ambition to become an alcoholic, a criminal, or a failure. Every alcoholic used to be a moderate drinker; every criminal thought that he could cheat and steal without being caught, and people who commit social sins always try to hide them.

Harmful and eventually destructive habits do not assault your character brutally. If they did, you would immediately reject them. They begin with a minor and harmless gesture that has pleasant results. As the pleasure increases you may think that you are still in control, until you suddenly realize that it has become impossible to resist the temptation in your own strength.

It is important to identify an addictive habit in advance. This is also where the acceptance of the living Christ is invaluable in your life. His Holy Spirit gives you the perception that makes you sensitive to the habit-forming powers of the Evil One, and He also gives you the spiritual power to enable you to say "No!" to the slightest indication of evil.

When temptation beckons the first time and offers you illicit pleasure, pause a moment and ask yourself where this will lead eventually. Don't become involved in matters that could cause your downfall. Reject them while you still have the strength to do so, and remain true to God as well as to yourself and those who love you.

Holy Spirit of God, I know that I can only resist and
conquer temptation through Your immanent presence.

GOOD INTENTIONS

Do not merely listen to the word, and
so deceive yourselves. Do what it says (Jas. 1:22).

If all our good intentions were fulfilled, the world would be a wonderful place. Unfortunately words have no power if they are not expressed in deeds. Good intentions are seldom fulfilled, and the good that could have been achieved remains undone.

Be realistic when you express your intentions: keep them within the realms of possibility and leave flights of fancy to those who dream dreams knowing full well that they will never be fulfilled. Begin with the simple things. If you planned to write a letter of condolence or apology, do it now. If you are aware of someone who is in need of encouragement and you are in a position to provide it, why not do it immediately? If your intentions don't turn into actions, they are meaningless.

Spiritually, the failure of good intentions is evident in the lives of many people. We will only know in eternity how many people "intended" to follow Jesus at some time or another. They admire and respect Him, but they withhold their full surrender to Him. In the meantime everything remains only good intentions, merely serving to quiet their conscience.

The Master demands of you as a Christian to execute your good intentions in practice. If not, the vision you once had of the good you could do will die.

Living Lord Jesus, through Your wisdom and power
all my good intentions become glorious realities.

FROM APPEARANCE
TO REALITY

When Jesus saw him lying there and learned that
he had been in this condition for a long time,
he asked him, "Do you want to get well?" (Jn. 5:6).

It's amazing how much energy people waste in pretending to be what they are not. They go through life and interact with their fellow human beings, all the while holding up a façade to make them acceptable to others. Behind their masks they may hide feelings of inferiority, frustration, or suppressed anger, but all these emotions are obscured by a veil of pretense that is only lifted for brief moments.

Of course, if everyone expressed their true feelings, the world may be an even more unpleasant place. However, life can become extremely stressful for those who hide behind masks. The answer to this unfortunate situation is that your inner character should be of such high quality that it would be unnecessary to live a life of pretense. The outer and inner person must form a close unit.

The teachings of Christ proclaim the completeness of the human personality. It emphasizes the fact that the inner person must be in complete harmony with the heavenly Father. If a person's soul is in harmony with the Holy Spirit, it becomes unnecessary to pretend, because your outer life will be nothing more than a reflection of your profound spiritual experience of Jesus Christ.

Merciful Lord and Master, in Your strength and
with the aid of the Holy Spirit I undertake to be as
devoted to You on the inside as I am on the outside.

CONQUER DEPRESSION THROUGH FAITH

"For you who revere my name, the sun of righteousness will rise with healing in its wings" (Mal. 4:2).

Depression and pessimism are ailments that destroy the soul. Apart from the fact that depression is an illness of the mind, it also affects your physical and spiritual well-being, limits your vision of the future, and negatively influences your general attitude to life. The causes of depression are numerous and include fear, anxiety, illness, financial instability, and loneliness, to name but a few.

You may attempt to fight the condition with man-made medicines, but their effect will only be temporary. Sooner or later the effects will wear off and your condition will return, often with a vengeance.

The only way to fight such an emotional disruption effectively is to turn to Christ and to open yourself to His love and healing influence. Accept Him as the Lord of your life and unconditionally put yourself in His care. This will require immense faith, but when Jesus takes control of your life and guides you on the path you have to take, you will find that, because of your obedience to Him, you will be filled with a sense of self-confidence and well-being that only He can give you.

I cling to You like someone who is drowning, Lord Jesus, in the knowledge that nothing in this life can disturb me as long as You are with me.

SPIRITUALLY UNDERPRIVILEGED

*"What good will it be for a man if he gains
the whole world, yet forfeits his soul? Or what can
a man give in exchange for his soul?" (Mt. 16:26).*

The average person wishes to achieve something with his life and wants to feel that his life was not in vain. To accomplish this aim he sets certain goals for himself and works towards achieving what he believes is success. He accumulates everything that might award him money and prestige. But in spite of all this, many people who have surrounded themselves with all the good things in life cannot get rid of the nagging suspicion that they have missed out on something significant.

Any person who has neglected his spiritual life, irrespective of how successful he might be in the eyes of the world, is short-sighted and foolish. He has convinced himself that gold (and everything it represents) is more important to him than God; that the visible things are more important than the invisible; and that a false balance sheet is preferable to integrity and honesty.

No person who pushes God from his life can be truly successful. Only when our spiritual life is in harmony with God and when we continually grow towards a fuller and richer maturity will we have a sound understanding of the meaning of life. To rob your spiritual life of the awareness of Christ's immanent Spirit is to live under the spiritual breadline. Then you are truly underprivileged.

*Heavenly Father, I realize the importance of my
spiritual life and know for certain that Your
Holy Spirit achieves purposefulness and depth in my life.*

YOU ARE WATCHED
CONTINUALLY

A good name is more desirable than great riches (Prov. 22:1).

Unless you are a hermit you constantly live under the scrutiny of many people. You are part of a family circle or of a business world in which you deal with different kinds of people. You live as part of a community and you may even be part of a sports group. Wherever you are and whatever you do, there are always people who are forming an opinion about you, and therefore you are constantly busy building up a character.

There are people who say that they don't give a hoot about what others say about them, but this is often nothing more than a shield for a bruised spirit and feelings of inferiority. Serious and sensible people, however, are deeply aware that reputation is a valuable asset and work hard at making their name synonymous with truth, honesty, and integrity.

Establishing and developing an honorable name seems like a time-consuming and tiresome task to some people. The values of society make it appear to be an impossible task and an unattainable ideal, but the truth of the matter is that it is the most rewarding task you can ever undertake. It creates a feeling of well-being and brings you peace of mind, because such a life is pleasing to God.

Make honor more important than profit; honesty more noble than cheap popularity. Remember that a good name is worth more than great riches. Then you will make the exciting discovery that an honorable life is the most rewarding life that can be lived, because it is to the honor of God.

> *Holy Lord and Master, help me always to hold my character and reputation more dear than wealth and popularity.*

THE PATH OF PRAYER

"When you pray, do not keep on babbling like pagans, for they think
they will be heard because of their many words...for your
Father knows what you need before you ask him" (Mt. 6:7-8).

Stereotyped and repetitive prayers may be a good discipline to contain the spirit of prayer, but the Master makes it abundantly clear that prayer becomes ineffective when it deteriorates into the mere recital of pretty phrases. Many prayers have failed because the beauty of their phrasing exceeded their actual substance.

True prayer is more than words. It is an orientation of spirit and mind that reaches out to the eternal God. When you pray, you must be convinced in your soul that you are trusting God in all things.

Too often we lay our needs before Him and then disappear from the scene, instead of remaining ready for, and sensitive to, hearing and obeying His voice. Prayer is a two-way process. You tell God what you want from Him and He reveals to you what He expects from you.

Prayer is not a series of empty words that are divorced from life, but rather an increasingly profound relationship with the heavenly Father and a sincere desire to do His will. When He reveals His will to you, you will be moved to the kind of praise and worship that will be reflected in the quality of your life.

God and Father, grant me the true spirit of prayer so
that my communion with You will become more
and more profound and meaningful in practice.

December

Holy God and our loving Father in Jesus Christ,
we look forward to another Christ-feast.
Let our perspectives on Christmas be pure and Christ-centered.
Cleanse our spirit from all bitterness and hatred;
our will from unworthy motives,
and our soul from practices that dishonor You.
Let each gift be accompanied by true love and let each greeting card
profess our faith in You.
We long, O Father, for the simple beauty of Christmas:
unadorned by the tinsel and shiny lights of the world.
Give new meaning to each familiar Christmas melody.
Let us rejoice in the knowledge that God became man—
a child in a humble manger—
so that people could be reconciled with God
and call Him Lord once again.
May it also bring reconciliation between people.
May the peace of which the angels sang not remain
a vain dream or impossible ideal to us,
but become a glorious reality to the honor of God.
Grant that the goodness and tenderness of Christmas will not only
remain in our hearts for a brief time, but that it will stay there
when we return to the harsh realities of life.
We pray this in the name of Jesus who came to be our Savior;
Immanuel—God with us!

Amen.

THE GOSPEL IN A NUTSHELL

*"God so loved the world that he gave his one
and only Son, that whoever believes in him shall
not perish but have eternal life" (Jn. 3:16).*

Jesus Christ had an exceptional ability to express the gospel in the most basic terms possible so that even the simplest person could understand it, and yet, the profound nature of the message was never lost. The main topic of His message was always the eternal and constant love of God: "God is love. Whoever lives in love lives in God, and God in him" (1 Jn. 4:16).

In order to be allowed to share in this love, we must first open our hearts to Him: "If anyone loves Me, he will obey My teaching. My Father will love him, and We will come to him and make Our home with him" (Jn. 14:23). Love for God overflows into obedience to Him and allowing His Spirit to reign over each aspect of your life and to be central to your thoughts and deeds.

To declare, "God is love!" is much more than a simple and possibly sentimental confession of faith: it requires a particular way of life which has to be a confirmation of faith in the immeasurable love of God that was confirmed by Christ's death for your sins on the cross.

Consequently we must once again ponder the birth of our Savior during every Advent-time; we must purify our festivities so that it will truly be a Christ-feast, and we must once again devote ourselves to the Child of Bethlehem.

*Jesus, I want to joyfully experience this Christ-feast
in the knowledge that You are my Savior and Redeemer.
May this impart a special character to my Christmas joy.*

CLOSE TO GOD THROUGH JESUS CHRIST

You who once were far away have been brought near through the blood of Christ (Eph. 2:13).

Christmastime is Advent-time! The term "advent" derives from the Latin word "adventuske", which means "arrival" or "appearance." In the terminology of the church it is used to refer to the four weeks preceding Christmas: the joyous time when we commemorate the coming of Christ to this world of humanity.

Christ became "flesh," but without sin. We are also flesh, but in our case the word carries the blemish of our "sinful nature." From the Word—and from experience—we know that the flesh is in a constant battle with the Spirit. Paul says in Romans 8:7 that the mind set on the flesh is hostile to God.

For Christ, however, the blemish of sin falls away. As a human being He was without sin, but still human and in the tarnished form of a servant. He became our equal in everything except in sin. This is the glorious message of Christmas: Immanuel! God with us! God visits man personally. He descended from heaven as the man Jesus Christ to prepare the way for humankind to be restored in the favor of the Father. He came to be the Redeemer of a lost world.

First it was God above, God far from us, then it became, in Christ, God with us, and then, through the Holy Spirit, God in us.

This is the secret of the divine Christmas Eve and the reason for our inexpressible joy at Christmas. May the time of Advent truly be a feast of Christ for you.

Heavenly Father, my mind reels before the mystery of the incarnation in the flesh of Your Son, my Savior, Jesus Christ.

THE PROMISE OF A NEW LIFE

A shoot will come up from the stump of Jesse;
from his roots a Branch will bear fruit (Is. 11:1).

A long time ago the royal house of David stood in the center of the entire country like a proud tree-trunk with a high top. But all this beauty was felled in the fullness of time. The house of David was dilapidated, and its glory had waned. All that remained was found in Mary, in whose veins the ancient, noble blood still flowed, but who was reduced to such a state of humiliation in the world that she could not believe that God would esteem her enough to make her the mother of His Son.

And yet, through God's omnipotence and mercy, a shoot came up from the meager remains of the once powerful house of David. This "shoot" that Isaiah prophesies of is no one else than Jesus Christ. This humble shoot became an ineradicable and mighty trunk which spread out its branches to the ends of the earth. The Child in the manger grew up to become the way, the truth, and the life. He brandishes the scepter over the entire earth, and His reign knows no bounds.

With the approaching Christ-feast we must once again assess our personal relationship with Christ. We must first humble ourselves over our spiritual decay and confess our sins before the Lord. From the stump of Jesse He brought forth new life, a new dispensation, a new period of spiritual growth for those who had back-slidden: "He who was seated on the throne said, 'I am making everything new!'" (Rev. 21:5).

Lord God, in these days bring forth new life
from the half-withered stump of my spiritual life,
to Your glory and through Jesus Christ.

LIVE LIKE ROYAL CHILDREN

You did not receive a spirit that makes you a slave
again to fear, but you received the Spirit of sonship.
And by him we cry, "Abba, Father" (Rom. 8:15).

There is a world of difference between confessing that you are a child of God and living a life as a child of God. Many people profess faith and yet live in constant fear. They suffer from a destructive sense of inferiority and are unable to deal with life's problems. There is such a gap between what they should be and what they really are that they tend to become despondent and abandon their principles.

When God called you to become His child and when you reacted to His call with joy, a new life began for you. Your sins were forgiven and since then you have stood in a new relationship with the King. Through His grace you became part of His kingdom. Because His Spirit now lives and works in you, your behavior towards people and your total way of life have been revolutionized.

The Advent-time reminds you once again that you should face life with conviction and without fear. Your Father is the King of all kings. Knowing that He loves you and cares about you should give you inner peace. The steadfast faith that He will guide you safely, as you obey Him and return His love, should be your comfort in life. Through Jesus Christ He invites you to call Him "Father."

Father, thank You for the indescribable grace of being
allowed to talk to You, which Jesus Christ obtained for me.

YOUR SALVATION IS HERE!

The LORD has made proclamation to the ends of the earth:
"Say to the Daughter of Zion, 'See, your Savior comes!'" (Is. 62:11).

During the Advent-time we commemorate the coming of Christ. However, we must never forget about the coming of Christ to our souls and
into our hearts. His appearance in the flesh was not everything. We
must never be content simply to testify that He came to take the curse of
our sins upon Himself as Lamb of God. It is a glorious testimony, but it
is incomplete if we don't call people to personally share in that salvation.
Then it is a Christmas carol sung out of key. Then it is only a feast around
us, never inside of us.

If we want to experience the joy of Christmas in the true sense of the
word, Christ has to arrive in and inhabit our hearts with His salvation and
peace. Christ's coming to the world is the external event; His coming to
my heart, the internal. We thank God that His coming can be a subjective
reality in the heart and life of everyone who believes in Him.

He came to find and redeem what was lost, and He gave everyone who
accepted Him the right to become a child of God (see Jn. 1:12). Do you
believe this? Do you believe that He comes to where you stand worried
and overwhelmed by your own sin? He comes to you with His hands
filled with grace and forgiveness and blessings; He comes to convert your
sadness into joy. Christmas is essentially a feast of salvation, because
your Savior came!

Jesus, my Savior and Redeemer, thank You that I may relive the
all-surpassing joy and happiness of someone who has been redeemed.

OUR FEARS
ALLAYED BY A CHILD

The angel said to her, "Do not be afraid, Mary,
you have found favor with God" (Lk. 1:30).

With this message, God wants to free Mary—and through her all of humanity—from fear, and to replace this fear with exultant joy. That is why the angel said on that first Christmas Eve, "Do not be afraid. I bring you good news of great joy" (Lk. 2:10).

This world has become a maze of fear. And it all began with the Fall when Adam said, "I was afraid...so I hid" (Gen. 3:10). And on the day of judgment sinners will still plead in a last, terrified prayer meeting "they will say to the mountains, 'Fall on us!' and to the hills, 'Cover us!'" (Lk. 23:30).

Fear is not merely a figment of man's imagination. From the cradle to the grave it remains a terrible presence. We fear the unknown as a child fears the dark. We fear for our health, for loneliness, for old age, and then for that fear of all fears: death. Everywhere and in everyone there is a constant fear for thousands of threatening things.

At Christmastime God once again sends His messenger to bring us tidings of great joy: the love of God expels all fear because the source of fear, namely sin, was conquered by Jesus at Bethlehem. In each terrifying storm of life He is with us to tell us, "Don't be afraid. Immanuel, I am with you!"

Shepherd of my life, even though I walk through the valley of the
shadow of death, I will not be afraid, because You are with me.

CHRISTMAS: FEAST OF CHRIST

She gave birth to her firstborn, a son. She wrapped him in cloths and placed him in a manger, because there was no room for them in the inn. (Lk. 2:7).

At Christmastime we all become children once again. In our hearts we relive the timeless adventure of unquestioned faith, where all things are immediately possible and where the child Jesus is in the center of everything. The stable is transformed into a palace, and kings from the east kneel in worship before the King of kings.

For a short time, as in a dream, we leave our predictable way of life and walk the path of rich imagination, of amazement and exciting joy, while we freely rejoice in the immeasurable love of God. Even the staunchest spiritual realist experiences stirrings in his heart upon hearing the age-old tale, imagining the fragrances of incense and myrrh.

On the other hand, Christmastime is also as real as the gifts that we give and receive; as real as the candles we light and the lights that charm us; as real as the bread we break in love with our dear ones; as real as the songs that we hear everywhere during this wonderful time. In experiencing the mystery surrounding Christmas, as well as the concrete reality thereof, we are all touched by the wonder of God's love—and all our dreams of peace and joy are rekindled.

If we have forgotten how to experience Christmas like a child, with joyful and excited expectation, we have to learn anew how to discover the enchantment of Christmas.

I thank You, Lord Jesus, that I may experience the remembrance of Your birth like a child and that I can therefore see the gates of Your Kingdom open before me.

CHRISTMAS: A FEAST FOR THE ELDERLY

Moved by the Spirit, he went into the temple courts. When the parents brought in the child Jesus to do for him what the custom of the Law required, Simeon took him in his arms and praised God (Lk. 2:27-28).

The pious and just Simeon was already an old man when he held the Messiah in his arms. He could talk to God and listen to God. In fact, Simeon's name means "the one who hears." God blessed him with the sight of the Messiah because he had been faithful in his meetings with God. Because he was present in the temple, he could take the Christ-child in his arms. In so doing, Simeon received God's wonderful gift and, by implication also accepted Christ as his Savior and Redeemer.

In old age you and I should also learn to wait for God, to listen to His voice, so that we too can receive His wonderful gifts. You must know that Christ was also born for you. That is what faith is: being able to see the invisible every Christmas. This is the type of faith that will compel you, like Simeon, to proclaim the message of Christ with jubilation in your old age: "a light for revelation to the Gentiles" (Lk. 2:32).

This is the miracle that God works with Christmas: He puts the Child of His love in your arms. And with this you receive His love, His salvation, His blood, His body—everything that is necessary for your redemption. What an incomprehensible gift this is. But with Christmas we also have to do something from our side. We must embrace Jesus and accept Him just as Simeon took the Child in His arms.

> *Help me, O Child of Bethlehem, to take You in my arms and heart as the aged Simeon did, so that Christmas can truly become a Christ-feast to me.*

IT IS ADVENT-TIME

"Behold, I am coming soon!" (Rev. 22:7).

The first Advent was when Jesus came to the earth in the flesh as mankind's Savior. He descended from the glory of heaven to the indignity of the manger and the cross. His earthly path would pass through great depths so that He could elevate a lost humanity to the heights of salvation as His glorified children.

His work, which began in humility during the first Christmas Eve, will be completed with His glorious second coming to harvest the crop. It will be a triumphant coming in majesty and honor. It will be the day of all days, the great Advent awaited in supplication by the true congregation of Christ. At Christmas-time we once again hear His voice saying: "Yes, I am coming soon" to which we answer with a deep yearning: "Amen. Come, Lord Jesus" (Rev. 22:20).

There are four Advent-times in your life: the coming of Christ in the flesh to earn redemption for you; a coming in the Spirit to give you a personal share in His redemption; a coming in your death to transfer you from the sphere of time into eternity; and finally Christ's second coming in glory to conclude the history of mankind, which will be followed by eternal life.

Hence, Christmastime is rich in divine consolation. We see Christ always and everywhere: in His struggle to save us; in our hearts where His grace worked; in our hour of dying that gives us victory in Christ; and any moment in the second coming of our Savior in glory and majesty.

I praise and thank You, holy Master, for the great blessing of the Advent. Make me ever ready for Your second coming.

DON'T STOP AT THE STARS

After Jesus was born in Bethlehem…Magi from
the east came to Jerusalem (Mt. 2:1).

The Magi persevered in their search for the King whose star they saw. God called them in a special way and in terms of what they knew: through the appearance of a star. They were, after all, astrologers, magi, learned priests of their people. Their fatherland was Mesopotamia, situated between the Euphrates and the Tigris, the old land of paradise from which Adam and Eve were expelled. Now they are following the star to worship and bring homage to the second Adam, Jesus the Messiah.

To them the star was the beginning of the light, because they were still children of darkness. In obedience they followed the star and God prepared for them a vision of what was previously unseen by human eyes, unheard by human ears, and unknown to the heart of man.

The star enchanted them so that they could find the Child. God indeed calls and searches in many ways: He calls the wise men with a star; He calls the shepherds with heavenly choirs. God's love for sinners gives us stars to guide us, and we thank God for these stars. But we may not remain standing in amazement before these stars. They are only the beginning of the path of salvation. We must proceed from the star to the Word; from the word of God in nature to the Word of God in Scripture.

God of creation, please also guide me to the Jesus-Child!

FROM THE STAR
TO THE WORD

Your word is a lamp to my feet and a light for my path (Ps. 119:105).

The wise men were initially guided by a star, but when they arrived in Jerusalem, the Word of God lighted their path to Christ. In Jerusalem everyone was expecting a King, but they did not know where to find Him. The teachers of the law were reflecting on the meaning of the Word of God. This must have seemed like regression to the wise men: away from the shining star to the moldy study of books.

We find the wise men with their star but without the Book, and the people of Israel with the Word but without their King—a King without an address. So they returned to the Word with its irrefutable authority. In Micah 5:2 this particular prophecy is presented: "But you, Bethlehem Ephrathah, though you are small among the clans of Judah, out of you will come for Me One who will be ruler over Israel." To Bethlehem then—to the small city of great things.

The star is therefore subservient to the Word. When the gilt is gone, the truth and reality is still there in the Word. Emotion and romanticism evaporate, and the Word of God triumphs. Hence the final journey to Bethlehem is always a journey based on the Word of God.

We love the stars and it is hard to part with them—but we must! We need the Scriptures: the, at times, disillusioning, provocative, tormenting, but always purely prophetic Scriptures. The stars without the Scriptures leave us with an insatiable longing for eternity and without the correct address of our King. The Word guides us to the true gold-reef, to Bethlehem, to the stable, the manger, and the King.

Jesus of Bethlehem, keep me from becoming so enchanted by the stars that I lose the address of the manger.

CAN YOU TRULY CELEBRATE THE CHRIST-FEAST?

Then they opened their treasures and presented him
with gifts of gold and of incense and of myrrh (Mt. 2:11).

The Magi from the east finally understood the true meaning of Christmas: to give. God gave with Christmas: He gave His best, His most valuable, His Son. He gave out of love (see Jn. 3:16). And the Child of Bethlehem also gave: He gave Himself; He continued giving even in His death on the cross.

You must first learn to forget what you did for others in order to remember what others did for you out of love. You must learn to forget what you expect from others and rather ask what you can do for them. For once you have to rid yourself of the idea that the world owes you something and start to think about what you owe the world. You must be able to relegate your demands to the background and place your responsibilities prominently on the foreground.

You must discover that your fellow man is as sincere as you are and be able to see the heart hidden behind the exterior—a heart that yearns for love, friendship, and compassion. You must be able to close your book of charges and complaints against life and look around you to find places where you can sow seeds of happiness and love.

If you are willing to do these things, even if only for one day, then you have brought your gold, incense, and myrrh. Only then can you truly celebrate the Christ-feast.

Loving Master, I begin this Advent-time by giving myself
to You anew so that You can use me as and when You please.

ATTITUDES SURROUNDING THE CHRIST-FEAST

Then Herod called the Magi secretly and found out from them the exact time the star had appeared (Mt. 2:7).

Christmas is first and foremost an attitude of the heart. There are many people who share in Herod's attitude. He is the prototype of those people who live in sin and in enmity with God; people who would like to eradicate the Good News; people with strong personalities and many talents but who want to banish Christ from their lives. They hide their disapproval behind a mask of hypocrisy. They also want to go to worship the Child. They also celebrate the Christ-feast, but in reality their hearts do not belong to Him. Their motives are impure as they search for the Child: they want to use religion to advance their careers and to keep the crown on their own heads.

The Advent-time proclaims the following message to these Herods: Christ can be found in Bethlehem, but only by those who have the right attitude in their hearts and whose worship is true in spirit.

This is the attitude of the wise men. They came from a distant land, in the same way that we have to come from the distant land of sin as lost sons and daughters. They persisted in their search and did not allow anything to distract them from their purpose. Jesus Himself promised that those who seek Him will find Him. The wise men stipulated no conditions. They expected a palace and a golden cradle—what they found was a stable and a humble manger. Like them, everyone who seeks can experience the joy of finding what God intended for each of us during this Christmastime.

I thank You, O Holy Spirit, that I not only found the stable and the manger but also the Child of Bethlehem, my Savior and Redeemer.

CHRISTMAS AND CHILDREN

"I tell you the truth, unless you change and become like little children, you will never enter the kingdom of heaven" (Mt. 18:3).

Christmas is the pre-eminent feast of the family and the child. It is difficult to express the excitement and expectations in the heart of a child during Christmas. Grown-ups are different: we are mostly negative—we expect to fail, and then we do fail; we expect to be unhappy, and then we are; we always anticipate the worst, and then it happens.

Advent is a time for recovering the lost glory of our faith in life and eternity. It is a time to believe that God can work the miracle once again: that Christ can be born again in our life and thoughts. It is a time to devote ourselves anew to God and to rejoice in the fact that His Spirit wants to live in us.

Christmas allows us to obtain new insights into the place of the child in the family. On that first Christmas Eve a Child was at the center of that holy tableau. Similarly, Jesus taught us that the child is at the core of the family. We are not allowed to remove the child from the center simply because we have other interests and responsibilities.

The Christ-feast repeatedly brings us back to the secret of true happiness and joy: mother, father, child—and God! May Christmas lead us to a renewed resolution to maintain the sanctity of the family which will bring you the happiness and peace of family bliss.

We praise You, Lord Jesus, for bestowing a new and particular significance on the family.

ADVENT JUBILATION— WITH A FALSE NOTE

"Say to the Daughter of Zion, 'See, your Savior comes! See, his reward is with him, and his recompense accompanies him'" (Is. 62:11).

At Advent-time we commemorate the coming in the flesh of Christ to the world. However, we must not forget the coming of Christ to our souls, to our hearts. We dare not stop at the material appearance of Christ in the world as if this is the only important event. We must not only testify with our mouths that He came to the world to take the burden of our guilt and curse upon Him as Lamb of God. It is a wonderful testimony, yes, but what good does it do if we do not truly partake thereof? Then it becomes a Christmas jubilation with a false note.

It may be a celebration around us but never inside of us. If we truly want to experience the joy of Christmas, Christ has to come to our hearts with His salvation, peace, and joy, and completely inhabit us. Martin Luther clearly states this: "Even if Christ has been born in Bethlehem a thousand times, but not yet in my heart, then I am lost."

Christ came to this world so that His love and grace could become a reality in the heart of everyone who believes in Him. He came to find and save those who are lost, and everyone who accepts Him has the right to become a child of God. Do you believe this? Do you believe that He comes to where you stand, overwhelmed by your own sin? He comes to you with His hands filled with grace and forgiveness. He comes to convert your sadness into joy; to take the false note out of your Christmas joy and to make you sing the pure song of salvation.

Heavenly Father, we are on our annual pilgrimage to the manger in Bethlehem. Satisfy us with the true Bread and Water of life.

THE SUN SHINES, BUT I AM BLIND

"For you who revere my name, the sun of righteousness will rise with healing in its wings" (Mal. 4:2).

The sun shines in glory and majesty, high in the sky, far and inaccessible in its reign. The eye cannot look at it directly without being blinded. As the sun is, so is our God. Elevated high above the earthly turmoil, He reigns over the entire world. Even though I try to shield my eyes from His splendor, He remains there.

Like the sun that brings light, warmth, and growth with its comforting rays, God also comes to us in the Advent-time. But unlike the sun, God is also still close to us in spite of His untouchable splendor.

We cannot go to the sun, but the sun can reach down to us. God sends His light to illuminate our dark minds, warm our cold hearts, and turn the night of our sins into the day of His grace. In Jesus Christ the sun of justice descends upon us. God from God, Light from Light.

Zechariah sings the praise of the Child of Bethlehem by describing Him as the rising light that visits us to shine on those who are overwhelmed by darkness and the shadow of death. So many are lost in the dark maze of sin. The sun shines, but they are blind. But, says Malachi, there is healing in His rays. He takes our ailments upon Him and carries the burden of our grief.

After Christmas, we must return to everyday life and carry the light we receive from Him into a dark world.

Sun of justice, thank You for reminding us in this Advent-time that we have a calling to be the bearers of light in this world.

THE TRUTH
OF THE CHRIST-FEAST

This is how God showed his love among us: He sent his one and only Son into the world that we might live through him (1 Jn. 4:9).

The most astonishing truth about Christmas is that God loves us. God is love and He loves us with a love that gives only the best and most valuable, as with Christmas when He gave us his Son. He also loves us with a love that forgives and cares. We dare not leave such love unanswered.

"Since God so loved us, we also ought to love one another," says the apostle John (1 Jn. 4:11). Love must triumph in our everyday lives: in our marriages, in our home lives, and in our relationships—not only with words, but with deeds of love.

However, it is also true that Christ did not remain in the manger; He grew to become a Man of sorrow in Gethsemane and at Golgotha. Therefore we, as His followers, may not remain infants in faith or become stuck in a faith centered only on the stable. We must grow to spiritual maturity.

Like the shepherds we must also be loving witnesses and praise God for everything we have heard and seen. We must proclaim the wonder of love: redemption, grace, and peace. The gate is always open to everyone who wants to enter—this is the love-truth of Christmas.

Loving Father, thank You for revealing Yourself and the fullness of Your love to sinners like us at Christmastime.

"SOUL, DO YOU HAVE ROOM FOR JESUS?"

"In my Father's house are many rooms; if it were not so, I would have told you. I am going there to prepare a place for you" (Jn. 14:2).

She gave birth to her firstborn, a son. She wrapped him in cloths and placed him in a manger, because there was no room for them in the inn (Lk. 2:7).

Had the people of Bethlehem known who these visitors were, they would probably have tried to "make" room for them. Mary would become the mother of the Messiah generations of Israel had been waiting for. Every devout Israelite would have been honored to give up his own room for Him. But God did not come to this world in greatness and splendor; He came in the shape of a servant and was placed in a manger.

Will this Christmas once again reveal to you that the Lord could not find a place in your life either? If this is the case, then your guilt is more so than that of the people of Bethlehem. After all, we know that He is the Christ, the Savior.

We dare not be Christians who have no room for Christ. The wonder of God's grace is that He does not repay us according to our sins. Although there was no place for Him on earth, He went to prepare a place in heaven for every repentant sinner. A "no vacancy" sign is never posted.

Our Christmas deed should be to make room for Christ in our hearts and lives. Then we will have nothing to fear because we know: a place has been prepared by the Lamb Himself for us, so that we may take our place at the feast of the Lamb. Hallelujah! Praise the Lord!

I want to make room for You in all spheres of my life, Lord Jesus. I thank You for the room You make for me now and in eternity.

NATURE, SCRIPTURE, AND FLESH

The Word became flesh and made his
dwelling among us. We have seen his glory (Jn. 1:14).

Of all the ways in which God reveals Himself to us (in nature and in the Scriptures), the revelation of God in the flesh is the most wonderful. This is the source of all our Christmas joy: Christ became man!

The Christmas drama reaches a climax when the Magi bow down to bring homage to the Child. Now, for the first time, they see God in the flesh. Up until this moment they searched for Him in nature, in the stars. But the enchantment of the stars is past. The light of God shines through triumphantly when they finally stand before the incarnate Word: the shining Morning Star!

Together with the Magi we have to look beyond the stars to the Word in the stable, where we surrender ourselves unconditionally in worship: the gold of our love; the incense of our prayers; and the myrrh of our offerings. In the stable we learn what the stars cannot tell us: that the earth became the center of the universe on Christmas Day.

And when the stars die out one day, the eternal day of God will dawn. Then God will no longer address us through the stars, nor through the Word, but will speak to us eternally and uninterruptedly through the incarnate Word: Jesus, Immanuel!

> *Holy and awe-inspiring God, guide me beyond the stars*
> *this Christmas, through the holy Word, and to the Child*
> *in the manger, so that I can worship in spirit and truth.*

CHRIST-FEAST!

*"Do not be afraid. I bring you good news of great joy
that will be for all the people" (Lk. 2:10).*

To many people Christmas has become a feast without Christ. He has been subtly eliminated to make room for other things. It is the task of the Christian to right such a wrong.

We must confront the worldly tensions of Christmas as mature Christians. We must guard against all God-dishonoring commercializations of the feast. It must not degenerate into cheap tinsel, shining lights, and superficial emotions.

We must not allow ourselves to be swept up in the mad rush before Christmas that it leaves us so exhausted on Christmas Day that we are unable to sing a song of praise in His honor. We must penetrate beyond the exterior trappings and get to the core of Christmas, so that the Light of the world can become a reality to us.

We must contribute to making Christmas a true Christ-feast. This does not mean that we should be spoilsports; Christians do have a reason to celebrate, as the fields of Bethlehem resounded with joy on that holy night. Without Christ there can be no true Christmas joy.

We must experience the true glory of Christmas in our hearts and not look for it in shops and places of worldly entertainment. At Christmas the world must clearly see who we belong to: in our Christmas cards; in our Christmas tree that points to the tree of the cross; in our worship; in our gifts to people and our offerings to God—our gold, incense, and myrrh.

*Holy Spirit of God, guide me this Christmas past the external
trappings to the true inner joy that can only be found in Christ.*

BETHLEHEM: HOUSE OF BREAD

"You, Bethlehem Ephrathah, though you are small among the clans of Judah, out of you will come for me one who will be ruler over Israel, whose origins are from of old, from ancient times" (Mic. 5:2).

As Micah predicted, Christ was born in Bethlehem—a small town approximately thirteen kilometers south of Jerusalem. It was also called Ephrathah in ancient times. The name Bethlehem means "house of bread." The town is situated among fertile wheat farmlands, which makes this name very appropriate.

Bethlehem has a long history. Jacob buried his wife, Rachel, there and erected a memorial pillar next to her grave. Ruth was living there when she met Boaz and married him, and on a clear day she could see her country Moab across the Valley of the Jordan. Bethlehem was also the town of David's youth. David yearned for the water from the well of Bethlehem when he was a fugitive from the wrath of Saul.

From the ancestry of this David, God would bring forth His Son to become the Savior of this world. He would become the Bread of life for millions; the fountain of living water to quench the eternal thirst of humanity.

When a pilgrim wants to enter the birthplace of Christ in Bethlehem today, he has to bend down low to pass through the opening that serves as a door. Similarly, all of us will have to bow down during this Advent-time before the Child of Bethlehem so that we can bring Him the true homage that belongs to Him.

Come all you faithful, cheerful and with joy, O come in the spirit to Bethlehem! Praise that Child born for our salvation—come kneel there in worship before Jesus, the Lord.

TENDER COMFORT
AT ADVENT-TIME

When anxiety was great within me, your
consolation brought joy to my soul (Ps. 94:19).

There is a lot of sorrow surrounding Christmastime: some people are gravely ill; others have to come to terms with the effects of old age; for others Christmas will never be the same again because the family circle has disintegrated irreparably through separation or death. There is much grief because death performs its grim task mercilessly, on our roads particularly, during this period.

There are parents who long painfully for their children who will not be home for Christmas because they have emigrated, live too far away to be able to be home for Christmas, or because estrangement has set in, threatening to break the hearts of parents.

There are countless reasons why these days hold little joy for many. One of the most terrible is the loneliness of those who will miss a loved one this Christmas due to death. Who can truly express or comprehend this longing?

The Child of Bethlehem had to travel these dark roads Himself as a man on earth, and therefore He is one with us in our grief and pain. He too had to sob for His loneliness at one time. He cares for you and He understands. He is mighty to touch your heart with consolation. Remain close to Him and you will experience the joy of victory, because His love will pull you through.

God of the lonely and sorrowful, thank You
for also bringing us comfort for our pain.

THE SIGN OF GOD'S LOVE

"This will be a sign to you: You will find a baby
wrapped in cloths and lying in a manger" (Lk. 2:12).

As with the arrival of a baby in a family, thousands of people yearned for the coming of the Child of Bethlehem: the prophets and the Old Testament believers; His parents and the devout people of His time— Simeon and Anna; Zechariah and Elizabeth. Similarly we look forward to the annual commemoration of His coming with the honest prayer: "Grant us in these days a true Christ-feast!"

God speaks to man in a thousand voices: on Sinai the thunder roars; in Sodom and Gomorrah God speaks with fire and brimstone; in the life of Job God speaks through loss, illness, and tribulations. But at Christmas God speaks through a Child who beckons us back to the heart of God from a mother's arms and from a manger. God becomes a child and speaks to us in a language everyone can understand.

The Child of Bethlehem speaks to us about God's immeasurable love and tells us exactly how much God loves the world! Will this love not compel us to love our children more and to desire their salvation? Having children always places before us a choice: to love and comfort them, or to neglect and sadden them. The Child of Bethlehem puts before us the same choice: will we love Him or will we sadden Him?

Holy Father, I gratefully accept Your miracle
and my heart chooses You as King for all eternity!

GOD WITH US

"They will call him Immanuel"—
which means, "God with us" (Mt. 1:23).

Christmas reminds us of the fact that God is with us, so that our imperfect love may be purified. Christmas teaches us the truth of self-sacrificing love. Christ came to earth and His people rejected Him. Nevertheless, He gave everyone who accepted Him the right to become children of God.

Although there was no room for Him in the inn, He guarantees everyone who loves and follows Him a place in His Father's house.

Although He was despised and deserted by people, He invites everyone who is exhausted and burdened to find rest with Him. He had the power to come down from the cross and destroy everyone who mocked Him, but instead He died on the cross for all our sins. Although the vengeful world begrudged Him His life, He lovingly and mercifully promises eternal life to everyone who believes in Him. This is the language of Immanuel—God with us.

There is so much lovelessness and hatred in today's world. It sours the relationship between man and God, and between man and man. But Christmas repeatedly tells us that love will triumph. Because God is love, He sent us His Son. If God loves us so much, we must also love one another. Let us profess our love anew this Christmas: to God, to our parents, to our marriage partner, and to our fellow man. Then it will truly become a Christ-feast.

Thank You, God of love, for allowing Your love
to be embodied in Jesus Christ. Give us even
more love through the work of the Holy Spirit.

CHRIST IS BORN!

Jesus was born in Bethlehem in Judea,
during the time of King Herod (Mt. 2:1).

It is an irrefutable historical fact that Jesus was born in Bethlehem. Through this physical birth God revealed Himself to all of humanity. The fact that humanity found it hard to accept this fact, however, does not affect the authenticity of the event.

He who was born in Bethlehem more than two thousand years ago is still being born in the heart and life of modern man. This simple but overwhelming truth is often lost in the agitation of our busy lives.

In spite of the world's festivities around Christmastime, it remains true that if you have not experienced the birth of Christ in your personal life, you will never know the true joy and peace of Christmas. Only Christ gives depth and peace to the joy of Christmas. The birth of Christ in Bethlehem is a mere historical fact and nothing more than that until He is born in your life. Then you not only know Christmas but also the Christ of Christmas.

If you want to experience true Christmas joy, Christ must be born in your life, and you have to place Him in the center of your entire life. When His holiness permeates your life, it becomes "a merry Christmas" in the true sense of the word.

I thank You, holy Child of Bethlehem, for being born
in me so that I can become part of Your Spirit, and
so that my entire life can be a celebration in Your honor.

THE AFTERGLOW
OF CHRISTMAS

The shepherds returned, glorifying and praising
God for all the things they had heard and seen,
which were just as they had been told (Lk. 2:20).

The shepherds from the fields of Ephrathah witnessed the miracle of that first Christmas Eve. Each of us experiences something of the miracle of Christmas every year, in the Christmas carols, colorful lights, and in the gifts that we receive. There is a spirit of love and goodwill everywhere. However, the spirit of Christmas discarded on the garbage heap, together with the wilted Christmas tree, is useless. It makes a mockery of the deeper meaning of the Christ-feast.

Would it not be wonderful if we could preserve the special Christmas spirit in bottles, like seasonal fruit, and then open one bottle a week for the entire year? After the song of the angels has died down, after the star has disappeared from the skies, after the wise men have returned to their home in the east, and the shepherds have returned to their flocks, only then does the real work of Christmas begin.

Because we were at the stable in Bethlehem and relived the first Christmas Eve, because we met the Christ-child, therefore the afterglow of Christmas must remain in our lives. With the glow of love in our hearts we must continue to have compassion for our neighbor even after Christmas. We must continue to help rebuild the world, to bring peace among people, and to fill the world with the music of His eternal love.

We worship You as the God of the Christ-feast,
but also of each day of the year. Help us to continue
singing the love song of Christmas throughout the year.

LIBERATING INTROSPECTION

Search me, O God, and know my heart; test me and
know my anxious thoughts. See if there is any offensive way
in me, and lead me in the way everlasting (Ps. 139:23-24).

It is once again that time of year when we have to take stock and do introspection. It is only fitting that we pray the above prayer together with David during these days.

Some prayers make no demands on the one who prays. They lull the conscience. However, to pray meaningfully and in such a way that pleases the Holy Spirit, a prayer must be truthful and accompanied by a sincere willingness to engage in thorough introspection.

Requesting God to know your heart and to test your thoughts can be an experience that completely re-creates you. It strips you of all egotism, superficiality, and hypocrisy. You see yourself as God sees you, and you may not like what you see. It is humbling, but it also liberating.

Testing and evaluating your spiritual life is an urgent necessity. It is the condition for service: if we cannot pass God's test, He cannot employ us in His service. Only when the Holy Spirit compels us to do introspection do we become useful instruments in the hands of the Lord, and only then do we work for His honor. Then we no longer fear the future, but we place our weak hands in His almighty hand and walk purposefully towards the unknown future.

Holy Father, make me willing to submit myself to the
testing of the Holy Spirit, and shape me for Your service.

JOYOUS CHRISTIANITY

"My soul glorifies the Lord and my spirit
rejoices in God my Savior" (Lk. 1:46-47).

Many people view their religion as a heavy and sometimes even unbearable burden. They easily frown upon any semblance of light-heartedness in spiritual matters. They stoop somberly under the heavy burden of their spiritual conscience. This is definitely not what God intended.

The faith of the Christian should be a joyous experience. Your Father takes joy in and is interested in your life. He is happy when you are happy; He consoles you in sadness and grief; He supports you when the burden becomes too much for you; He helps you up when you stumble over obstacles; He enjoys your successes as you enjoy them yourself.

Christianity does not eliminate joy and happiness from life. On the contrary, it returns happiness to your life. Through your communion with the living Christ you realize the blessing of His presence every day. The more you praise and thank Him, the more happiness you glean from your spiritual life.

Happiness is the fruit of the Holy Spirit (Gal. 5:22). Your surrender and devotion should be such that the joy of the Lord is revealed across the entire spectrum of your life. Then every day becomes a joyous Christ-feast.

Dear Lord Jesus, I continually delight in
the knowledge that You are always with me.

CHRIST IS ALWAYS AVAILABLE

"Surely I am with you always, to the very end of the age" (Mt. 28:20).

One of the glorious truths of the gospel is that Christ is always available for his followers who need Him. This is a comforting knowledge in these last days of the old year, when we are often overcome by an inexplicable melancholy.

The comforting truth is that the Master is with you wherever you are. While you strive to get to know Him better and while you try to break through your doubt and uncertainty, He is at your side in your struggle. It is as if He wants to tell you: "Stop struggling with your self-made doubt and fear and come to Me. I am the One who will give you calm and peace."

Christian pilgrims know that if they accept this merciful invitation, they will have to relinquish all their pet sins, which have become part of their lives. Unfortunately, there are those who want to claim the presence of the living Christ on their own terms. This can never happen though, because His presence can only be experienced and enjoyed if you meet His requirements.

The basis of your Christianity is your acceptance of the living Savior. Without that your faith has no foundation and you will be unable to venture into the new year. Together with Christ you also accept the Holy Spirit. Through the working of the Holy Spirit you become aware of the presence of Christ with every step that you take.

*Thank you, loving Father, that You are always available
and that I may experience Your presence every day of my life.*

GOD'S PERFECT METHOD

"He has done everything well" (Mk. 7:37).

Most people want to conclude the year that has come to an end in the presence of God, and enter the new, unknown year under the guidance of His merciful and loving hand.

God speaks to us in many ways, but He speaks most clearly to us through His Son and through His Word. With the Word before us, we have to look back on the road we have traveled and beg His friendly light to illuminate the road stretching out ahead of us. On New Year's Eve we are not allowed simply to contemplate the transience of life—the mere thought of our mortality is enough to upset us—but the content of the year behind us is much more important than its duration.

In the past year the Lord has done so much in our lives, giving it meaning and quality. All of this is undeserved grace. We do not deserve what we have achieved. We can merely confess: "Everything He does is good." The year did not bring only joy, but that is not necessarily bad. Sometimes God tests us with grief, but this too is for our own good.

When we reach the end of the pilgrimage, as we have reached the end of this year, we will clasp our hands together in amazement and humbly confess that He did everything well. With this knowledge we can take our leave of the old year with peace of mind.

Leader and Finisher of my faith, I rejoice
in the knowledge that through Jesus You work
everything that happens to me for my good.

PEACE UNTIL THE END

*"I am the Alpha and the Omega," says the Lord God, "who is,
and who was, and who is to come, the Almighty" (Rev. 1:8).*

And so we reach the last day of the old year, through His grace. There are many things we are ashamed of, but there are also many things we are thankful for. There are many reproaches for missed opportunities, but we have also received so much grace from God. The year brought joy, but also grief; victory, but also defeat; sunshine, but also storms.

However, we may still call God "our Father," the biggest privilege a humble human being can expect. Let us therefore count our blessings today, in the knowledge that He remains constant—yesterday, today, and in all eternity.

You are richer today than you were yesterday if you smiled often; could give something of yourself to others; could forgive your enemies; make new friends; convert your problems into opportunities. You are richer today than you were yesterday if you made time to notice God's handiwork in everyday things; if you learned to distinguish the essential things in life; if you had a little more patience with others' faults.

You are wealthy today if a small child smiled at you, or if a stray dog licked your hand; if you sought out the best in others and if you gave the best of yourself to your fellow man and to God. Then you begin the new year secure in His love.

*Eternal and immutable God, I thank You for guiding
me through another year and for giving me the
knowledge that You will never abandon or forsake me.*